Bloody Murder On The Dog's Meadow

Building a straw-bale grand design in France

Mark Sampson

For: my wife, Debs, a gently glowing pink pearl light in times of darkness; our dear daughter, Tilley, who now feels much more positive about our 'new' family home than she did at the time; Alfred Lord Sampson, a dog supreme; and Bret, my trusty cohort, without whom...?

Introduction

'Barking!'

That was one TV guide's considered assessment of our grand design in straw when first aired on Channel 4.

I rather like that. Like many an Englishman abroad, I like to be considered a little eccentric. It's part of our culture and heritage. *So Breeteesh*, the French might say. *Is* it crazy to build your house of cereal stalks, when you know nothing about such matters and have no aptitude for things practical? Was it daft to sail the ocean blue when the horizon was thought to define the edge of the world?

Well, this is an account of a year of living dangerously on the dog's meadow, where our future house was conceived and hatched, painfully. Twelve months of sound and fury, during which it often felt like I'd booked my passage to Bedlam. Others point to the challenge and satisfaction of such an endeavour, whereas I would have told enquirers at the time that the experience ranked with divorce in the Misery League Division 1. Almost as long-running and every bit as relentless.

Certainly a lot of barking went on. Mainly canine but occasionally human. Our daughter, who was eight at the time, named the plot of land on which we built this house *Pré du chien*. The dog's meadow. To this day, Alfred Lord Sampson, our *labradoid* dog, patrols his meadow and proclaims territorial rights. He barks at people who rootle for mushrooms in the wood that shades this house from the summer sun. He barks to protect us from hunters, who come to shoot anything that moves during the autumn and winter months.

And he barks at any threat to our safety from the air. This plot of land, you see, commands a magnificent view: the most compelling reason for buying it and putting ourselves through the torment of construction. The panorama once belonged to the venerable Viscount of Turenne, whose eponymous seat sits floodlit on summer nights on the northern horizon. His former territory extends roughly from the valley of the Tourmente directly beneath us, a tributary of the Dordogne, to the foothills of the Massif Central in the east. On clear days, you can see the mountains of the Cantal. On moist mornings, the whole plain is swaddled in a thick duvet of mist. Hills rise out of it like islands in some great inland lake and the Viscount's ruined chateau appears to sail towards us like a Spanish galleon. It's a feast for the eyes that consistently uplifts the spirit.

Much barking has gone on since that auspicious day when a friend from my days as a volunteer DJ at a tin-pot local radio station helped us move to a virgin meadow any personal effects that we hadn't boxed up and deposited in friends' barns. Later that day, my wife and I left our former claustrophobic village in two cars stuffed to the gills with paraphernalia. We moved from a dark stone farmhouse that would never quite be finished to a caravan – with a set of drawings depicting a light and airy straw bale house that would one day, money permitting, be finished. Moved from the hills and the steep-sided valleys of the Corrèze – where folk who have never set foot outside the *département* might challenge you to duelling banjos – to the limestone Lot, where the water wrecks your kettle, but the countryside opens out like a double-page spread, inviting you to fill your lungs with refreshing air.

So: are you sitting comfortably? Before we begin, there are a few things that you might find helpful to know. Bits of the story that don't always fit into a journal of this kind.

*****

I was not reared to take risks. The eldest of four children, I was brought up to be nice, steady, helpful and responsible. Even as an apprentice hippy, I never quite managed open rebellion. I grew my hair, drank Strongbow cider and listened to Van der Graaf Generator, but collected all my 'A' grades and went to university at a time when tuition fees were funded by the state.

I learned to be careful with money and turn off lights

when not in use. Two reasons, I suppose, why I ended up wanting to build a straw bale house. People said that they were cheaper to build - and certainly cheaper to run. My Pavlovian impulse to switch off evolved into a desire to respect what little remains of our natural environment. A straw bale house represented an opportunity to do something positive, to make a statement. Show people that you don't have to use the nasty overpriced materials that the construction industry promotes as the 'traditional' way.

A third reason was my wife, Deborah. Or Harri, to use her stage name. An erstwhile actress (who once dressed Kevin's wounds as a non-speaking nurse in *Coronation Street*), she started off over here as a back-street aromatherapist: working from a spare room in our house while she tried single-handedly to take on the medical mafia and a Kafkaesque bureaucracy. Despite being denounced to the authorities on a couple of occasions (in this area of France, staunch resistance to the Nazis could be undermined by betrayal), she stubbornly went on massaging oils into the bodies of locals seeking alternatives to prescription drugs. Now she has a successful practice. Doctors and psychiatrists send her clients, and she has a lilac-coloured plaque on her door. Which may not seem such a big deal until you realise that, as a *non-professional professional*, she could at any moment be tried for treason.

Anyway, that's just to suggest that she has guts and determination (and a remarkable ability to talk me into doing things that, deep down, I'd really rather not). And, had she not happened to have a sister near Flagstaff, Arizona, we would never have found ourselves at a party in a straw bale house on the edge of the Navajo Reservation. It was a beautiful house built in the indigenous adobe style, with huge comely ochre-coloured walls. We experienced that famously intangible sensation of well-being, and decided that, since the dragon lady at the *mairie* had told us that we couldn't build a wooden house on our new plot of land, then we would build one of straw.

Change requires an impetus. The original impetus – though she had little say in the matter at the time – was our daughter, Tilley. Without her, we may never have left our cosy terraced house in Sheffield and migrated at the end of September 1995 in our hand-me-down Golf. We'd bought our farmhouse in the beautiful unspoilt Corrèze five years earlier. Just the right environment in which to bring up a child. What a head start it would give her to grow up bilingual. Full of the joys of an exceptional autumn, we began our new lifestyle adventure, giddy with hope and expectation.

After eight years in an ailing house in a sick village nicknamed *Les Balkans* in recognition of its internecine tendencies, we decided that it was time for another change. It was not, as the programme suggested, that life was intolerable and we had decided to give France one final chance. We were simply ready to move on, and wanted to live with more natural light in a more energy-efficient house.

For me, though, moving on is easier said than done. I'm not like our daughter, who seemed quite un-phased by the prospect of graduating to a school ten times more populous than the village school she was leaving. I seem to travel through life in a Spectrum Pursuit Vehicle (or SPV to fans of *Captain Scarlet*): in which you sit the wrong way round as you move forward, surveying the road just travelled. I had to be prised out of my nest – in the same way that I was dragged, kicking and screaming, from our terraced house in Sheffield. A typical Libran – if such a thing exists – I hate change, because change means choice and there are always so many legitimate considerations on both sides of the scales. Give me good old gradual, slow, organic, non-contentious evolution any day of the week. The faster the deadline for moving approached, the more I convinced myself that all was fine with the current situation. Wasn't there something safe and cosy about living in a village where the devils you know pass by and say hello and stick together to ward off unwelcome strangers?

Nevertheless, we made it in the end. Only 15 years or so after we'd started our vague search for a new life remarkably near to this very spot, a circuitous route brought us to a caravan on the dog's meadow. 15 years before, we had looked at an old restaurant in the nearby town – but failed to spot the opportunity. Instead, we opted for the hills, deliberately far from any whiff of a British ex-pat. We gave it our very best shot, but even partial integration would prove too steep a learning curve.

In roughly 12 months, the house was built. As near as damn it. This isn't a technical how-to manual that will show you how. There are plenty of good textbooks available. No, it's more of a human-interest story: a kind of antidote to *A Year in Provence*, which proved ultimately, I believe, a disservice to anyone contemplating selling up and moving to France. It's sometimes a great notion, especially if you've got a decent pension. But life here is not just a glass of wine on the terrace at the end of yet another balmy day, and the locals aren't all amiable rogues, who leave baskets of walnuts on your doorstep but never turn up to fix your leaking pipes. So I wanted to suggest the day-to-day reality of life here for those who aren't, financially speaking, particularly well endowed: people like us, who live by their wits and hustle to survive. A journal seemed the best way to convey the flavour of this hustle.

It's a book of 'c' words, like change, choice, construction – and conduct crass and unbecoming. I just hope that it will prevent anyone about to embark on a similar venture from making the same mistakes.

Finally, I am mindful of (and grateful to) one particular French *bricoleur* (DIY enthusiast), who guided us around the two straw houses he had constructed with his own bare hands. Going totally against national type, he started by admitting all the mistakes he had made. (Over here, you learn that there is no such word as *sorry* because it denotes individual weakness, which undermines collective rectitude.) Nevertheless, he was able to show us his creations with touching pride in his achievement. Here was an individual with perhaps fewer skills than I have. Yet, for all the off-kilter verticals, he had managed to construct two solid edifices that will – probably – outlast his earthly tenure. He showed me where and how to start. I may have gone home with a heavy heart at the thought of all the disruption to come, but he also gave me a shot of much needed confidence. If he could do it, so could I.

It's bloody murder, building a house. But if I can do it, so can you.

Prelude: June 2003

Exactly one calendar month to go. 30 days hath… 'My deepest sympathies, darling,' my mother says on the phone. 'I do *so* wish I could be there to help you pack.'

A silly-hot Saturday afternoon. We drive to Limoges for the *Foire de Limousin.* A kind of Ideal Home Exhibition. The place is packed and stifling. We drag Tilley from one stall to another, from one verbose salesman to the next, in search of materials for the house. And there's the wood-burning stove that we have come to see – but the salesman who is temporarily minding the display drags us over to see his Jötls. *Na, you don't wanna look at those; come and see these.* So much for honour among thieves.

On the way out I spot the son of Madame du Monde from the village. I've waved at him in his Ford on days when he goes to visit his mother, alone in the spotless house that her dearly departed husband probably built for them, but we've never before talked. A softly spoken man with a beard and the sallow complexion of a smoker, I take his card in case we can, some far-off day, afford one of his swimming pools.

*****

After the customary Sunday morning coffee-and-Gauloise, and the parental call from home, I ring our new neighbour. He's posh, efficient and friendly. I arrange for him to ask his local farmer to cut our knee-high grass before we move to the land. He tells me that it is a farmer's duty to keep the countryside tidy. Something to do with the exorbitant stipend they receive, courtesy of the insane Common Agricultural Policy. On no account offer any payment, he warns. It gives them some obscure entitlement to ownership.

Then I speak to another farmer; a friend of a Dutch friend. He confirms that we will harvest the straw bales towards the middle of next month. Gingerly he puts it to me that I should pay 1.10 euros per bale. The additional 10 cents for stocking them in his *hangar*.

After lunch, I take my laptop over to Bernard's. He is watching the Monaco Grand Prix on his day of rest and I feel wretched about asking a favour. I wish I understood more about computers. I depend on them for my livelihood, yet am helpless in the event of something untoward. He mumbles inaudibly (in French) as he tinkers about with the speed of a disdainful expert. He installs some software for me and I take the machine away with my usual feeling of inadequacy. Dependency does little for your self-esteem.

On the way home, we meet up at our local lake for a swim. This man-made *plan d'eau*, created as a leisure facility for the families of the workers from the big armaments factory in Tulle, like the bigger lakes made by damming the local rivers for hydro-electric power, has arguably enhanced the work of nature. I have come here some mornings with the dog, when a gauzy mist is rising off the surface of the water like steam from a bath, and the peace and beauty and solitude have filled me with wonder. Once I watched a heron glide just a few feet over the water from one bank to another. And I realise that such epiphanies help to make it all worthwhile.

In this heat it's like sinking magnificently into a warm bath. Alf doggy-paddles beside his mistress across to the other side and back, while Tilley swims through my legs and revels in her piscine talents. She desperately wants to swim to the other side and back. To someone her age, it must be like crossing the Channel. I can only marvel proudly at her ease and regret that I still panic whenever I haven't, as she puts it, *got foot*.

Young Melissa turns up with a pile of *crêpes* that she distributes to the stragglers. She made a mountain for a village fair, which was so poorly attended that she's only sold a handful. Driving home, the three of us reflect on how much we will miss our lake. We must remind ourselves that it's only really for three months of the year that people emerge to socialise here. The rest of the time they seal themselves up behind closed shutters.

The weekend concludes with a *Crack-er-jack!* of a storm; a real *son et lumière* spectacle with lightning flashing around the hills. *Lord, may it not be the harbinger of a troubled leave of absence.*

*****

Tilley is very tearful about me travelling to the UK by plane. Since 9/11, she equates air travel with death and destruction. Bin Laden became the bogeyman at her school; he occupies the same space in her subconscious as Cruella de Vil once did in my sister's. I promise to phone home on touchdown.

It's the first time I've done the new Limoges to Stansted route. I prefer to take the train because these cheap flights are a subsidised con. What about the **real** costs to our environment? But because of the latest round of strikes, I have no choice. My eight years of travelling back and forth to the UK have been plagued by industrial action. Every trip becomes a stressful drama of will-he-won't-he-get-there-or-back? God knows what this latest round is all about. The French are such a paradoxical bunch: they take the pills that their doctors prescribe and live life according to the rules of the little black book with which they are issued at birth, yet they will take to the barricades at the merest hint of some unpalatable new legislation.

Apart from twenty worrying minutes in a traffic jam at Limoges when all seemed lost, the journey passes without incident. I am pleasantly surprised to learn that you can still park the car for free at the airport. Fortunately it's but a few steps from the terminal, because I have to run back and leave my mini Leatherman in the car when I discover that I won't be allowed onto the plane in possession of such a deadly weapon.

Stansted is (like most airports, I guess) a blot on the landscape. Concrete city, devoid of charm. I take the overland route to Southend, by means of country buses, and discover that Essex isn't quite as awful as I had thought. Change at Chelmsford. Just time to pop into the Post Office and deposit a cheque or two into my Smile account. Then a late-afternoon wander around the shops of Southend's city centre. Still my first instinct on arrival in the UK is to shop. It must be a national characteristic. I once heard a *yoof* in the back of a Eurolines coach at Dover explain to his French companion that *England's great, man, if all you wanna do is fooking shop.*

Down to the sea for a look at the mighty pier and the old Kursal where my grandparents would go dancing during their courtship. Before or after my grandfather went off to fight for King and Country? I drag my bag along the esplanade, all the way to Westcliffe-on-Sea – where the two of them grew up independently – and the hotel where my sponsors have billeted me for the night. My first time here by the estuary, but the ghosts of ancestors are everywhere. Alone in the restaurant at a table by the window, I ask the waiter if he knows what the place is with the big power station across the Thames. 'Kent,' he opines helpfully.

I linger too long over dinner and arrive at the nearby Pavilion Theatre half an hour after Ladysmith Black Mambazo have started their set. When do *pop groups **ever*** start their sets at the scheduled time? I guess it's the last leg of their nationwide tour and they are impatient to get home. *Moi aussi.*

*****

Home. I'm still not entirely sure where that is. When I travel to the UK, it's like going home. Yet, when I return to France, it's like coming home. Home is where I lay my pork-pie hats. Home is my wife and daughter. But it's not as simple as that. Every time I 'land' in France, I have to remind myself that I actually live here. It still doesn't seem quite right.

However... I am glad to be home. After the tawdry hotel in Dover and the constant stream of lorries rolling off the ferries, followed by a night at Stansted with all the other uncomfortable travellers waiting for inconveniently early flights, it's great to be back at South Fork. The old stone walls are now solar storage heaters and the house is as warm as I have ever known it. There is a rich familiar aroma of aged chestnut beams.

This will probably be my last homecoming to this particular venue. Sometimes, when I look around at the solid walls and the big swathe of open-plan parquet and the baronial *cantou* fireplace, I have to pinch myself. Did we really make a proper functioning home of this place? Many moons ago we turned up early one evening in the pouring rain to take possession of it. Debs had driven all day in her orange Beetle to get to the *notaire's* office in Argentat in time to sign the contract. The vendor poked his head through the door of the waiting room to glimpse the mugs who were paying him fifteen grand for the house in which his marriage had failed. So we signed a contract we didn't understand and drove up into the hills with a bunch of keys furnished by our dubious estate agent. Not one of them would open the front door. The rain was coming down in rods and everyone was tucked up behind closed shutters next to their stoves. We drove off into the wooded hinterland to find a hotel. And the only one we found was closed for the winter. God, what had we done? What kind of a place was this? Yet it became our home, and our marriage set fast as our daughter grew up, and now I see it as a repository of memories. Most of them happy, some grim. How will I feel about coming home to a caravan?

The girls get up at five to go down to the *Salle Polyvalente* to join the other 'communards' for a coach trip to Futuroscope. Now that we are finally and reluctantly a two-car family, I can turn over and go back to sleep. The annual communal jaunts are organised by his worship, our match-chewing mayor, as a sweetener to the voting populace. (Paid for with all the money he doesn't spend on genuinely communal ventures like a children's playground. *La-di-da, la-di-da.*) Last year it was my turn. Tilley the Kid and I took an interminable trip in the rain to some dull spot on the unremarkable northern edge of the Massif Central, to take a few *fun-rides* and view the melancholic animals in some benighted theme park.

I drive over with Alf to the land for a spot of upkeep. It's horribly overgrown, but each time I behold the wonders of that view, I feel an invigorating sense of relief. No, we haven't done a nonsense. It's beautiful where we are, but there's something claustrophobic about all those deep-cut, densely wooded valleys. Up here you can fill your lungs and stretch out your arms like the man in that radiant painting by William Blake. *Glad day!* Yes, it will be lovely to build on this slope that falls away then plunges over the bluff to the plain below. Even if it faces the wrong way. (North by north-east.)

Just then, a little push-me pull-you train rumbles along the line that skirts the road to Quatre Routes. I follow it till it snakes around the bend and away. As a boy, I yearned to have one of those panoramic papier-mâché landscapes for my Blue Pullman train set. Now I have a real one of my own.

In the searing heat, I don visor, ear-muffs and face-mask and fire up the strimmer. But the foul-smelling weeds that are growing all the way up the drive like an outbreak of John Wyndham's imagination are too tough for the nylon thread. I need the blade – which is back home. By chance, I check out the water connection and realise, to my horror, that we don't yet have a counter. One more thing to arrange before the move.

After lunch with Thompson & Thompson, watching the sheep in the field engage in synchronised stupidity from the blissful shade of our friends' oak tree, I drive to the abandoned hotel by the roundabout at Bretenoux to record another exciting broadcast of *Musique pour Armageddon*. All alone down in the tomb-like basement with only the sound of your own footsteps for company, I half-expect Jack Nicholson to peer round the door with axe and manic leer. I haven't found time to prepare the show and it's one of the worst ever. All the elementary mistakes I used to make at the outset – like talking into a microphone that's switched off. Why do I bother? I'm not being paid, not even reimbursed for my diesel. I feel trapped by a self-inflicted sense of responsibility and a silly fantasy of fame. Does the ego trip of playing my chosen music to a handful of anonymous listeners justify the time and effort? Is it really likely that Atlantic Records will send me their entire back catalogue to review, or that some scout from a hip Parisian radio station will discover me? (Mental note: *knock this little charade on the head toot-sweet*.)

*****

Pentecôte. Don't ask me what that's all about. Most French public holidays are a complete mystery and designed to catch you unawares. In the scorching heat, a gaggle of villagers congregates outside our gates. Either you ignore them and risk opprobrium, or you tag in on some witless conversation and waste valuable packing time.

Mirianna, our Belgian refugee, is staying with us for the umpteenth time. She came once to do a magazine feature on our still-born *aromatherapeutic* holidays. We liked each other at once, she fell in love with the area, and she has been coming to recharge her batteries ever since. She arrived on Sunday evening in some shiny black 4x4. It's short and dumpy: a perfect *objective correlative*. Don't even ask about the fuel consumption, she warned me. Since the apartment looks like Citizen Kane's box room, we put her up this time in the *gîte*, where she sleeps till half past noon.

Debs fills me in about Futuroscope. A concrete wasteland, apparently, and slightly disappointing exhibitions. As usual no special catering arrangements for two vegetarians. It's as if we're punished every time for daring to be different. The same thing at Tilley's canteen last year. The *cantinière* – a friendly, grandmotherly sort – simply refused to make any allowances for her. If all her friends were eating, say, meat and green beans, then Tilley would eat beans. Unaccompanied. No grated cheese, no nothing. No wonder she would come home so tired and listless. Picking her up at midday disrupts the working day, but vitality once more courses through her veins.

'And what would happen if there were a Moslem child in the class?' Debs in her frustration once asked the mayor of that particular commune. He merely shrugged his shoulders and implied *tough*.

Over her futuristic lunch of inevitable omelette, she sat with Fat Nat. I am immensely proud to hear that she made some kind of peace with her. 'I want you to know that I don't hold anything against you,' Debs told her. 'If I've shut myself away, it's nothing personal – it's just that I've learned that it's what you have to do to survive here.' We were so naïve when we arrived here, full of the joys of our Big Adventure. We would answer people's questions openly, because we had nothing to hide and it's how we were used to living. Sheffield folk call a spade a spade, but after Debs was denounced on two separate occasions for trying to start up her business from home, we learned circumspection.

Fat Nat, too, was denounced. For neglecting her children. (Which prompted a campaign of social rehabilitation. She became an impresario overnight: stage-managing a children's *spectacle* at the *Salle Polyvalente* – and directing her husband to build a Wendy house out of old wood panelling on the scrap of land where he used to burn plastic-sheathed wire to salvage (and sell) the copper.) With admirable restraint, Debs said she wasn't interested to know who had done the dirty on her. The woman burst into tears and confessed the problems that she's having with their neighbours, who are taking her to the tribunal over some nonsense about parking rights. No wonder they are so keen to sell up and leave their house and its fake Victorian streetlight.

By the end of lunch, Fat Nat was talking nostalgically about the evening the *young mums* and children had shared a pizza in our house (during one of my many initial business trips). I guess she'd have liked to be a friend of the foreigners. As it was, she and her husband turned into smiling back-stabbers. How sad it all is; how twisted we can become. This couple once sent us a pair of baby's sheets and pillowslips to mark our daughter's birth. Those tears, were they tears of self-pity or regret?

*****

My giddy aunt! The month is already half over. Still no reply from the digger driver, so I phone an alternative and am pleasantly surprised when he doesn't laugh in response to my tentative suggestion that work might start, maybe, possibly, during August. I've arranged to meet him at the land this Sunday. Meanwhile, my attempts to recruit someone to tow the caravan to its new berth have been in vain. Geordie Mark is willing, but his 4x4 is disabled. Two weeks to go and nowhere yet to live.

Yesterday was possibly the hottest day I have ever lived through. Anywhere in the world. The thermometer outside the Parisians' holiday home was registering 37 degrees. I managed some change-of-address letters on the computer, then simply had to join Debs for a siesta. We slept too long and woke up disorientated and even hotter than before. Nothing for it but to go for a late swim. Incredibly, Mirianna's first time at the lake. Her rapture doesn't help. *How could we contemplate leaving behind such a beautiful spot?*

It's great having her to stay – she cooks wonderful Italian meals for us, picks up Tilley from school, pays for her massages and generally exudes a reassuring calm. But my stress levels must be sky-high. My left ear is bunged up. It last happened in Jersey. Striving to meet deadlines while clearing up the mess of a colleague, whose ex-public school, ex-army credo was: *never admit to any fallibility; always exude confidence e'en in the face of blind incompetence.* Maybe something to do with the Eustachian tubes.

*****

Father's Day. Tilley the Kid gives me a poem that brings tears to my eyes. I get to lie in while Debs walks the dog. At the fountain, she encounters Claudine and Fat Nat, who embraces her warmly like an old friend. The Futuroscope trip is discussed. Debs tries to suggest disappointment without provoking an incident. 'A little soulless,' she ventures. 'Too much concrete.' 'Ah yes,' says Claudine. 'But it's scientific.'

Apparently, it's 39 degrees in the valley of the Dordogne. Mirianna prepares a sumptuous farewell meal for us and our mutual friends, Régine and Bernard. We eat outside between the house and the pond on the only vaguely flat bit of garden. Tilley entertains us with songs from *My Fair Lady.* For a while it's very funny. Like most kids, though, she doesn't know when to stop. Just before she goes to bed, Claudine's niece joins us at the table in her bikini, which shows off newly acquired rolls of puppy fat. Like her sister before her, she's losing her looks with the onset of adolescence. She just sits down at the end of the table uninvited. We look at her with amiable perplexity. When she asks me whether she can bring her friend, who's hanging around by our gate, I suggest politely that perhaps really she should maybe leave. Odd behaviour. *Darling, these hillbillies have* **no** *social graces.*

We eat and drink on till after night falls. Bernard leans back too far and falls off his chair into our mallow bush. Shuffling its solitary way across the garden, a passing hedgehog sends Alfie ballistic by hissing in response to his inquisitive nose. As tiredness sets in, we have the usual comedy of Régine berating her narcoleptic husband. 'I'm resting my eyes, Régine,' he mumbles in his sleep.

*****

Fast approaching the longest day for yet another year. Usually I go into a state of mourning for the passing of the seasons. All down hill from the 21st June. This doesn't accord with my wife's upbeat philosophy, so she does what she can to dispel my melancholia. This year, however, it won't worry me. I want the time to pass as quickly as possible: fast-forward to a time when we are installed in our new house, when all the misery is behind us. Just a bad dream fading into history. I am comforted by how rapidly the time has passed between the shortest and the longest days. Six months have flashed by in a blur of activity. Pages torn off a calendar, spinning into the void.

Mirianna leaves for Brussels on the same morning that Debs takes Tilley over to see her new school. Tilley will be sorry to see her go; she's like a favourite auntie, a big sister even. She loves going into her domain for a *girlie chat*. Debs is very impressed with the headmistress and optimistic that things will work out well. No doubt trying to make light of the ordeal of changing school, Tilley is singularly under-whelmed by the whole experience. I am still concerned that she will be thrown out because she doesn't have the compulsory vaccinations. (*Sorry, can't work, must educate the child at home. 'Annual expenditure...' Penury. Starvation. Ruin.*)

Meanwhile I'm here hanging by the telephone most of the day: fielding phone calls from Debs's clients, while she waits for a phone to be installed in her new clinic; arranging for France Telecom to hook up the caravan without revealing that it's a caravan (and thereby incurring added expense); failing to cut through the water company's corporate inefficiency; discovering that the digger driver still hasn't provided an estimate, that Geordie Mark's 4x4 has expired, that the standby driver is snowed under with work. I spend an hour talking to my contact in Southend about the work that I'm trying to negotiate while all this is going on. My current

lack of fax facilities is embarrassing and I have to give him
Régine's number at the restaurant. Doesn't exude a
professional image. My friend from the radio, however,
phones to say that he thinks he's found a roofer for me.
Hosanna in excelsis. Ever since the 1999 hurricane, a ready
roofer is worth two platinum birds in the bush.

Then my sister phones from her new summerhouse at
the bottom of their garden. She's feeling tearful and
frightened about the side effects of the post-masectomy
drugs. The treatment has plunged her into a full-blown
menopause. No time to prepare yourself, but WHAM!
Straight in there. And her sessions with a faith healer must be
compounding her disorientation. During the first, the healer
told her about someone who was watching over her and
described – in perfect detail – our grandfather. Then, at the
second séance on a hot afternoon, she told her about a female
presence showing off her beautiful fingernails. My sister's
best friend, who recently died of cancer, was always
apparently very proud of her nails. Are these genuine
visitations or can the healer tune into the psycho-energy of
my sister's memories?

No sooner have I put the phone down to ponder the
question than Tom from the TV programme is on the blower.
What's happening? How's it all going? I do my level best to
mask my panic. Sometimes I wish I led an ordinary nine-to-
five life. Occasionally I look back wistfully and see myself
walking home from work in Sheffield. *Hello-darling-I'm-
home.* Put the kettle on, clear the head. Enjoy the evening
without dwelling on what tomorrow will bring. Something to
be said for the Civil Surface.

*****

During my morning walk with Alf, I dwell on the irony of
being too pre-occupied to enjoy the best summer since '76
(when my friend and I were swanning about in Guernsey:
scruffy students with nothing in mind except sea, sun, girls
and weed). I conclude that I don't enjoy life often enough –
even though I would never describe myself as an unhappy

person. Happy marriage, lovely daughter, beautiful surroundings, privileged western lifestyle. Nevertheless, life over here sometimes does seem to have been a lurch from one crisis to the next.

On this scorching day, Tilley travels with a coach-load of school kids for a day-out at Vulcania: the theme-park they have created in the middle of the volcanic Auvergne. The culmination of her class project on… volcanoes. I go to pick her up at the end of the day. While hiding from the sun's gaze, chatting to fellow parents, a car passes us and I recognise Olivier, the Parisian artist who comes down here now and then to recharge his batteries. Last time he was here, he skidded on some ice and ended up in a ditch. He had to call me on his *portable* to come to the rescue.

Olivier is the cadaverous man's cadaver. In comparison, Keith Richards is positively fat-faced and in the pink. Something to do with his heart condition. My mother would itch to paint his portrait (as once she wanted to paint Charlie Watts). He gets out of the car and we embrace and he introduces me to a friend from Paris – '*un sacré bassist*' – who makes Olivier look radiant. When I moan about the problems of moving the caravan, without hesitation he offers us his house down here for the duration. We have had our share of problems since up-sticking to France, but we've also encountered many such gestures of warmth, friendship and generosity.

Tilley the Kid's coach is late, so I turn into an old mother hen. When it arrives, she makes straight for the car and won't come over to say hello to Olivier. I tell her off on the way home, only to discover that she has wet herself and is too embarrassed to see anyone. We had given her a big bottle of water to drink, but they wouldn't allow her to go to the loo after a certain hour. What you get for trying to be responsible parents.

*****

The longest day comes and goes in the company of the Squirrells. I have been dreading their arrival because it means that it's really time to go. They have come to claim the house that they've had on deposit now for eight months. Ingrid saw our advert on the internet and thought, *Oh that looks nice.* She phoned up Debs to arrange a time to come over and see it. Debs being Deborah suggested that they stay next door rather than go to a hotel. It would let them *get a feel for the place.* My intuitive wife had one of her good feelings. So they came, they saw, they purchased. Ingrid simply fell in love with the house. Ours was the only house they looked at. Living in a cramped house in Lewes, it must have been all that space. The dream of having her own studio where she could make her wonderful idiosyncratic sculptures of women and birds. People have called us courageous, but it's nothing compared to what she's doing. Starting a new life at sixty with an incapacitated husband (who can barely speak following a stroke) in a land where she knows no one. In the few days left, we resolve to pass on as much knowledge as we can. *Le Handover.*

When they roll up in a Citroën AX stuffed with boxes and bubble-wrapped sculptures, we are in the middle of working out our electrical requirements for the new house. You're supposed to take months over such decisions, but I have arranged to go to the land again the next morning to meet the electrician and the reserve digger driver. So it all ends up in the usual rush and flurry of snap decisions.

While chatting and exchanging news, the retired teacher next door pops round to say goodbye in her customary puckered manner. She has to go to Clermont-Ferrand for an operation on her troubled stomach. Hopefully they will remove the large cork from her back passage at the same time. The usual moans about the village. Hard to sympathise when you know that she'll be moaning about us to someone else tomorrow. She will almost certainly be as glad to see the back of us as we are relieved to see her departing Fiat. Ingrid knows now to look but not to touch. You don't want to influence people's judgement; on the other hand you don't want them to make the same mistakes.

20

They smile it in your face, all the time they want to take your place, the back-stabbers...

*****

Early Sunday morning on the land. From the valley below I saw a raw patch of yellow on the hillside – like a cornfield by van Gogh. And when I drive down the track and park beside the electricity box, I find that the farmer has indeed cut the grass to a golden stubble, as crisp underfoot as a Ryvita. One less thing to worry about. Before I fire up the strimmer, equipped this time with the blade, and tackle the foul-smelling tough-stemmed John Wyndham weeds, I imbibe the sound of birds in the trees and the soothing *pock-pock* of tennis balls from the court beyond the trees next door.

The reserve digger driver drops by as promised, rumbling down the track in a big low silver car that smacks of Money. A fat man with the familiar look of glaucoma, he gets right down to business and warns me about the need for some kind of *terrassement* to prevent storm waters pouring down the track and straight into the house. One more thing to worry about.

Paul, the electrician, comes by soon after in his plush white van. We sit underneath the dead walnut tree to shelter from the merciless sun, going through our requirements and talking about the expatriate life. He is busy but not burdened. He leaves work at a sensible hour so he can get home to enjoy the last of the sun with his wife and young boy. In England, he would be stuck in a traffic jam and developing ulcers. He shows me stuff about a vacuum system, which releases you from the drudgery of Hoover bags. You plug the nozzle into various locations throughout the house and some central motor sucks up the household dust – and takes it, no doubt, to some vast subterranean dust sack. To be emptied every six months or so. Asthma City. I nod enthusiastically and make the right noises, but it is not a priority.

Late that afternoon at the lake, the rumble of distant thunder flushes the multitudes out of the lukewarm water.

Rummaging for our car keys, I can't understand why Michelle is looking at me so strangely. Then I realise that I am rummaging in her basket and not ours. My mind is elsewhere. An evening trip to Tulle to see *The Hours* in *version originale* gives it a short vacation. *Tense nervous headaches?* Nothing works faster than a damn good film.

*****

Somehow I got talked into a round of golf. Only a week to go and the first wet day for aeons. Golf, I am now quite convinced, is a game for masochists. 34 euros it costs to traipse through wet grass in shoes that would better serve as sponges, dragging my beaten-up golf bag with its few spavined clubs through a ceaseless Correzian drizzle, slicing my iron shots, nagging my subconscious to watch the friggin' ball and, all the time, listening to Tim, with his posh bag and flash clubs (now with new enlarged sweet-spots) belly-aching from one hole to the next about his swing. As if I should give a god-damn, when all I really want to do is to talk about foundations and digger-drivers. Watching him address the ball, legs apart and bottom thrust out, I can't help but think of the Reeves & Mortimer characters who speak through their arses. (Mental note: *never again. Plus jamais.*)

That night, the long awaited storm arrives. Not with a whimper, but a big, big bang. All evening long, we see it coming. No *son* but lots of distant *lumière*. When it comes our way, the ferocity gets us out of our beds to huddle by the sitting room window and watch the wind thrash the silver birches and shake the remaining cherries off the cherry tree. Each thunder clap is an explosion and the lightning flickers like a faulty celestial strip-light. The storms here are not of the puny English variety, but the tense tumultuous type featured in *Key Largo*. When there's an appreciable gap in the proceedings and we are fairly sure that the house isn't going to blow down, we go back to bed for the storm's quieter coda.

*****

Normally such storms clear the air. But by ten the next

morning, it's Gas Mark 8 once again. The storm has snapped my rustic arbour that previously supported the vine. I feel responsible, but tell myself that this is the Squirrells's problem now.

Debs and I toil all afternoon while Tilley is at school, carting endless boxes of books from the Citizen Kane box room to Victor's attic across the road. Up the path, through the former dingy kitchen of Mad Sad (where once we had sat with our old former neighbour and her cantankerous departed husband, eating Madeira cake and looking at the x-ray photos of her arthritic back), up the cluttered stairs to the expanse of wasted space under the roof. The young couple who bought the house use it now as drying space for their laundry. I fear for the glue that binds our books. Beggars, however, cannot choosers be.

Our driver is finally available to tow the caravan to our land. At the tail end of the day, I lead him and his burly 4 x 4 over to Mike and Hazel's, where our new home sits forlornly outside their new home. They have left their jobs and house in Croydon and come out here at the behest of a mutual friend: Monsieur Fromage, as Tilley once christened him, when he came to work on our house – the first English person we had met since landing in the Corrèze. Mike and Hazel's French is even worse than ours when we settled out here and I keep thinking of a neighbour's words when we set off from Sheffield that chilly September evening. *Well Mark, you've got it all ahead of you.*

Mike hitches up the Swift *Conqueror* to the 4x4. *Take 'em to Missouri, Matt!* I lead the way in my little 205 along by the river and up the hill to the terrain. Helped or hindered by our frantic hand signals, the driver backs the caravan down the track and onto the land, swings it round and lands the south-side wheels dead square inside the slope-compensating hollow I have excavated. He asks for twice the sum that I had divined. I guess he has five children and a 4x4 to support.

My handiwork, as usual, proves anything but. My

hollow is nowhere near deep enough. Unless dead level, Mike explains, the fridge of our *look-sherry cara-van* won't work. Only with chocks, jacks, stabilisers and elbow grease do we re-dress the one-in-five gradient. Next – a management training game. *Take these rods and canvas and assemble an awning. Without tears.* The caravan, our new home, appears to list one way, while the awning definitely lists the other – as if some leviathan has tried to tear them apart. I try to put on a brave face as Mike gives me his *50p tour* of the Conqueror and hands me a file full of instructions to read. Do I not like gadgets.

*****

What, meanwhile, is going on inside our daughter's head? Kids are infinitely adaptable, they say. They take it all in their stride. She is apparently sanguine about the prospect of leaving her best friend and their village school and starting out in September as the new girl in a school of ten times as many pupils, but Debs and I keep reminding ourselves that she must be harbouring all kinds of anxieties. Disturbed nights: a sure sign of distress. Involving her in the practicalities of the move, I commission a signpost for our land. Handing her a tin of white gloss and a brush, I request the name she has given it – *Pré du chien* – in her best writing on a piece of old chestnut salvaged from the remains of a barn struck by the *tempête* of 1999.

So, the day after the Swift is moored, I am back on the land, trying in vain to hammer the new sign into the concrete earth while waiting anxiously for the Man from France Telecom (who will surely take one look at the caravan and refuse to connect us to the telecommunications network. *No telephone, no work. No work, no pay. No pay, no food. Ruin, starvation, death. Bad move. Should've stayed put. Didn't I tell you...?*) I move inside to convert a couple of English sockets – and the heat is asphyxiating. Sweat pouring off my forehead, I can barely see to screw. When we bought our caravan, we talked about the winter cold, but didn't spare a thought for the mid-summer heat. How can we possibly survive at such a temperature? *Discuss*.

As it transpires, the Man from France Telecom doesn't blink an eye at the caravan. There I am, acting the charming, daft Englishman, telling him that the line is for the house, the caravan is just a temporary affair... and I know that he knows. So I just keep my mouth shut and pull on the flex when he shouts. By now, the sun is a little lower in the sky and the place is alive with insects that I have never seen before. Droning around the caravan like little Lancaster bombers. Not the vicious horse flies that have been attacking us unprovoked since the start of the drought, but some kind of flying beetle or solitary bee, attracted perhaps by the newly mown grass.

With the telephone installed and tested, I am ready to head for Baladou to deliver some boxes of winter clothes to Sue, who will lodge them there in her garage. The Diaspora of Sampson family artefacts is underway. But I waste precious minutes trying in vain to lock the caravan door. Defeated by a plastic lock. On the point of telephoning Mike and asking him to talk me through the process, I give the door an exasperated heave and find this time that the lock engages. Brutality, as is too often the case, seems to be the key to success.

From Baladou Sue's bungalow and her disconcerting dog, who tries to hump my leg at every turn, I drive to Thompson & Thompson with more boxes of tapes for my music library under their stairs. I find our friends relaxing by their pool at the end of the working day and join them for a blissful swim before driving home for an early-ish night. Debs thinks we should build a pool before the house. Maybe she's not so crazy, after all.

*****

The Sunday before the move. A party at seven that evening in our honour. Organised by Michelle, who works in the *Bibliobus* that drives around the Limousin, lending books to schools and isolated householders. Hers are long but leisurely working days: people like to hang around inside the bus for a chat or drag her inside their homes for coffee and cake. Michelle was one of our first friends here. We discovered, a little late in the day, that she is an *élu* (or *elected one*) of the commune, which means that she has the mayor's ear. Michelle will listen sympathetically to our problems or proposals and then talk to the mayor, who will do nothing about it. Before, we would talk directly to the mayor, who would chew his match and pontificate and do nothing. A kind of progress after all these years.

The party is at *La Maison Ethnobotanique*: the house that Jean-Claude, her untamed husband, bought as a ruin and restored virtually single-handed as a venue for his *classes vertes* and exhibitions of Corrèzian apples, gnarled fungae and the like. The original wild man of Wongo – short, strong, dark moustache, hair cut in the style of a 60s schoolboy – you wonder whether he runs on all fours. He takes classes into the woods and shows them how to survive on nuts and berries. He also likes to get his kit off at the drop of a hat and the family has taken to spending summer holidays in naturist camps on the coast. Perhaps it was this proclivity that attracted him to aromatherapy. One of the first people here to give Debs any practical assistance with her profession, he lent her exhibition space for her oils and creams at his *ethnobotanic* house and organised a course at the ex- school in our commune. It proved a salutary lesson. Someone reported the English witch doctor to the official medical body. A representative was despatched to speak to Jean-Claude and shut down the course. After such treachery, Debs became more guarded. She is still a backstreet aromatherapist, but her burgeoning reputation now confers on her a quasi-legality. Moreover, she pays her taxes and her exorbitant social charges, so the authorities are happy to let sleeping dogs lie.

We turn up in a Berlingo brimming with more boxes of our artefacts. Jean-Claude is busy tending to a gooseberry bush and Michelle is setting out the food. The little house round the back that he is busy restoring looks great. Last spring, in the middle of a barren spell without work, Jean-Claude employed me to rake out the joints for pointing and carry piles of chestnut shingles up onto the roof. A pittance. But cash-in-hand and no questions asked. It was my introduction to the fabled black economy.

Foolishly, I have imagined an acre of free space under the roof. But he has restored the first floor now: brand new computer in the main room, with a magnificent triangular window and a view over to the distant blue hills. So I feel rather embarrassed emptying the car of its clutter, which Jean-Claude magnanimously slots into any dead space he can find. And all the time, he is itching like an impatient child to play table tennis outdoors. But then the guests turn up and all the children insist that we open our presents. A pair of collages to help us remember our time here: one for Tilley, one for us. And a basket of local produce. A genuinely touching moment.

Finally, with ping-pong bats at the ready, a meteorological phenomenon chases us all indoors. Although we can see and hear the storm arriving, the sky over the house is still blue. Suddenly the children come running towards us, chased from the other end of the house by driving rain. It reaches us after a magical hiatus – a scene from a cartoon film, almost – during which half the house is lashed by rain and the other half bathed in sunshine.

So we move indoors and Jean-Claude lights a fire in the *cantou* (the traditional wallk-in fireplace). All the food is set out and everyone is hungry, but we have to wait for Christine and Jean-Luc, who make the best goats' cheese in the *département*. True to their reputation, they turn up around an hour late, with one of their beautiful daughters and their son, who always takes the piss out of my French accent. They say that husbands and wives grow alike over time. I have never seen the pair of them together before and am fascinated by their physical resemblance. I also find myself staring transfixed at Christine's varnished toes. Never, before or since, have I seen a woman with such long toes. So long that each toe seemed to fold in on itself as if abashed by such prehensile length.

We eat well of course, but in groups rather than round a common table. Michelle has commissioned a cake with a map of the Corrèze scanned onto the icing, and Jean-Luc tries hard to inject some humour into the evening by pushing a child's nose into it. Jean-Claude does one of his celebrated disappearing acts long before midnight: driving off without a word of farewell and leaving his wife and children to find their own way home. A nice *do*. But, as always, though warmed by the occasion (and the fire), I leave feeling slightly sad and frustrated. That inability to communicate anything profound. Chitter-chatter I can manage, but, when it comes to something really meaningful, I'm usually – literally – lost for words. These are good friends, but I know precious little about them after all this time.

*****

The next day, Michelle drops by to say a personal goodbye. She bursts into tears and she and Debs hug each other and promise to stay in touch. After all, we'll be just over an hour away in the next *département*. To many, though, it's as if it were a foreign land.

Later, we travel down to Beaulieu with the Squirrells for our appointment at the *notaire's* office. The day of reckoning: signatures, transfer of money, no turning back. Our charming, elegant *notaire* prints off x copies of the contract, we sit around her office and do our best to make sense of it. We point out any obvious mistakes, she corrects them and prints off some new sheets. We approach the desk by turns and sign our names to each sheet of the master copy – and hey presto! The house now belongs to the Squirrells and we have a caravan and 146,000 euros in the bank. Plus plenty for the government, plenty for our *notaire*. How come the careers master didn't tell me about the cushy profession of a notary?

After the ceremony, I go over to the land alone for one last time before tomorrow's move. We have as yet no water and no electricity. Driving down the track, the caravan and awning combined look not much bigger than a van. With a heavy heart, I see that, despite countless calls, there's no promised standpipe in position. This is what you often find here. You speak to someone, who may be gruff, who may be charming – and it's always the same old story. '*Je vais m'en occuper, Monsieur.*' Leave it with me; I'll look into it; it'll be done this week; I'll send someone tomorrow. '*Merci, monsieur,*' and you know it's about as likely as seeing God in a burning bush.

Paul, the electrician, turns up in his spanking van and wires us up to the grid. If nothing else, I can plug in my computer. And then I wait. *Für der Wassermann.* And I hope. And I worry. How can we live without a supply of water (like most of the world's poor)? *How many more phone calls, Lord, how many more?* I pace around and do some futile jobs in the caravan. And I wait and I hope and I project melodramatic scenarios in my head. Come six o'clock and it's surely too late now. Bastards! On the point of getting into the car, another white van backs down the track. Can it be? Can it possibly...? Yes! *The water-man cometh.* God is merciful after all.

'You have a nice view here, Monsieur.'

'Yes,' I beam. 'It's not bad, is it?'

July 2003

The bells are ringing for me and my dog. It's early Saturday morning: the first Saturday of a new life. Are the church bells ringing in celebration – or is it yet another public holiday?

Alf and I stop in the nearby hamlet to admire the stunning view below. The valley lies under a quilt of early-morning mist and the rising sun is a fiery orb suspended over a great lake. The muffled rumble of an unseen passing train fills the space with some fleeting noise.

In the hamlet, I stop to talk to a farmer with bushy hair and terrible tartar. The French national tooth is not a pretty sight. I ask him if he's seen Dexter, our ginger cat, who ran off while following Alf and me the previous morning, spooked by a barking dog. When I tell him about our plans, he points out the house he built and explains that they had to use explosives to make the *sous-sol*, or cellar.

*****

We've been here now for less than a week. We finally left early on Tuesday evening, having already made one return journey in both cars packed with boxes. In the end, it wasn't so hard to drive away. Not like the wrench it was leaving

Sheffield. Both of us were touched, however, by the parting gift of the young couple who bought Mad Sad's house. They hardly know us, but they're housing some of our belongings and they presented us with a book of photos of the Corrèze.

When we got to the land, we liberated the animals, buttered the cats' paws and went straight to bed, exhausted. Tilley found it all rather exciting, sleeping in her own little section of the caravan, which you can close off with sliding doors. How lovely to be so young and full of life, when everything unusual seems part of a great adventure. When my family moved to Belfast from London back in 1961, I took it all in my youthful stride. I don't think it even occurred to me what my parents must have been going through.

For the last few days, I have been trying to make sense of our awning. The unexpected rain has meant that I've had to move things around under cover of canvas: a cramped and exasperating game of musical boxes, stacking them this way and that on a makeshift floor of old pallets crudely levelled with chunks of limestone. I've created ersatz wardrobes using our flimsy rails-on-wheels and hangers suspended from reinforced sections of this lean-to. The girls have made positive noises to encourage me, but the traveller's life is not for me.

After spending yesterday at my wife's *cabinet médicale* in a fairly fruitless attempt to find the peace and quiet I need for work, I ended up making our first major purchase for the new house: our double-glazed doors and windows. My heart sank when they told me that they have stopped making the models for which I have budgeted. What's more, they tried to palm me off with a 10% discount, rather than the 20% I had previously negotiated. I had none of it and stood my ground like a redcoat at Rorke's Drift. I insisted on seeing the manager, explained the situation – and he agreed to the additional 10%. Little triumphs like that make you feel like a real man.

*****

We have, it would seem, our *permis de construire*. I don't read all the technical stuff, but just enough to learn that no modifications have been stipulated. Our chain-smoking architect has done his stuff. *Glad day!* I am ready to strip off in imitation of William Blake's little pink happy man, spread wide my arms and shout my relief from the highest hill. Our daughter would be mortified.

Instead, I go over to see Christophe, our young farmer friend, to discuss the harvesting of the straw. There is a slight problem with the old baling machine. It won't take the blue recommended plastic twine that I have bought. We're going to have to make do with sisal, which will eventually break down. By then, however, the bales will be sandwiched between two thick skins of render. Christophe suggests that we can go ahead in the next few days. Hopefully, it will coincide with the projected visit of the TV man. Despite the recent rain, the fields from which the straw will be cut look like they've been scorched by a desert wind.

In fact, the call to bales comes during the weekend. We'll be ready to go Monday morning. The weather is ideal: silly-hot and dry as a ship's biscuit. The short notice necessitates some urgent child-minding arrangements. After delivering said child, I roll up chez Christophe with Alfred Lord Sampson in the back and a sense of nervous anticipation.

My Canadian friend, Bret, is there to help us. Despite majoring on computer repairs, he always seems to be, if not sensible, then certainly practical. The more I get to know him, the greater the reassurance I feel in his company. I'm even beginning to think about asking him to help me put up the straw walls. A computer technician and a dunderhead: it could work.

Christophe drives us to the nearby field, which has been drastically shorn. The bales are dotted around like out-size golden Weatabix. They are clearly bone-dry, which is a big plus, but a little looser than I would have wished. Still, balers can't be choosers – and I can't hang around ruminating on degrees of compaction. There's work to be done before the midday siren. Christophe manoeuvres the tractor and trailer; Bret runs around like a blue-arsed fly, gathering up bales; and I totter around on the trailer, taking each bale and quickly trying to fit it into the most economical stack we can manage. Too often, I manage to get it wrong and Christophe has to call out, *No, not like that! Other way round*.

Once the trailer is full to capacity, Christophe drives us back to his hangar for the delicate business of arranging the bales in such a way that the hangar will by the end of the day accommodate 450 bales in one neat weatherproof stack. I have come with a diagram of a beautiful Rubick's Cube-type of construction. Pretty soon, though, theory gets stomped all over by practice. There simply isn't time to create anything pretty. It's about all we can do to get the bottom row sitting off the ground on palettes in a way that's level enough and strong enough to support all the bales above. Bret clowns about and keeps us all entertained with jokes and asides in his singularly quirky French, but I blanche as we trample over my building materials, manhandling the bales and bashing them into tight niches. *Have some respect fellas*, I want to call out, *this'll be my house, you know*!

By lunchtime, we've gathered and stored two lots of roughly one hundred bales. True to his apparent pillar-to-post existence, Bret goes off to fulfil another commitment, but Eric, my Dutch farmer friend, will be taking the afternoon slot. So I join Christophe for lunch at a farmhouse kitchen table also populated by his charming wife, Chantal, their two impish sons and miniature toddling daughter, whose eyes are almost as big as the rest of her body. One day she will be as naturally beautiful as her doe-eyed mother. It's a chance to chat and get to know them better, but as usual this entails fairly detailed explanations of why we chose to come here and, *yawn*, why we should choose to be vegetarians. So I pass on the home-reared, home-killed pork, but compensate with two slices of Chantal's renowned walnut tart.

After lunch, we trundle off down a particularly rocky track to a further-off field. This time, I take Bret's role, running around gathering bales by their sisal ties, while Eric stays on board and stacks. This suits me better, as it's clear that he knows what he's doing. My only problem is the heat. I'm partially protected by peaked cap and handkerchief hanging down over my neck, but the sun is relentless. We've already had weeks of this and it's getting too much. I've always said with typical British bravado – possibly born of years of frustration with the unstable British climate: *Oh, I love the heat; the hotter, the better.* Now I'm not so sure.

Bouncing back over the stones to the farm, Alf throws up what looks like bile. The heat must be getting to him. So, before we head off for the second hundred of the afternoon, I tie him to one of the hangar's posts and leave him with a bowl of water in an attempt to enforce shade on him.

By the end of the day, we have finished our labour and I am utterly and comprehensively knackered. My legs, too, are lacerated by the straw. I look like I've woken from a restless night in the brambles. Shorts were maybe not the most suitable option. Our daughter, on the other hand, has been frolicking in her friend's pool all afternoon, so she doesn't grasp why her father and her dog are so listless.

Looking up at our land from the road that winds across the flood plain, I can see an unfamiliar white vehicle. It turns out to be the van of the farmer who sold us this land. He has brought Tom from the TV team to talk to me about the project. On the phone I envisaged someone with gravitas in, say, his late 40s. The still bright light of late afternoon reveals him as a young whippersnapper. A mere minion. Nevertheless, his deep hazel eyes and aristocratic accent are enough to intoxicate our daughter, who flirts overtly with the dishy young man. If she's like this at age eight…!

*****

Back in the studio for another exciting instalment of *Musique pour Armageddon*. Maybe just maybe (but probably not) that talent scout for Radio Nova will be touring in the Lot and turn on the car radio to catch the last few minutes of Fela Kuti's 'Equalisation of Trouser and Pant' and experience one of those *sacré bleu* moments...

The studio is a dingy room in the basement of a large near-derelict hotel on a busy roundabout. But down in what feels like the bowels of the earth, it's blissfully cool and I think of my wife and daughter, left behind in our asphyxiating caravan to get ready for a weekend away with friends in Montluçon. Were it not so spooky down here, entombed among empty concrete corridors, I might have suggested that they come here with me.

With the headphones on, I can concentrate on the job at hand, free of such distractions as: how to stay cool in a tropical heat wave or *canicule* (as it is becoming known); or how to entertain our daughter and keep her happy enough to compensate for the upheaval of the move; or how to prepare a healthy meal in a kitchen no bigger than a packing case.

Later at the caravan, a cool breeze blows up, flapping our canvas awning and agitating the wind chimes we have hung up inside to ward off evil spirits. Sunset bruises the northern sky above the village of Turenne and all is beautiful. My sister phones and describes the water-retention and myriad other side effects of her medication. She has been to see a faith healer, who has been trying to clear out the baggage related to previous incarnations on earth. My sister is apparently *an old soul*. Rather her than me. The thought of another round of existence horrifies me. I've been so fortunate this time round; next time I'm sure to come back as a one-legged street urchin in the slums of Calcutta. Or Kolkata. Or worse. Despite all her troubles, she has found the time and consideration to send her niece, our daughter, some Barbie-ish dolls: a pair of preppy twins who go by the names of Mary-Kate and Ashley. Tilley the Kid has taken them both to bed with her.

*****

Le quatorze juillet! Or Bastille Day. The French still

celebrate the day, over 200 years ago now, when the revolutionary mob set free the prisoners of the *ancien régime*. 'A'-level History seems almost as long ago now as the French Revolution itself.

We're staying with friends in their elegant rented town house in Montluçon: a one-horse town in the geographical centre of France. Isabelle was my wife's first aromatherapy client in France and our daughter's first teacher. And me, I've been attempting to give her husband English lessons by telephone. He tells me that they've been useful, but I'm never convinced and feel a bit of fraud in taking the company's money. Silly really. He works for EDF and they're not short of a euro or two.

It's wonderful to be in a house again. It's the lap of luxury to sleep in a real bed. Even better to sit on a real loo, knowing that you can simply flush things away without worrying about where you're going to empty the contents of the slop-canister. I've insisted on bringing with us not only our dog, but also the expensive wine that has been spoiling underneath our caravan. Some substitute for a cellar it has proved. The heat has forced the corks half-out. Debs was embarrassed when we handed our friend, the wine connoisseur, two double-size bottles of once-best Bordeaux. He poured some into a glass, carried out the usual ritual of slooshing, slurping and swilling – and pronounced it one of the best Bordeaux he had ever tasted. Vindicated!

Montluçon may be a dump, but drive 45 minutes south to the foothills of the Massif Central and you're in the heart of glorious countryside. It's never too far away in France. We spend half a day in kayaks trying to negotiate the rocks of the beautiful river Sioule. Normally there's enough water in this river to make it navigable, but the drought has transformed it into a nerve-wracking obstacle course. As Chief Man in our kayak, I manage only to steer us round and round in circles and to run us against every available rock. Isabelle is too polite to voice any criticism, but my daughter cannot hide her displeasure. She does not tolerate fools gladly and it's dispiriting to feel that she thinks of her own father as a fool. It's only when Tilley and I join forces with Pierre-Jean that we go forward. I am quite happy to follow the lead of Man *numéro uno*. In this magnificent setting, we paddle like crazy to avoid one rock and then another as we hurtle through rapids and spin round eddies. The women folk have a terrible time of it with a very perturbed dog as their passenger. Periodically, he leaps into the water rather than teeter on the edge of a glass-fibre projectile.

At the end of our weekend of comfort, we eschew the motorway home for the scenic route across the under-populated Creuse and the seemingly uninhabitable Plateau de Mille Vaches. A storm threatens all the way back. Tucked up later in our caravan, we hear the rumble of distant thunder. But there is still no rain. *How long, Lord, how long?*

*****

A sudden bout of visitors and dinner invitations has compounded the disruption caused by heat, premises and child-minding duties and made it almost impossible to work on my e-learning project. Last night, for example, Smiffy – our friend, the tree surgeon – dropped by with his friend, Chas, the cabinet-maker. We sat outside to chat and drink beer and watch day become night as the stars came out and the lights went on in all the little houses dotted around the plain. I talked to Chas about the plans for the house in the hope that he might be interested in, say, the interior carpentry, but he couldn't commit himself.

Dinner at the Jacksons means another late night. A small price to pay for the joy of not having to cook a meal in the caravan, which is the equivalent of trying to boogie in a straightjacket. It's always a pleasure to talk to Steve and listen to that lovely South Carolinian drawl of his. We discuss a future book project: the true-life stories of people who have moved to France and survived (or not) the hard way. In other words, without a pot of money and a heap of business connections. *You know what, Mork? Ah reckon people lurve a bit of suffering and misery – so long as they don't have to go through it themselves.* Ah reckon he's right. One great bonus in dining with the Jacksons is that our girls are of a similar age, so we were able to leave Tilley with Ione and go home with one less person to worry about.

Friday night is music night. Debs is happy, or so she says, to stay and look after our daughter, while I go swanning off to Souillac for the jazz festival. I'm going on a freebie with the Radio team to see Bireli Lagrène's Gypsy Project. My price of admission is to interview the celebrated guitarist, who plays in the tradition of another *gitan*: Django Reinhardt. I have my questions prepared in my little blue note book. The other real cost, it soon becomes apparent, is to endure the bickering of my two colleagues. He is 34 and she is 57 and they are apparently an item. Yet they take any opportunity to bitch about the other to anyone available to listen. After a while, I manage to switch off and concentrate on the event. We sit in a kind of arena behind the magnificent Roman abbey. As night descends, the swifts that probably nest in its eaves swoop and dive about. The band swings relentlessly and Bireli Lagrène beams throughout, visibly touched by the warm ovations of the big crowd. We hang around till after midnight, but learn that the press interviews were all concluded between 6.00 and 7.00pm. Despite my irritation, I'm secretly rather relieved. I drive my bickering colleagues back to their car in Martel. Both of them have been drinking beer all evening. I don't give the relationship long.

The next morning finds me at Jan and Eric's sort of market garden. In return for lodging our video collection, I have offered to help Jan dig potatoes for a morning while Eric mans their market stall in Brive. Being organic farmers, they can't use pesticides and herbicides, so the rows of spuds are choked by weeds, which makes it difficult to gauge where to sink the fork – and I spear a few precious tubers. I also follow Jan's lead in squeezing Colorado beetles to death. *Dis-gusterous*! When one splatters my face and sunglasses with its bodily fluids I'm ready to throw in the towel. I toil for three hours or so in the extreme heat. Later I learn that it was 42° in the shade and 51° in the sun. *Fiddly doe, fiddly dee, the farming life ain't for me.*

Sunday is a proper day of rest. We seize the opportunity to relax and enjoy each other's company for what seems like the first time in ages. I spend part of the time massaging Debs's neck to alleviate the whiplash she seems to have incurred in the kayak. Later, the three of us troop over to our British neighbours' lovely house for an aperitif and a chance to get to know them. I doubt if we share their politics, but they seem a pleasant and very decent couple. They were so ravished by the view, they tell us, that they bought their house without having seen inside it! As neighbours, they are not too near to be on top of us, but near enough to be a reassuring presence. What's more, they have a tennis court.

*****

Despite the distractions, things seem to be on the move. A phone call from dishy young Tom confirms that the TV programme wants to follow our project. American Steve, a shrewd cookie, urges me to find out what the production company can do for *us*. We are cleaning up his glass-blowing studio and re-arranging his junk in order to accommodate some more of our junk. His work is stunning and I rashly (in terms of our budget) commission a pair of wall lights for the new house. He tells me about a couple he has read about, who are restoring an old manor house somewhere in the wilds of the Limousin. Their project is also to be part of the TV series and they have obtained the use of a JCB in return for the publicity opportunity. What if I can score some geothermal heating equipment and/or some solar panels, for example? Suddenly I have myself a distinct project.

I take a detour on the way back to check out the sawmill Smiffy recommended. It's run by a woman, whose husband died horribly and tragically in the course of his work. The wood seems rather twisted and buckled, but the woman is pleasant and helpful and I want to give her some custom. Maybe the roof battens. I've seen a map with shades of red to indicate the prevalence of termites. There's a red patch in the Lot and they found some in our very own commune. So I am becoming obsessed by wood-devouring insects. She tells me that it's hardly worth treating the battens; they'll eat through anything. All you can do is to be vigilant.

The next day I drive down to Cahors, the departmental seat. Moving department within France is not easy. But what *is* in this bureaucratic country? We have to change the matriculation of both cars – or risk a fine. I've phoned up twice to check which papers to bring with me and have taken just about everything official I can find. However, the dragon at the 'welcome' desk informs me that my wife must sign the forms for both cars. I tell her about my advance phone calls and the time and money it has cost to drive down here *blah blah…* She refuses to look me in the eye, but simply turns away to address colleagues and leaves me to fume.

'OK, what if I sign the documents for my wife?'

'Monsieur, you can do what you choose, but I can't tell you that it's OK to sign on behalf of your wife.'

I test the ambiguity of her statement by taking another ticket, then boldly marching past her and through the double doors into the bowels of the Prefecture. The woman I see in the *cartes grises* section is reasonability and understanding itself. She lets me sign both documents on Debs's behalf without any fuss. As I walk back past the dragon in triumph, I am tempted to give her the finger, but don't wish to get her pragmatic colleague into trouble for defying protocol. *Au revoir, Madame*, I rehearse in my head. *I was a civil servant myself for 15 years. It's a privileged position. You have a good job and a good pension. So why is it necessary to be rude to the people who pay your salary? I bid you good day and poor health, Madame.*

Before leaving Cahors, I learn at the plush EDF offices by the station that there are no more grants available for geothermal heating. So that's one rather expensive option that appears to be *hors question*.

*****

When Didier, a friend from the Corrèze, delivers his younger daughter and Tilley's best friend, Juliette, he scans the horizon with his Bausch & Lomb binoculars, impressed and maybe more cognisant of why we moved away.

It's a shame he's not still here to witness dawn breaking the next morning. A hot-air balloon and the rising sun, like a big red Japanese orb of fire, hover above the mist below as if painted on a theatrical backdrop. From the sublime... I trudge off with Alf, equipped with bog-roll and plastic bag. I have taken to *going commando* in the woods. If he can do his business there, so can I. The sordid ritual just about beats using the caravan's sani-loo, then emptying the canister in some out-of-the-way corner of a foreign field.

With Juliette here, Tilley is occupied and I can get on as best I can (given the mess and the enervating heat). Like many a single child, she's very good on her own and adept at occupying herself, but it's lovely to hear her playing with a friend. The pair of them seem to cope better with the heat than I do. As I survey the suffering trees, I see desertification and rising global temperatures, which fills me with visions of hardship and suffering.

My wish for rain almost does the trick that night. Woken by the distant thunder, Debs and I get up to bring the washing inside the awning and to flush the girls out of their tent. They join us inside the sauna. Despite the lightning that flickers around Turenne, dramatically silhouetting the northern horizon, no rain beats down on the plastic roof of our shelter.

In the morning, my heroic wife drives off to work with Juliette in the passenger seat for safe return to her parents. It's just The Kid and I once again. How does she do it? The idea of massaging even one hot, sweaty body in this heat defies belief. On the occasions that I've worked in her waiting room and witnessed her unfailing good humour and care for all her clients even when dead on her feet, I've felt like an intruder, like a stranger at a birth, someone who has no right to be witnessing such intimate moments. She is my strength. I know that things must be bad if and when she ever feels downbeat. I am wracked most days by anxiety at the moment; a man living in Limbo, waiting for the phoney war to end, wondering what's going to happen and worrying about the way our outgoings exceed our incomings. It doesn't seem to worry my wife at all. She has this almost religious faith that everything will turn out fine. I could do with a dose of whatever she's on.

*****

As July segues into August, there is a sense of winding-up all over France. It seems extraordinary that here we are in one of the world's most advanced industrial nations and the whole country still shuts down for the month of August. I thought we'd long ago seen the last of the *urban weeks* – when Blackpool and other holiday hotspots would suddenly fill up with thousands of factory and mill workers and families for a week or even a fortnight. I remember the red alert among the staff in the Butlins holiday camp in Filey because Glasgow week was due to start on Saturday.

Towns are emptying of their natives; Paris becomes a mere shadow of its bustling self. The roads here are busier than ever – with the influx of tourists and holidaymakers. It will be even harder to pin people down and get things done. There is now just over a month before everything is officially scheduled to kick off. I'm still frantically reading books in an attempt to become an expert on every facet of building. My friend Tim, who will be overseeing the building of the base on which the house will sit, phones to say that he's back in residence. He has organised a meeting for later in the week. I'm excited and intimidated by the prospect: it's the point of no return; decisions must be made.

With no sign of the local digger driver whom Tim has lined up for the build, I go to find him at his nearby yard. It's lunchtime, theoretically the most likely time in which to find someone here. The yard is deserted and I am surveyed by a bevy of hunting dogs that bay at me from behind their caged runs. I knock on the back door and am greeted by an old man who explains that he is the Digger Man's dad. His son lives in the modern house across the main road. Families are close-knit in these parts; the children don't tend to stray far from the ancestral home. I leave him with a hand-written message for his first-born. *Tell him Sampson was here. Tell him Sampson is waiting for him on the land. Tell him to come unarmed and pronto.*

My daughter has a day without friends and is probably glad of the chance to play quietly on her own. I marvel how a child of eight can be so self-reliant, but then think back to the hours I would spend at that age, drawing idiosyncratic Westerns. ('*Meanwhile...*' and there would be a picture of a removal van steaming down a motorway, even as a bunch of baddies would be holding up the First National Bank. How glorious to be so free from rules and logic.) I take advantage of her absorption and an unexpected dip in temperature to the low 30s to put together a proposal for potential suppliers of materials for the house. After months and months of reading and reflecting, I suddenly find it's rather difficult to explain succinctly what the *project* is all about. It will be even harder to translate it into French, and probably harder still to convince a French company to sponsor an *anglais*.

I nip down to the *Mairie* to pick up Tilley's bus pass for the next academic year. Smiling sweetly at the dragon-secretary, I mention the pile of wood rotting by the roadside near our drive. Predictably, I am told it is not their problem; it is the adjoining commune's. I want to tell her that it'll be everybody's problem if it attracts a colony of termites. But she'd no doubt simply earmark me as a madman. I tell my daughter, but know I shouldn't, that it's an example of why the world cannot resolve its collective problems.

*****

On the last day of July, under an uncommonly grey sky, the Digger Man arrives with a rotund henchman (who will, in fact, be driving the digger). Both of them seem very pleasant if challenged by the customarily bad teeth. They wander about, ponder and exchange a few mumbled sentences, but there is no particular reason for alarm. Certainly no need for dynamite, which immediately dispels subliminal fears of some *Wages of Fear* scenario: a pair of trucks with volatile high explosive on board, bumping down our *chemin*. One false move and they blow themselves – and us – to Kingdom Come.

As usual, I'm over-anxious to impress upon them that we've been here in France for eight years now and aren't just a bunch of rich Johnnies-come-lately. That is: we know the ropes and are not soft targets. It probably makes not the slightest bit of difference, but the mere fact that we can communicate reasonably intelligibly must surely count for something. What I gather is that it's up to Tim and me to mark out the foundations on the terrain before he comes back to dig out the trenches.

'And you're OK for the middle to end of August?"

'Mmm. *Plutôt le fin...*'

He chuckles, we shake hands and they head for the yellow van.

Now what, I ponder, *am I to make of that laugh...?*

August 2003

The hot weather returns with a vengeance. August is often too hot here and tainted by a sense that after August comes September, after September comes the autumn, and after autumn comes the winter. And after the *quinze août*, the French head back for work in dribs and drabs.

Early in the day, I have to cancel my meeting with Tim, the *maçon*. (It's a term in frequent use here, but one that seemed to die out in the UK after the great cathedrals were built.) The cancellation is due to the fact that my wife has driven off to Brive with the keys to both cars. We have an ongoing battle about keys. I advocate depositing them in a specified drawer. She prefers the laissez-faire drop-'em-anywhere approach. For example, her pocket.

Later, however, our architect, Gilles, turns up on site astride a scooter. I don't recognise him under all the clobber, but as soon as he removes his helmet, I see the trademark plaited beard. We sit side by side with Alf on the slope to admire the view and discuss the coming project. It's actually the first time he's seen the terrain, which still seems a little peculiar, but I'm growing more and more fond of this quirky man. He's en route to see another English client near him, so I ply him with as many questions as I decently can, and try to make sense of his answers. The timbre of his voice has been roughened by far too many cigarettes and he peppers his phrases with quips and argot, which generally escape me, but I hang on in there and gather some nuggets of wisdom. I don't manage, however, to explain *rubble trench footings* adequately. I've read about them and am sure they will work, yet no one seems to understand what I'm on about. Without the courage of my convictions, it looks like I'll have to accept reinforced concrete.

Before leaving, he presents me with my book on bale-building, which he previously denied having. It was only by standing my ground for once and insisting that he hadn't returned it to me that I've succeeded in getting it back. It's not a big issue; it isn't the best of my textbooks. Nevertheless, it's irksome. So is the fact that there is no word of apology. Clearly, even the alternative French don't do apologies.

Debs gets back from the Corrèze in the evening, having delivered our daughter to our friends from Lille, who are back in their Espagnac home for a few weeks. After trying for a few years to hack it in *France Profonde*, they went back *oop north*. Alain has got back his sensible job in local government after an unhappy time of being effectively ostracised by Corrézian colleagues. The five children are growing up, not unexpectedly, but still apparently as differently as it's possible to be. The oldest girl is training to be a nurse now; the blonde Arian oldest boy looks destined for the Hitler Youth; the middle boy is a mad professor in the making; the youngest boy is a future sporting superstar; and Tilley's former best friend from nursery school still appears to be from another planet. When I see them together, I can't help but picture them singing 'Edelweiss', conducted by their proud father and clapped on by their spaced-out vacant-eyed mother. It's odd to think that we were friends and indicative really of how desperate we were for company.

While performing my favourite task of emptying the chemical canister underneath the caravan's loo, I contrive to do my lower back in again. It's a bonus to have a masseuse for a wife. Prone and *en plein air* on her bench, listening to Cassandra Wilson's wonderful *Belly of the Sun*, I watch the sunset dim and the moon come up over the trees of our wood as the last of the local trains sprints along the single-track rail to Brive.

Because of the heat inside the caravan, we try sleeping in a tent. It's cooler, but we both keep waking throughout the night. It's either Alfie tearing off to bark at some unseen nocturnal visitor, or it's the need to haul our bodies up the 1-in-5 gradient. Better, I decide, to sleep horizontally inside a sauna than to sleep on a slope.

*****

While on our own, we experience what must be the hottest days of the year so far. 40 degrees centigrade and counting. That's over a hundred in old money. The needle on the dial must be just a millimetre away from the danger zone, the point when everything starts vibrating crazily just prior to the cataclysmic explosion. The caravan has undergone a metamorphosis from sauna to furnace. There is a slight odour of putrefaction, which seems to come from the loo or from the fridge – or both.

While trudging up our *chemin*, bound for the woods with bog roll in pocket, I encounter a man standing by the side of the road, looking across the landscape through binoculars. We engage in what might loosely be termed *conversation*. A speech defect allied to a heavy dialect makes it hard going. I think he tells me about fires in Portugal; how everything could go up here, too; how he built *his* house nearby. As I slip off, a few hesitant steps at a time, he kindly offers any help he can usefully give.

Later, while checking our green tin mailbox at the top of the lane, I encounter another stranger. This is the man who owns a little strip of wooded land bordered by our wood and that of our British neighbours. When he opens by telling me that his brother is dying of cancer and that he himself is hoping to build a swimming pool for his retirement and that he wants to recoup his money *blah blah blah*, I sniff a rat. Yes, the situation here is wonderful. Yes, you can travel quite easily to Paris – and thence to England. No, I don't want to buy it for the very reasonable sum of 12,000 euros (which represents roughly four times as much as we paid per square metre for our land). He's not really interested in the money, of course. He wants to sell it to someone who is interested in conserving nature. Mere minutes later he's talking about putting Round-Up down to eradicate the brambles. As Tony Hancock would sneer, *Good luck!*

In the night, we are awoken by the sound of rain beating on the caravan roof. We both run outside and dance naked in some weird re-enactment of an ancient ritual. But it lasts no longer than half and hour. Strangely, the parched grass feels immediately dry under foot. One of my wife's clients has told her that the heat is due to continue for another couple of months. It's something to do with the alignment of Mars – the planet associated with war and fire and God knows what else. In such temperatures, any concrete poured would go off far too quickly. And what if there is no water with which to mix it? It is already frequently being cut off between 10am and 7pm.

*****

The Kid is back with us in our temporary family home. She wakes up this Saturday morning and beams with delight because she thinks it has rained in the night. But she is wrong. Within a couple of hours, the heat is once more unbearable and she is whimpering piteously, *Why won't it rain? Why won't it rain?*

Why won't it, indeed? Each time I take our dog for a walk, it seems that there are more and more trees whose leaves are withering on the branch. The colours are autumnal and rather spectacular, but you can't derive any pleasure from them because you know that all is not well. By the time autumn really comes along, there will be no colour left.

Is it the heat that has profoundly affected our collective mood? I suspect that Debs is depressed, which intensifies my own depression. Yesterday evening we attempted to peg out the footings in the crepuscular light. A big fat yellow moon was laughing at us from over the top of our neighbours' wood. We have to get this done by hook or by crook, because the Digger Man cometh now in mid- rather than late August (due, inevitably, to *les vacances*). But the all-important diagonals are out of kilter. We are bemused, deflated and irritated by our ineptitude.

Monsieur Fromage the carpenter drops by to compound my depression. The girls have gone to the river with Alfie in search of some respite from the sun. When his white van pulls up, I am working naked at the laptop in the caravan, the sweat pouring down my body. Hastily throwing on some clothes, we go up into the woods to discuss his estimate – which is for considerably more than I had hoped. Moreover, he has grave doubts about being filmed for TV, because his reputation is at stake and there are so many risks associated with this build. He can't work out from Gilles' drawings how to construct the central mezzanine. How will we find beams that are 7 metres high, for example? How are they to be tied in to the rest of the construction?

His doubts and fears hit me like a mortar shell. I have always looked upon this man as a rock. Ever since he first turned up at our old house, courtesy of his ad in *France Magazine*, to do some work for us and, in the process, become our first English friend and earn our daughter's affectionate appellation, he has seemed capable of anything. Up until now, nothing has ever phased him. By the time he leaves, I want to curl up into a permanent foetal position. *Our Father, who art in heaven, what the hell am I going to do?* I've been counting on him to such an extent that I haven't even approached other chippies. Even if I knew of any, it's getting very late in the day. I can't let the schedule slip; not now that I've signed the TV contract.

I decide to work to take my mind off it. Isn't that what

a Joseph Conrad hero would do? Mark-kind cannot bear too much darkness. Better to compose and despatch more e-mails to prospective sponsors. I take my stuff into the woods, but am driven back to the four-wheeled oven by the tormenting flies, there to perspire the whole morning long in splendid isolation.

The postponed meeting with Tim happens in the afternoon: a summit meeting under the lime tree by their pool. Clutching my folder full of stuff I have gathered together about alternative footings and the like, there is fear in my belly as I wait with trepidation for our mason to retrieve his calculations. In under a fortnight, they'll be *pulling out the trenches* (as the pros say).

Sotto voce, my wife and I discuss our fears like guilty conspirators. We are concerned that our values and principles are being compromised by people who know better than we do. Everyone seems to know better than we do. There's a danger that, unless we take hold of the reins, it won't seem like our project any more. Our feeling of isolation and vulnerability is probably part of the uprooting process that we're still going through. We're like a pair of cuttings waiting to take. Debs no longer has her little network of *helpers*, like Michelle and Nadine, both of whom have daughters of a similar age. We miss the society of our local lake. It's arid and dry here, while the Corrèze still seems like a green and pleasant land.

While we conspire, one of our friends' holidaymakers stops to chat en route for the pool. An American from upstate New York, she tells us with tears in her eyes that they are still suffering the pain of 9/11. Apparently our misdirected rain has been falling almost non-stop in their state.

Despite our mutual concerns, we come away from the meeting feeling lighter and rather more reassured. Following the visit of Monsieur Fromage, I have been seriously toying with the idea of abandoning it all, selling up and going back to the UK. Buy a small cottage in Westmoreland with what's left of the money. Or, at the very least, postpone things while

I gather some more estimates. But then it could drag on for months. The family needs a proper home, not a caravan.

Tim's estimate seems *correct*, which casts the carpenter's in a still more dubious light. Moreover, he has helped to diffuse some of my paranoia about the foundations. It won't be a matter of whole battalions of lorries dumping energy-intensive concrete into our footings, as I have been picturing, because the trenches will be fairly shallow. We are, after all, sitting on a seam of bedrock. I am aware, of course, that he has skirted the whole issue of using rubble, like a seasoned politician, but then no one really knows how you would do it – and I certainly don't feel brave enough nor confident enough to direct the operation. I feel I have given it a decent shot.

Buoyed by a positive meeting, we dance until the wee small hours at Dutch Eric's 40th birthday party. It's an outdoor affair, with the area between their charming farmhouse and the big barn lit by fairy lights. Eric has rigged up an old turntable in the barn and we play some old vinyl records all evening long. Achim, our towering German friend, hammers away in time to the music on his congas. The food is good and the company is as warm as the evening itself. Jan gives her present to Eric – an airline ticket to India for the trip of his dreams – and he is so moved that he bursts into tears.

Debs and I drive back home rejuvenated. Dead to the world, our daughter sleeps slumped against her seat belt in the back of the car. It may be the norm in France, but 2am is far too late for eight-year olds.

*****

Mid August already. The savage searing heat has abated, but it still seems like the Serengeti here. Those bovine shapes on the plain below could even be water buffalo. I am *alone again... naturally.* The girls left at 5.30 am, gone with Tilley's friend Phoebe to The Ocean for a few days' respite in the holiday home of our friends, the kayakers, from Montluçon. It's a converted schoolhouse from an era when primary boys and girls were kept apart. Utterly charming and just a 20-minute cycle ride to the majestic beaches and foaming sea of the Atlantic coast. Ceaseless white-capped breakers and mile after mile of sand so fine that it squeaks underfoot.

I am staying on to feed the animals and supervise the digging of our trenches. After our confirmation that the footings were now pegged out and the diagonals were (apparently) *in* kilter, Tim met up with the Digger Man to mark out the lines with fluorescent paint. I overheard some disturbing snippets of their conversation. It was like that early Hitchcock film, *Blackmail*: single words highlighted at the expense of everything else. *Knife... knife... knife...* Something about concrete cracking because of the heat. I resisted the temptation to chip in. *Ah well, you see, you wouldn't get that with rubble-trench footings*. When Tim talked him through the schedule, I was amused to witness the man's double-take about the walls. *En paille!!??*

Yesterday was the infamous *quinze août* or *Assomption*, the day when Mother Mary was *assumed*. Whatever that entailed, it became the excuse for another public holiday. We took the opportunity to go back to the Corrèze. Lunch with the Squirrells in the old house. While bizarre to be back, it was refreshing to see that Ingrid has put an individual stamp on the place. So at least it now looks like theirs rather than ours. It's good to know that we have sold to someone prepared to invest some time and love. Later we went to the lake to swim in a warm bath. Alf stayed touchingly close to Ron, no doubt sensing his vulnerability post-stroke.

The call comes from the Ocean and I can relax. The girls have arrived. I decide to indulge myself: a *grasse matinée* of reading Richard Russo's latest novel and listening to Kenny Burrell and some of the other musical bargains I should not have snapped up in this summer's sale.

Later, at the local garden centre, I locate the bamboo stakes I'll need for pinning the bales. However, to buy the quantity I require would cost more than the bales themselves. Clearly, some other source is demanded.

On my return, Dishy Tom from the TV programme phones to say that he and the director will be arriving on Sunday evening to film the first cut of the JCB. *Am I excited*, he asks? Excited? I'm bloody terrified. It's the end of the phoney war at last. We will see just how wide the chasm is between theory and practice.

*****

At last. I note the date in my desk diary: 18th August. The Big Day does not, however, get off to a propitious start. Tim comes over, reluctantly, to double-check our measurements and the chasm between theory and practice is soon exposed. He starts by telling me off about the sticks we've used to mark out the house. Apparently, they're not right – though I've not previously had any tuition about the right type of stick to use. I feel like a child exposed to the irrational ire of a parent. To compound matters, our two diagonals don't quite match, with the result that the two widths are slightly out. He says it doesn't really matter at this stage, because the digging out is only approximate. But I'm of the view that it's vital to get this right at the beginning. I'm mystified and disappointed that we seem to have got it wrong – and not a little indignant that it was left to two such incompetents as my wife and me. Surely the builder should be doing this himself.

Despite bets to the contrary, the Digger Man rolls down the track in his mustard yellow van bang on time. Half an hour later, his henchman, Gerard, reverses a lorry down and drives off the *tractopel*: a lumbering monster of a machine on caterpillar tracks with iron claw.

Tom and Sasha have arrived to film the great event and to capture our thoughts. Despite previous assurances that dynamite shouldn't be necessary, I'm still secretly convinced that the iron claw will hit solid bedrock and everything will grind to a halt. Nevertheless, I try to simulate calm for the sake of the camera. Tom prowls about with his toy, complying with Sasha's suggestions for shots and angles. She will be our director for the duration, which is encouraging as she's unpretentious and rather cuddlesome.

Tim is soon convinced, though, that the pair of them are hatching some kind of plot. He bases this on the premise that they have asked him, *Do you think you'll still be friends at the end of this?* A valid question in my view. I'm not sure how I would answer at this point. The cracks are beginning to show. Probably suffering from the realisation of what lies ahead of us, we're both over-sensitive to minor irritations. I'm still licking my wounds after this morning's parental lecture about the flaming sticks. Little things like this have made me begin to wonder whether we are properly friends and whether it's really a good idea to involve friends in this kind of enterprise. What do you do when something goes wrong – as it almost surely will?

(We were certainly still friends at our mutual friend's bash for his 40th birthday last Saturday night. Our mutual friend is French and it was therefore a sit-down event based heavily around food. It was significant the number of people who bought him bottles of wine. I bought him *The Best of the Gladiators,* since I know that he likes reggae. His wife rushed around serving dish after dish to the assembled multitudes and she was probably quite glad of a foreign presence, because Dutch Eric, Tim and I got up at the earliest opportunity to dance. If the French just want to eat, the Brits *just wanna have fun.* The poor woman must have been glad of the break. But come 3 a.m., when I went home to bed and the wonderful sound of rain drumming on the caravan roof, she was serving onion soup to the revellers.)

There is actually no need for dynamite. Progress is remarkably swift… until midday. From 1.30 onwards, I prowl around our deflowered terrain, glancing disbelievingly at my watch. Gerard doesn't return till after three. Ah, these French and their frigging food. How the hell do they compete in such a cutthroat world?

Nevertheless, by day's end the work is done. I wait

until Gerard's departure and then take a couple of measured laps like a sentry with guard dog around the perimeter. It feels good. The big push has started. We'll be hanging out our smalls on the Hindenburg Line by Christmas. I try to envisage our eventual house. The two long sides seem remarkably long and the two short sides remarkably short. Not unlike living in a hospital corridor?

*****

A little R&R in the company of Tom and Sasha after the crucial goings-on of yesterday. We drive across the sun-scorched *causse* to Figeac, there to interview Gilles, the whacky architect.

On home territory, he's on fine form. I watch Sasha nod with desperation as he goes off on some crazy tangent about global warming and the Americans' refusal to ratify the Kyoto treaty. It must be easier to interview a politician. At least they speak a form of English.

I take the opportunity to quiz the beaded-bearded sage about our carpenter's misgivings concerning the mezzanine. As usual, I understand what he says to me in reply, but don't understand what he means. The idea of trying to relay all of it to Monsieur Fromage is farcical. If only I didn't need to pinch pennies. I could hand it all over to Gilles and come back when the house is ready for habitation.

Tom and Sasha drop me off at the caravan and we take our leave of each other for now. Alf has not slipped his long leash, but is there to greet me, his tail gyrating in sheer pleasure. I feed him, walk him and take him over to Tim's for a meeting to discuss costings. This is not something I am looking forward to, because I feel that I have been summoned to be sacked, or something. We sip wine by his manorial pool and the new figures aren't quite as bad as I have been dreading – the cost has gone up, but not by much, largely because of his recalculations for the concrete involved – but this time I feel that it's not so much a parent/child encounter as a Squire/tenant one. *This year, Sampson, I will let you work the east field in addition to the middle one, but I want an extra three bushels of barley brought to my door before the summer sun has shone its last. Understood?*

Back home, I walk across the rocky track that joins our land to our neighbours to take advantage of their invitation to pick some figs. Alf barks suddenly and goes rushing off towards the bottom of their field. Peering into the late evening gloom, I spot three tan-bottomed deer racing off with a yellow dog in hot pursuit. My spirits soar to see such a sight.

I find time for an hour's begging at the computer. Some grand designer in England told me that he saved himself a cool 70 grand thanks to deals struck with sponsors. So far, I haven't managed to score even a tin of paint.

Debs phones just before I'm ready to turn in – to see if she can tempt me out to the Ocean. I hum and I hah, but feel that I am needed on the land. Someone has to be here to do the fruitless worrying.

*****

All is not quiet on the western front. I'm worried about the trenches. As I pace the perimeter of our house-to-be for the umpteenth time, it appears that they aren't deep enough. Though what, to be sure, do I know about it? The Digger Man has promised to drop by and take a look.

I'm also worried about how we will heat the new house. We've had a couple of estimates for a geothermal system that converts the temperature in the ground into calorific energy. The estimates have been very high – around €14,000 – and typically there is now no government assistance available. It takes wealth to be a pioneer in this country.

So I drive over to see the young plumber that Tim has recommended. It's not at all easy to find his converted barn, hidden away as it is in a clearing of the surrounding oak wood. On the phone, he has a soft, lilting accent, so I'm not expecting someone quite so brawny. He seems to like the sound of his musical voice and it's hard to get all my questions voiced, but he appears to know what he's talking about. Only around 40% of geothermal installations work as they are supposed to do here, apparently, largely because of the lack of water due to the prevalent limestone. If cartridge filter systems are indeed only around 30% effective (and only if you change the filters every six months), this suggests that we should buy a salt-based water softener, over which the opinion of health gurus is divided. And *so it goes...* One expense soon leads to another. There's something to be said for cave-dwelling.

Late in the evening, the girls return safe and sound from The Ocean. I've had progress reports relayed to me by mobile phone while Phoebe's mum and I sit outside in the dark, drinking peppermint tea, watching for shooting stars and discussing the quirks of our respective daughters. The returnees bubble and froth about the time they've had. It has been a little lonely without them and I really should have achieved more during their absence. Can one be a writer ***and*** a family man? Some have managed it, of course. Others, like Saul Bellow – who got through wives like cupcakes – clearly haven't. Sometimes it seems like a choice between fame and fortune on one hand and a happy family on the other. I recognise that I'm just not driven or ruthless enough to sacrifice the latter for the former.

The three of us all decide to sleep in the caravan tonight. They're too tired for tents. I tell them the news that our English neighbours have gone back to the UK to supervise the painting of the windows of their British home. During their absence, they have kindly offered us the use of their swimming pool. It will help us get through the last of this terrible tropical heat wave. So far, according my sources, it has claimed the lives of hundreds of old people in Paris, abandoned by their families during the annual exodus.

*****

The Digger Man cometh. He accompanies me on my well-trodden route around the trenches and I voice my concerns. *In my opinion*, he tells me, *they will support a block of flats.*

Word is already out that a straw bale house will be built on this site. Jean-Claude, our strange friend in Corrèze, the ethno-botanist, in whose *ethno-botanique* house some of our belongings are stored, has steered a charming young couple in our direction. They have plans to build a straw bale house of their own a little further south. Huddled together against the shadier side of our caravan, we discuss plans, decry the state of the world and exchange tales of our mutual friend, the Wild Man of Wongo, as he is affectionately known in this family. We marvel how he has forged his unique way of earning a modest living, harvesting grants from any official body willing to pay him to give classes on rare breeds of Limousin apples, or to take groups of people into the woods to learn how to survive on berries and fungi.

Debs has gone in to work. For the first time in ten days or so, she has a few clients. And she has undertaken to make some calls for prospective sponsorship. When she was an actress, she often had to do this kind of thing: to raise money or obtain props for this or that show. September is nearly upon us and we both hope that business picks up soon. She's gone out on a limb, opening for business in a town where she's not yet really known. She wanted to open her *cabinet* in Tulle, convinced that she could manage the twice-daily hour-long drive. I told her she was mad. Fellow therapists have told her that she will be snowed under in Brive. Anxiously we watch 'this space', knowing that if she doesn't make a go of things – and fairly soon – we are going to struggle, since I'm effectively going to be out of action for the whole year.

We took Tilley the Kid to the Corrèze yesterday. It's her last chance to enjoy the summer holidays before she starts at her new school. We met up with Juleitte's parents at the Etang de Laborde, a picturesque little lake near the picturesque town of La Roche Canillac. The Corrèze is its usual fecund self; the trees haven't been as badly affected as they have in the Lot. The familiar, slightly musty quality in the air made me feel very homesick.

While the adults prepared the picnic, Tilley, Juliette

and her older sister went in for a swim. All three wore goggles and looked like some exotic species of frog. Joining us round the table, the girls watched with barely disguised horror and fascination as a middle-aged couple carried their son down to the water's edge and propped him up against a yellow polystyrene tube with his feet dangling in the water. Juliette's mother knows them. Their son is in his mid 20s and he suffers from muscular dystrophy. He is as thin as a death-camp survivor. Apparently due to a lack of oxygen, his skin appears dry, red and angry. The parents' evident love for their suffering child was both pitiful and touching. If nothing else, it reminded me of how fortunate we are, for all that life feels so tough at the moment.

As if to diffuse the emotion, Alf spotted a group of dogs gambolling together in the meadow behind us. He ran towards them, barking confidently. As one, the dogs ran at Alf, barking menacingly. We watched our dog do an immediate U-turn to come running back to the sanctuary of our table, his tail between his legs and an expression of sheepish embarrassment. A moment to treasure that unified friends and strangers alike in collective laughter.

We were chased off by a torrential downpour that arrived with barely a warning cloud. So we finished our meal at our friends' house before leaving our daughter with her best friend. Childless, we dropped in on our old house, where we found the Squirrells enjoying the late afternoon sun under the vine. My jerrybuilt arbour, constructed from lengths of chestnut dragged out of the surrounding woods, snapped during a storm, so I felt guilty sitting there with them, keenly aware of the temporary prop. Change was evident everywhere. They've taken down the fence I built around the pond and it looked a whole lot better. And a friend of theirs has constructed a ramp and handrail for Ron's wheelchair over my precarious steps down to the terrace on which we sat. Ingrid is in the process of turning the apartment we created from bare cellar under the house into her studio.

While Ingrid prepared one of her customary sumptuous

meals, I swept the two chimneys for her and earned for my pains a proper shower – not the cramped plastic dribbling shower in the caravan, but a spacious, tiled affair under a real jet of soft water. A V.I.P. in a five-star international hotel never felt more pampered.

After dinner, Debs and I strolled around the village in the fading light of day, saying hello to the old crowd, stopping to exchange news, putting a positive spin on the experience of being exiles. It all felt so easy, so familiar. While I felt sad to be driving homeward at the end of the day, Debs said she felt relieved. She has broken with the past and can look forward. It will take me longer. But I did observe that some of my happiest memories of the old place are associated with driving away on trips to see friends at the Ocean or in the Alps. Maybe I'm making more progress than I give myself credit for.

*****

Today Tilley has gone to her new school. I watch her walk off wearing a brave face, with her long blonde hair tied back and a brand new pink *Hey! Arnold* briefcase, the cartoon we used to watch together. It's a new school, around seven times the size of her old village primary school. She seems so brave and matter-of-fact, but I wonder what terrors she may be feeling inside. I phone my wife several times and we speculate about how she's getting on. How will she cope with the new canteen, for example, and the customary problems about being a vegetarian?

The day before Juliette's mother came over with her two girls and handed back our daughter into our safekeeping. Tilley and Juliette took themselves off into one of our two tents for a heart to heart about undying friendship, or *coeur d'amitié* as they call it. I felt bad about getting cross with them when it was time for mother and daughters to head back to the Corrèze and they wouldn't emerge from their summit meeting. When they left, Juliette was in floods of tears and Debs and I gave her big cuddles to reassure her that she would always be welcome here. I'd forgotten about how important these kinds of trysts are for girls. Boys just say goodbye and go their own way and that's that. I still feel ashamed to think of the Saturday morning on Royal Avenue in Belfast's crowded city centre when I passed without a sign of acknowledgement an old primary school friend, who had gone to board at Dungannon Royal. Boys believe that they have grown out of all those foolish things. Girls know differently.

While waiting for our daughter's verdict at the end of her first day of a new life, we have our first delivery: a lorry load of gravel, which presumably will serve as hard core and aggregate for concrete. Otherwise, I work on the first article I've written for some time for *Country Smallholder Magazine*, a commission that accidentally put me back in touch with a dear friend from Exeter University. The e-mail response to my standard enquiry message asked, *Are you* **the** *Mark Sampson, who was at Exeter University in the early '70s?* It's nice to think of myself as **the** Mark Sampson, though it hasn't helped me secure any sponsorship deals as yet. My spirit is flagging; I need a *done deal* from some company or other to re-kindle my enthusiasm.

We go together to Martel to wait outside the school gate at the end of the academic afternoon. Our daughter emerges deep in conversation, holding the hand of the very girl whom Debs predicted would be her friend that day earlier in the summer when she took Tilley to look over her new school and meet her new teachers. Sometimes my wife's prescience is positively scary.

I stay on in Martel to meet the carpenter and his mate at the local PMU. I haven't a clue what the letters stand for, but there tends to be one in most settlements of any substance. They're a kind of café/bar cum bookies, where punters come to drink and place their bets and watch trotting and other arcane sports on the big-screen telly. Our local is a smoky, lacklustre affair and the food is rudimentary, to put it kindly. We can at least sit outside, where we drink cold beers and discuss the architect's additional drawings for the mezzanine. Our friend still has serious doubts. I'm a fairly hopeless go-between. The trouble is, Monsieur Fromage's French is meagre and Gilles's English is non-existent. But I dutifully annotate the drawings with questions and concerns, so I can fax them to our chain-smoking architect.

Mike, the chippy's mate, one half of The Carpenters, talks of his childhood in Croydon, where he saw such legendary bands and artists as Booker T. & the MGs, Sam and Dave, Carla Thomas and Otis Redding. The Stax-Volt tour of '64 or whenever it was. He was there; I just listen to a cassette recording. This is definitely someone I want to work on our house.

Late in the evening, inside our mobile inferno, the telephone rings unexpectedly. It's always worrying when the telephone rings late. This time it's the girlfriend of a neighbour from our old village. Her guy has got lockjaw or something obscure. Debs takes over. He can't shut his mouth, so she offers them a slot early the next morning at her *cabinet*. His father has an appalling reputation as the local brigand and the poor guy has been trying to repair the damage with acts of kindness. His family problems must be eating away at him from the inside out.

Outside there are rumbles of thunder and flashes of lightning over the horizon, but no significant rain falls. Debs tells me that the planet Mars is nearer to the earth than it has ever been before. Many of her clients seem to have been adversely affected: sudden relationship problems after years of relative harmony and so forth. I can't pretend to understand it, but all these personal problems, the excessive heat and the cataclysmic fires down south do seem to add up to something more than mere astrological coincidence.

*****

Rain, rain, rain – beautiful rain...

At the bus stop down the road apiece, I wait with my daughter in a humid steamed-up car for the school bus. The *transport scolaire*. We watch an adjacent car with horror and fascination. A mother with a car full of little children. She smokes her cigarette with all the windows shut until she opens one to chuck out her glowing butt. I think of the kids' lungs and of the forest fires raging down south, caused no doubt by some thoughtless smoker's discarded fag. Ah, the glories of humanity.

After seeing her onto the bus, I drive half an hour up river to Biars, where I shop at the local supermarket and then sit in my still steamed-up car, scanning the car park for the likely car of Bob Ze Builder. Christian at the radio has put us in touch. He's a young guy apparently who can turn his hand to most anything – including roofs. Since I've singularly failed to line up anyone for the roof, I'm hoping for a Godsend. However, the beaten-up Peugeot 205 doesn't inspire me with confidence. Bob himself looks like a New Age traveller down on his luck. We shake hands awkwardly and I follow him back to his flat on the wrong side of the railway tracks.

It's a dingy affair. There's a fading Bob Marley poster in the stairwell and the sitting room smacks of a squat. There's an Alsatian-esque mongrel, a pretty girlfriend and a baby asleep in a bedroom. Appropriately, the lyrics of a reggae song go round in my head, *Looks is deceiving, yeah/Don't underrate no man...* I feel ill at ease, sitting on an old car seat, unsure whether to use the second person singular or the polite second person plural. I choose the former because it seems so incongruous to be *vousvoying* someone who clearly doesn't stand on ceremonies, but am conscious of coming over as someone trying too hard to be hip; one of the boys.

I warm to Bob. He has a gentle, diffident manner and he tries hard to impress me with his range of skills. He tells me where I can go to view his handiwork. Moreover, he will have his *carte* in October (although it might be a blood donor card, for all I know and understand), which reassures me, as this will supposedly render him legitimate in the eyes of employment law. I earmark him for the roof and maybe the tiling.

On the way home, I do my good deed for the week by picking up a hitchhiker. I like to think that I'm helping to boost the entente cordiale (so often undermined by acts of crass thoughtlessness by Brits and French alike). The man's car broke down in the Cantal and he's been walking for 20kms. I drop him off at his home in Condat, hoping that he will spread the word that *les anglais* are decent coves.

Back in my *office*, I am buoyed by a reply to one of my sponsorship messages from a company that makes gas boilers. However, it's a French company, so there must be a catch. Perhaps my translation has misled them and they think I'm offering rather more in return than I can. Nevertheless, it's a tonic. I feel more connected with the world outside my caravan.

When Debs gets back from another day of massaging clammy bodies in her clinic, she tells me a tale that underlines the importance of picking up hitchhikers and other random acts of positive PR. A new client told it to her, an Australian woman who has bought an old chateau near our former home with her American husband. In Brive one day, she dropped in to see her manicurist and ask whether by chance she could fit her in at short notice. 'No,' the manicurist said, 'And for you there will never be time.' The client's jaw dropped to hear such unbridled xenophobia.

One has to ask, however, *Are there still people who pay for manicures in this day and age?*

*****

The end of August, as far as I'm concerned, is the end of summer. No matter how lovely September can be, I have always associated it with the return to school and the prospect of an interminable academic year ahead – before the next summer comes around. Much as I love summer, I won't be sorry to see the back of this one. It has put me off heat for life. There have been times inside the caravan when I've had the impression that my brain has been boiling inside my cranium. I hope there's no lasting damage.

September 2003

September is the month when it's all supposed to happen. The phoney war is over and the Luftwaffe's aloft. *Scramble, chaps, scramble!* I go to Leclerc in Souillac to buy beer for the anticipated men and drop a six-pack on my way back to the car. The auspices are not propitious.

Back on site, I find no promised men. Just two pairs of boots and a box of nails in the awning. I could go into Brive and finish painting the walls of my wife's loo, which I started on Sunday instead of going to the memorial service for Mad Sad, our dearly departed old neighbour, or... I decide to spend the day begging on the computer for sponsorship.

As evening starts to fall, with dinner prepared and my daughter doing her homework while we both await the return of our significant other from the *cabinet*, I drizzle used engine oil into the trenches, where the metal reinforcement now lies in readiness for the concrete, in an attempt to dissuade termites from choosing our future home. Guiltily, I attempt to disguise my work with a bit of sand. It would be clear, however, to all but a cretin that I have polluted my environmental credentials. Better perhaps than using toxic chemicals. Certainly better than a colony of active termites.

*****

We got ourselves a con-voy! Today is the day of the concrete lorries. It's a beautiful day for it: dry, but not too hot. Tim arrives with Geordie Mark in tow: the fastest brickie in town and a hard-drinking man with enough metal in his mouth to start a foundry. Just as I'm making tea for them, Dishy Tom and Sasha turn up with camera at the ready to film the preparations. No doubt the men find my form of assistance bothersome. Fussing about the metal work. Despite all my reminders, they have failed to leave the requisite rebar proud of the footings in order to tie in all the metal work to the northern corner of the construction. It's all to do with Faraday's Cage and electro-magnetic force fields. I don't profess to understand it all, but Debs is keen to avoid anything of that nature. If you can't rely on the professionals, do it yourself. I borrow Tim's huge Makita and an 80cm drill-bit, but retro-sinking a length of rebar into bedrock is an unsatisfactory business.

After lunch, the first two giant *toupis* come lumbering down our track and I'm despatched to the bus stop by the main road to look out for lorries #3 and 4. I stand there like a lemon surveying the hill until my quarry rumbles into view, then hop Le Mans-style into the Peugeot and lead them to the dog's meadow.

The first lorry has finished disgorging its contents and is busy washing out its insides, as the second is spewing its load into our future cellar. Tim and Geordie Mark are shin-deep in wellies, raking and levelling the slurry. Miked-up now by Dishy Tom, I am asked to provide some fatuous commentary, while mulling over the implications of what Tim has just told me. The Under-Digger Man, apparently, has dug out the cellar at too steep a pitch, which means that too much concrete is going in – which means at least another lorry-load (and more money). Moreover... he's dug some of the trenches to the middle of the marker posts rather than the outside edge, so they will have to adjust the block-accordingly. I'm not quite sure what this signifies, but the tone of his voice suggests that it's surely my fault.

Moreover, one of the drivers – the fat, grumpy one – manages to reverse his lorry into the telephone pole at the top of the track. It snaps like a matchstick. So all subsequent deliveries involve jumping on board to hold up the wire with a forked stick and pass it over the cab. The same driver managed to demolish an old well at Tim's place. Presumably the employment laws here make it impossible or just too expensive to sack him.

At the end of the day, I have to pick up The Kid and settle her inside the caravan with a snack, report a broken telephone pole, take a barrow load of leftover concrete up the drive to bed in our *Pré du Chien* sign, sort out a cheque for Tim and deal with a long phone call from a company apparently interested in supplying some materials. By the time I've cooked dinner and wetted the concrete to stop the wind cracking it, I am hugely relieved to see my returning wife. How do working mothers manage it?

*****

From bare foundations we've suddenly gone up four rows of concrete blocks thanks to Geordie Mark and Pascal. Our house is beginning to look like… an air-raid shelter.

It's a big day. The first *Kevin Day*. I am surprisingly nervous when he turns up with the full media circus. *Lights, action, sound!* But *yer man* is a real pro, who soon puts everyone at their ease. Conscious of the men at work on the new shelter, I slip into my most bedraggled rags lest I come across as a mere employer. Mr. McCloud and I go on a tour of the perimeter for a natural, unrehearsed chat that goes swimmingly. *Cut! (That's 'One-Take' Sampson, the TV hack.)*

Come the end of the day and we're joined by my industrious wife for a kind of round-table think-tank outside the awning. Even Tim seems happy and relaxed, freed from the responsibility of overseeing his team. I, however, snap wearily at our daughter when she refuses to co-operate for the camera.

By the time the crew has packed up and gone, evening is upon us. We dine late and retire late and it's all a rush the next morning to get our daughter ready for school. From the rear window of the caravan, I watch the girls get into the Berlingo and I can tell by the angle at which I had to park yesterday to avoid all the other cars that disaster is afoot. I try banging on the window, but it's made of plastic and they don't hear me. By the time I have unzipped the awning and waved my arms in warning, it's too late. Debs has reversed the car and caught the electricity box and in the process dented the wing of our once-pristine Citroën and the box is leaning like the Tower of Pisa. She is distressed not only by what she has done to the car, but also because our daughter is sobbing hysterically. What was it that Tim said about green being an unlucky colour for a car? Pah! Stuff and nonsense.

Mr. Media and I meet again at Christophe's farm to talk about the bales. I try to put all thoughts aside of whether our £500 fee for the programme will cover the damage to the Berlingo and for the possible replacement of EDF's electricity box in order to appear bright and breezy while chatting to a man who has just spent a restful night in the best hotel in Martel. *Bastard*! I could do his job. I could stay in hotels. *Oh Chollie... I coulda bin a contender*.

Give him his due, Kevin knows a straw bale when he sees one. There they are in all their glory, stacked up under Christophe's hangar. Kevin and I remove a couple for the camera and toss them about and talk like two experts at the Antiques Road Show. They're good bales: nice and dry, but maybe a little *too* dry and not dense enough to work with easily.

Evening finds me sitting in the cavernous Palais de Justice in Cahors, waiting for a friend's case to be called on an uncommonly uncomfortable wooden bench, witnessing the incomprehensible cross-questioning of some Algerian defendant before a panel of three judges who sit at a podium underneath a wooden cupola. My head begins to throb. Up on the ceiling and clutching their painted scrolls, bearded and bewigged judges of yesteryear look down upon us sinners. Black-cloaked advocates enter and exit by great wooden doors all around the tribunal room like extras in *Alice in Wonderland*. In front of us, a guy with a shaven head sports an Arsenal shirt that bears the name of Thierry Henry. Perhaps it's my headache, but the scar on the back of his pate strongly suggests a lobotomy.

By the time my friend's case is finally called, my head is ready to explode. Every magnified sound resonates and I feel like *Eraserhead*, trapped inside some new inexplicable nightmare dreamed up by David Lynch. Nothing goes as we discussed it on the way down to Cahors, but the panel shows leniency and surprising good sense. Effectively, he's handed a suspended sentence. A good, sensitive and caring man, he has suffered 18 months of torment that have stripped him of all self-confidence and *joie de vivre*. So I am happy for him, but by the time we emerge from the tribunal, it is night and I am in no mood to celebrate. A quick beer, I haggle, and then home.

*****

Last night I somehow managed to sleep through *The French Connection* car chase. It's usually my wife who falls asleep, but she stayed awake on the sofa beside me. We're staying in a friends' house for 48 hours of glorious refuge from the trenches. Our daughter can play with their two daughters, bilingual ex-pats all. They switch from French to English and back again without any discernible signal. It's astonishing to behold and it makes me feel like we made the right decision to come here back in 1995.

Staying here in their lovely house is a salutary reminder of what it's like to be a householder. One day we shall have a comfortable abode like this. Such knowledge gives you the strength to carry on.

It's raining heavily and looking out at the sodden hills beyond on such a grey day reminds me – improbably – of the beautiful North York Moors. *Hark! Is that a pang of homesickness I see before me?*

*****

Rain stopped play. Work, too. It has turned our clay-site into something resembling the Somme. Following Geordie Mark down our track this morning, after seeing my girl onto the minibus at the bus stop, his car skids down the slope and almost ends up in the trenches. We spend the next 20 minutes laying down sand in the steady drizzle to effect a tortuous and mud-splattering reverse back up the slope onto the limestone chippings of our drive. He reckons it's still too wet to continue and promptly buggers off.

Later Geothermal Man arrives. He represents a company that responded quite enthusiastically to one of my begging e-mails. I thought I'd hit pay-dirt at last, but now I'm not so sure. He's a typical sales rep: smart car, dark suit, poncy pointed shoes – which he prudently swaps for a pair of boots in order to wander onto site and take some measurements. It's clear, though, in talking to him that he's here to give us an estimate and the best he can do in terms of sponsorship is to *make an effort*, that strange French phrase that covers a multitude of sins and usually ends in disappointment. He assures me that the rocks in the soil will make no difference to the performance of the underground tubes that effectively pre-heat the water in our planned under-floor heating system. I am not totally convinced. He is talking a shed-load of money and I would need a rock-solid guarantee before committing to his system. His best effort proves predictably rather disappointing. 14 grand or so it would cost. Not what I understand by the noun 'sponsorship'.

So it's deflating news to deliver when the wife gets back that evening. She trades some shocking news. According to a client from our old village of ill repute, my omniscient spouse was right all along: our plants – the robust mallow, for example, which we'd brought with us as a cutting from Sheffield – were indeed poisoned. So whenever I question the wisdom of leaving our house of stone to build this house of straw, I shall think of that spiteful, hateful act and thank my lucky stars that I followed my wife's instincts.

*****

Our British neighbours are back from the U.K. They drop by during supper to assess the progress. Pascal, with his limited English, and Geordie Mark, with his execrable French, seem able enough to work together efficiently. The cellar wall has now reached its maximum height: ten rows of concrete blocks. The budget, however, has already begun its inexorable climb upwards. Tim has talked to me of the need to get the Digger Man back to flatten some more ground on the oak wood-side of the house and lay some more chippings to facilitate future deliveries. More expense.

We talk of the trees. They have been away during the worst of the summer heat, so haven't seen the vegetation in its most pitiful state. A local farmer told me the other day that the trees effectively shut down during prolonged periods of drought and may shed their leaves. The recent rain has revived them and some even seem to have grown some new leaves. It's a miraculous thing, Nature.

Debs 'fesses up about a cracked skimmer lid, which one of Tilley's friends stepped on when we took the girls swimming in their pool last month. She has been haunted by it ever since. The breach of etiquette. She offers them both a free massage some time and they seem absolutely fine about it, but we both suspect that they will never again invite the Sampsons to use their beautiful pool when they are not in residence.

Come 9.30 or so at night, when the washing up has been done in the diminutive sink, there's nothing else for it in the compressed world of our caravan but to go to bed with a book. We try to keep Alfie outside in the awning, but he just groans at the door and we end up letting him in to sleep on what's left of the floor once the beds are pulled down. I've started Don DeLillo's densely packed *Underworld*, but allow myself a read only after the accounts have been reviewed and totted up. The work on the car will come to €1,000 or so, but most of it will be covered by the insurance. I've had a reminder from the *notaire* about an unpaid bill that I'd hoped to get away with. We've just had a bill for the *taxe foncière* to be paid on our two plots of land here. I've had an unwelcome e-mail from Her Majesty's Customs & Excise, which suggests another delay on the project I have been working on, so I won't be able to expect payment just yet. They've started the grape harvest down in the local vineyards. Maybe I should take a few days off site to join in and earn a bit of extra money to cover the shopping. Worrying about it all does at least send me off to sleep.

*****

Sunday morning and Tilley is tired and tearful. She needs a real roof over her head. One forgets the needs of children sometimes. They are supposed to grin and bear it while their parents get on with the business of negotiating the pitfalls of life. *Don't complain. Don't ask questions. Consider yourself lucky.*

The night before, for example, we were invited out to eat with two of my wife's work associates: osteopaths from nearby Vayrac. We shared an aperitif in their barn with a hornet that buzzed around menacingly, so we moved out into the garden and tried to locate our caravan near the pylon on the western horizon. Night fell and Mars, the culpable planet, was clearly visible near the moon. By the time we finally moved inside for our late meal, our daughter was starving. She and I were not really privy to the medical and therapeutic chat and our minds were fixed firmly on food. Once she'd eaten her full, she went to lie down on the sofa with a book and mercifully fell asleep quite rapidly. I found solace in Rodolph's collection of CDs and picked out Terry Callier's *Live at the Jazz Café* as balm in Gilead.

While Debs stays behind to console our daughter and make sure that Harvey and Dexter the cats don't follow me, I take Alf out for his walk. There are hunters in military gear all over the place and I seem to spend my entire time hooking up his lead to rein him in. On the way back, I bump into the guy from up the road, on patrol with shotgun resting on shoulder. I am tempted to ask, *what did you kill, Bungalow Bill?*, but I doubt if he'd get the reference. As we talk, almost certainly at cross-purposes, I find myself transfixed by the sheer horror of his teeth. It's a relief to make my excuses and head home.

In the afternoon I drive over to Curemonte across the valley to help my friend Bret, the computer technician, with the mammoth task of re-pointing the house he and his wife are renting. An *immigré* from the west coast of Canada and a fellow writer by desire, he couldn't take the severe winters any longer. Snow and ice from October to April. *The horror! The horror!* It's clear that he is much more competent than I have ever credited, while I am considerably less so. His work is efficient and precise; mine frankly a mess. Level 2 NVQ would be charitable. Nevertheless, we have a laugh together and it reminds me of working with my brother: singing silly songs and speaking in exaggerated dialects and generally being puerile and daft. So I sound him out about the prospect of working on our new house with me.

On the way home, I try to track down a natural spring I have been told about in order to fill up all the plastic water bottles I have brought with me. The drinking water on our limestone ridge is like liquid chalk and it would be one less expense at the local supermarket. But I fail to locate it.

*****

Suddenly, my sponsorship campaign has had a welcome boost: three fairly definite offers (pending, of course, the counting of chickens). While staring at what might be up for grabs on the computer screen that Bret has lent me for my ailing laptop, two authors talk on the radio about finding fame and fortune via self-publishing. Opportunity *knock-knock-knocking* on Sampson's door?

At the end of the day, another lorry turns up with a delivery of more metal and more concrete blocks – for the platform on which the house will, eventually, sit. All this metal, though. We don't want to spend the rest of our lives here trapped in Farraday's cage. I jot in my to-do notebook,

Remind Geordie Mark about tying in the metal.

Monsieur Fromage still hasn't received the supplementary drawings from our architect. So I phone Gilles to remind him and he tells me that he will be phoning our man that evening. He also gives me some words of advice about the stairs up to the mezzanine level. Something about the angle of ascent depending on the type of insulation we choose to use in the ceiling. I don't understand what he's on about, but jot down another bullet point.

Despite my sudden buoyancy, my partner – my rock in times of trouble – has sunk into a depression. *If the girl's happy, the boy's happy too.* But if she's not, then the boy's seriously worried. A couple of nights back, we stayed with our friends the Jacksons again and spent a delightful evening playing Scrabble, followed by a night in a blissfully comfortable bed. So maybe it's the *caravan effect.* Maybe it's the pressure of having to keep HMS Sampson afloat. She's had a lot of cancellations this week. Someone suggested that all her clients have gone off to pick mushrooms. The sun has shone brightly and edible fungus no doubt is popping up all over (although I certainly haven't found anything edible).

*****

All summer long, our friend Sue has been telling us that things would get better for us from the middle of September once the influence of Mars has started to wane. Not normally one for astral charts and all mumbo jumbo, I am at the moment quite happy to derive comfort from the least likely of sources. The trouble is, Mars is still up there in the sky. Talking to Monsieur Fromage the night before about the wood situation, he told me that he'd got up in the middle of the night with a dodgy tummy. He'd wandered outside and looked up to see Mars shining down upon us all. What's more, the colours kept changing: from red to orange and even to green. (Something to do with the gasses perhaps. From Mars, that is, and not from his bad stomach.)

Any road up... after a mundane day of investigating

heating systems in Brive, I am invigorated by a commission from *Caravan* magazine. And then the wife gets back with news to dispel any depression. Without telling me, she has been focusing her positive thoughts for some time on an outcome that has dared not speak its name. After giving our neighbours their complementary massages that afternoon, they made her an unrepeatable offer. Would we like to use the little Wendy house in which they lodge friends and family while they are back in the U.K.? From October to April. Would we pass over manna from heaven!? We have bought the caravan to lodge us for the duration, but this summer has taught us what a naïve notion that was.

She checks out the premises that evening, while I drive over to see Monsieur Fromage with a whole load of papers and paraphernalia. Gilles, it seems, rather typically faxed him the wrong stuff, but he has sent a photo of a similar mezzanine construction, which clearly illustrates the type of joints necessary. When we report back later that evening, Debs tells me that our billet is not quite as 'teeny' as our neighbours have suggested. Tilley the Kid is ecstatic. There is a television and we have promised to pick up the box of her videos, stored in Jan and Eric's barn.

It's a funny thing. Here I am, a middle-class English child, a product of the stuffy '50s, raised never to ask but to wait until something is offered. Yet, here I am asking almost every day in some way. And *lo!* in many cases we receive. Our friend Jessica told us a story the other night over Scrabble about having to get back to the U.K. from the U.S.A. She had no money, so she contacted Virgin Atlantic and offered them a deal involving the glass products she and her husband make. They gave her the tickets without ever collecting on their part of the deal.

The very next day, the marketing director of a huge industrial conglomerate calls me to talk about the possibility of supplying our roof tiles at a substantial discount. There's a lesson to be learned there.

*****

Bad news follows good as sure as winter follows autumn. It has nothing to do with a brief trip back to the Corrèze with my daughter. We go to see the Squirrells, happily ensconced in our old house, for coffee and cake. I fill up our water bottles at the fountain, clean the chimney for Ingrid and take a shower in our old bathroom. Debs often points out my inability to let go of the past. Clearly I haven't yet let go of our old house.

I take Tilley over to see her old classmates at the little schoolhouse in nearby St. Paul and chat to her teacher while watching her run around in the playground. Afterwards, we pop into the bakery for a chat with Jean-Louis and his mother and a loaf of their finest spongy bread. I once went out on his delivery round and wrote an article about the bread man of St. Paul for *France Magazine*. He has put on weight and gone to seed. He seems to have given up running and cycling and probably all hope of finding a nice woman with whom to make a home and a family. He's a lovely chap, but bakers here are married to their trade. Realistically, what chance does he have to get out there and meet someone? Internet dating? I can't see it.

'Was it nice to see your old friends, poppet?' I ask on the way home.

'It was OK.'

With sudden clarity, I see how I have coloured the seemingly happy scene in the playground with my own nostalgia. Her truth is probably more one of having felt – as an English vegetarian – like a fish out of water throughout her earliest years in this land. She has already made some new friends at Martel and it's possible that this whole outing has been an unwelcome reminder of a chapter of her life that she yearns to put behind her. My God, what have we done? What traumas have we incubated?

The bad news has certainly nothing to do with the party at Bret and Corinne's the night before, where a German friend was playing the congas to accompany a friend of his from Heidelburg on the guitar. While Geordie Mark was knocking-back the beers and working himself into his customary off-duty state of intoxicated belligerence, I was eavesdropping on a fascinating conversation about suppositories. A British expatriate was telling another how much she had come to depend on suppositories for treating her young child's maladies. Now that, I decided, is a sign of integration beyond the call of either duty or common sense.

No, the bad news comes on site. Delivered by Tim, who is becoming a harbinger. At the party, his wife spoke of the stress he is under as a result of this construction. If so, the stress seems to make him act belligerently. Not the cartoon belligerence of Geordie Mark under the influence – *wanna fight?* – but the kind of hit-before-you're-hit belligerence that derives, I'm sure, from insecurity. Rather than sitting down with me and saying, *Look there's a problem and we need to talk about it*, he puffs himself up like Foghorn Leghorn and gives me a load of bluster – which makes me feel worse about the situation, worse about myself (because I recognise that I'm easily bullied) and worse about him (because he comes over as the bully). He always says that he doesn't like doing jobs for friends and I'm starting to understand why.

The bone of contention is the 13cm perimeter *fillet* to accommodate the level of the finished floor. On top of this *fillet*, Monsieur Fromage will fix his *toe-ups* for the first row of bales to lift them clear of floor level and any potential floods from within. So I get a spiel about his generosity and pairing his costs to the bone and how much a mutual acquaintance is charging some American clients for a similar platform, which is designed to soften me up into agreeing a solution that may be easier and cheaper for him, but isn't necessarily ideal for me. It involves me going to a local sawmill and buying some lengths of Douglas Fir to fix to the perimeter of our eventual platform. It means that the house will have a wooden ring beam, which we will have to treat with toxic chemicals to protect it from any kind of rot.

Meanwhile, the builder's merchant has underestimated

the number of concrete blocks required for the *hordis* that will bridge the walls and create our helicopter pad. More money. The estimate that looked reasonable is creeping up in value. His generosity doesn't come cheap. No wonder I'm feeling and probably acting disenchanted. I look at our faithful dog and think, *What's it all about, Alfie?*

*****

My wife has a close encounter of the unpleasant kind this morning in Martel.

She took our daughter in for her musical notation lessons in the magnificent Palais de Raymondie: towering medieval buildings built in the indigenous white limestone, enclosing a cobbled courtyard. The dragon who gives the class has arbitrarily changed the hour from 6.00-7.00 to 7.00-8.00, which means that the kids will probably be starving while they wrestle with their treble clefs. EGBDF: *Every good brat deserves feeding.* The reason for this arbitrary change is that one of the mothers doesn't like driving at night. When Debs points out that the few remaining kids in her class will be tired and hungry, the woman won't have it and accuses my mild-mannered partner of 'aggressing' her. She even brings our daughter into it – *You're not tired, are you Tilley?* – which is surely the quintessence of ignorance. Well, her class will be even smaller next week, because Tilley for one will not be going back. She can stick her semi-quavers up her... *Hush yo mouth!*

As foreigners, we have encountered enough ignorance and rudeness to last a lifetime. Being nice and considerate to others gets you absolutely nowhere. We've had to fight and get nasty just to get heard by some of the intransigent people we've come up against. And yet... and yet... That old intangible quality of life is still a notch or two above anything that you'd find in our homeland. We both still hope to spend the rest of our days in this area.

For example, this very morning I take our dog out for a walk early, while it's still dark. The sky is as clear as a Tibetan temple bell. The Plough is more visible than it ever is at night, because all the myriad supplementary stars – all the extraneous celestial 'noise' – have disappeared to leave only the brightest. When I get to the highest point of our walk and start our descent to the nearby village, the rising sun is turning the eastern horizon as red as a ripe peach. Such beauty *don't come easy*.

The dry weather following the recent rain has hastened progress on site. The concrete beams are spanning the walls now and soon we'll have a flat pad on which to land passing helicopters and set out our old garden table and chairs. During the morning, I encounter an old dumpy white-haired man in blue overalls. He owns the ruined house at the foot of the field here. His grandfather once owned this land and he, the dumpy chap, used to roll down it to amuse himself as a kid. He lives now with his wife near Tulle and knows of our old commune and the mayor's clan. We won't have any problems with neighbours here, he assures me. Minds are a little more open here. In the Creuse, apparently, a father killed his son rather than having him build a house on their land. Strange things happen in that deserted department.

The heat builds up to an unseasonable degree in the afternoon. I try chipping away at our concrete in order to expose some of the ironwork, but it's a fruitless business and I'm beginning to accept that Farraday must have his cage and we'll have to learn to adapt to geopathic stress. The men no doubt think I'm completely mad, but it pisses me off that they have ignored all my requests. Biting the hand that writes the cheques.

So I go out in the car with Alf in the back seat to source some Douglas Fir for the perimeter beam and some sheets of tin with which to fashion some kind of termite shield. My determination to stop those destructive bastards is perhaps turning me dangerously obsessive. They'll be carting me off to the loony bin on the other side of St. Céré before this build is through. Tim has warned me that the guy who runs the sawmill in Seillac is a little *spécial* – that damning French euphemism to suggest a multitude of shortcomings –

but I actually find him accommodating and likeable.

*****

The caravan is beginning to smell of old trainers. I'm hoping that it's our dog and not my *pedal extremities*.

It has been a day of high drama, starring another convoy of cement lorries. *Toupies* 1 and 2 arrive punctually and disgorge their load on the *hordis*. Needless to say, though, complications arise and Tim is tearing his hair out as he rants about the building trade. Poor chap really is under stress. His local builder's merchant has told him that two lorries will suffice. However… they get their sums wrong and a third one is needed. As a result of the delay – and I don't pretend to understand the mechanics of it all – some of the concrete dries up in the long prehensile arm resembling an immense elephant's trunk that swings out over the surface to spew out its grey porridge. The driver spends his designated lunch break clinging to the mechanical trunk and whacking it at various points with a hammer to shift the blockage. His humour is foul. When, at last, the plug is dislodged like a stubborn fishbone, we finish off quite swiftly.

There is just enough concrete to do the job – which makes a mockery of their calculations back at the yard. They've cocked things up a number of times now and I ask Tim why he continues to use them.

'They're all as bad as each other,' he tells me. 'All bloody useless. You can never trust anyone to make deliveries when they say they will. I'd go down and say something, but they'd never admit that they'd made an error. You know how it is. They'd make out it was our fault – the way we assembled the *hordis* or something. I've never known such a… such an ***indifferent*** race.'

It's a great adjective. *Indifferent*. That stereotypical Gallic shrug. Still. '*T'is done*. But I have no way of knowing *if 't'were well done*. You have to trust the pros. As I survey from our caravan window a terrain churned up and criss-crossed by the tyre-tracks of lorries, the smoke from Pascal's bonfire of old cement and lime sacks drifts across our land to complete a scene of devastation reminiscent of Paul Nash's famous painting of a WW1 battlefield.

Later I phone back a producer at the BBC. My friend Trevor, a PR guru, has tried to fix me up with a slot on Radio 5 Live with, among others, Jonathon Porritt of Friends of the Earth fame, to add my twopenny worth to a discussion on environmental issues. I will keep quiet about the burning sacks. I'd given my consent to the conflagration without realising that these sacks are lined with plastic. Of course! Isn't everything? It's all irrelevant, anyway. I'm too late. This particular window of opportunity has now been shut.

*****

The routine already seems relentless: help get the girls ready for work and school, walk the dog by the first light of day, greet the day and greet the workers, get them ready and motivated for the day, help out, make calls, fetch any missing materials, fire off more sponsorship letters, make more calls, help some more, pick up the daughter from the bus stop, wind up the site for the day and review what has been done and what's still to be done, walk the dog again, get changed and get washed, cook dinner, then update the accounts and read some technical stuff that will, I hope, give me just enough knowledge to keep me one step ahead of the game and enable me to carry out my appointed role of site supervisor and clerk of works. When my head hits the pillow, my brain shuts off and I go into a deep sleep until woken either by the need for a pee or the clamour of the alarm.

However... This weekend, the last in September, has been especially rich in terms of human society. On Friday night we dine with Monsieur Fromage and family in the house that he is building. It is a simple affair: Mike, who sold us the caravan, is there sans wife who is visiting their daughters in England. He and our hosts reminisce about the old days in London and we laugh at an old photo of Mr. F. with long hair and droopy moustache, looking for all the world like Gary Brooker of Procol Harum, with Sue at his side in short skirt and probably pink lipstick. We eat lasagne, the staple dish for vegetarians cooked by people who don't really grasp vegetarianism. It's very nice, though, and afterwards we watch Arsenal v Newcastle United on the telly, because our Mr. F., like my dad, is a diehard Gunners fan.

In a better humour after a good night's sleep, our daughter apologises for any brat-ish behaviour towards the tail-end of our soirée. When her mum gets back from her half-day Saturday stint in Brive, we pick up Tilley's Franglais friend, Ione, and drive over to Calès on the other side of the Dordogne to descend very, very carefully the rutted track that drops down to the Moulin de Latreille. It's the first time we've been to visit our friends, Fi and Giles, by daylight. Previously it has been for nocturnal parties and, in the darkness, it has seemed like a very bumpy ride into the heart of the earth. Lit up by fairy lights suspended from the spreading trees in front, the mill at the bottom looks like an illustration in a book of children's fairy tales.

By daylight, we can absorb its setting. This is the valley of the Ouysse, a languid river that flows mainly underground for a mere 45 kilometres to join the Dordogne at nearby Lacave. Spanning part of the river, between the right bank and a tiny island around which the mill-race is diverted, the mill looks out on a meadow broad enough to accommodate some kind of music festival. It's all locked in by the steep wooded slope we have just negotiated and the cliff face on the opposite side. It would make a perfect hide-out for outlaws. Squint and you can almost see the dust kicked up by a group of horsemen zig-zagging down through the brush on the opposite bank.

We find Fi outside playing table tennis with a friend who's over from Guildford. Our friend is slight and ethereal, with shoulder-length blonde hair, a cadaverous face, sparkling eyes and an impish grin. Giles calls her *Bubble* and it's perfect for someone who seems so light on her feet that she might, at any time, drift off skywards. She married someone with whom she bought this abandoned, extraordinary dwelling, but he proved unreliable and generally unsuitable. After the inevitable split, she stayed on here and met Giles, her good-looking good-time party-boy, who looks and sounds like a relative of Mick Jagger. Together they've been renovating the place, little bit by little bit according to circumstances and cash flow, and spurred on by a dream of one day running courses and *chambres d'hôte* down here in Dingly Dell. Winter is on its way and winter brings the cold – and it can be uncommonly cold inside the stone walls of their mill. But today the sun is shining and it's a golden autumnal day and all is smiles.

We meet Giles's godmother, a florist from Carcassonne, who has lived in France for 30 years or so. And we meet Dickie, the handyman, who has been staying with them while helping Giles with a pair of elegant tiled bathrooms destined for paying guests. Underneath the arbour that the pair of them built, overlooking the leisurely river, we drink wine and eat salads, while Tilley plays with her friend and Alf runs around with their two dogs. I discover that Fi's friend Nicky shares my birthday. Bizarrely, it transpires that she knows my brother. Nearly 20 years ago, she shared a house just outside Guildford and she has, apparently, been nurturing a soft spot for him ever since. She has a young daughter and in many ways she would be perfect for him. If only...

As the sun starts to go down over the yardarm, prematurely in their valley at this time of year, Nicky and Dickie go off to build a fire in the meadow for the evening's barbeque. I sound out Giles about hiring Dickie once work is suspended here. He's exactly the kind of person I need to have around for sound advice and skilled help. If only...

*****

Stark reality takes the form on Sunday morning of a brimming slop jar under our caravan loo. I've never had to clean out latrines in a Japanese P.O.W. camp, but emptying this is pretty damn wretched and why I still prefer, largely, to disappear into the woods with a wad of loo paper.

Reality also takes the form of a hideously long to-do list for the week. Our friend Helen has written back to tell me that the enquiry letter for my book proposal is excellent, but what it really needs now is a detailed synopsis and a couple of sample chapters in case the letter hooks a potential publisher. When in God's name am I going to find the time for all that?

Our friend Jan comes over with her dog, Nadia, and the girls take both hounds out for a long walk while I get on with my admin in the caravan. A guy from along the crest drops by to introduce himself and wish me luck with all this. He owns the beautiful house that dates back to the 13th century, half way between here and the bus stop. He tells me about how rich is the alluvial soil in the plain below. The farmers from Martel used to lead their cows down there to graze by means of one of my wife's favourite dog-walking tracks. Soon and for much of the winter, he adds, it will all be be covered in mist until about 11.00 in the morning.

Winter schminter. In another few short days I will be 49 years old. In a little more than the time we have spent in France so far, I will be sniffing 60. It makes you think. And shudder.

October 2003

Standing on our new heliport, waiting for the men to arrive, I survey the familiar plain below. Sure enough, it's covered in a thick blanket of early morning mist. Apparently, this is the time of year to see it at it's breathtaking best. The small private chateau opposite, tucked up among the trees, peers across the great white lake of cotton wool from the edge of the rocky outcrop where supposedly the Romans suppressed the last of the Galls' stubborn resistance. Gazing out at this scene, I feel like the modern equivalent of that frock-coated gentleman with a stick, staring across at a Gothic-ally sublime landscape of mountain peaks swaddled by clouds, in the famous painting by Caspar David Friedrich. Or Wandering Siegfried, who has lost his bearings, with everything that is safe and familiar lying somewhere swaddled in mist.

My head must have been lost in a mist yesterday when the Under-Digger Man finally turned up – after a couple of frustrating non-appearances – to pull out the drainage trenches and the channel that will take the electricity and telephone lines into the house. I had a meal to prepare and I let him get on with it. I figured that he would, of course, remove the earth that he excavated, so didn't want to annoy him by stating the obvious. But before I knew it, he'd driven off and left all the earth to form impassable levees by each of the trenches. Just to put the old tin lid on it, we had a downpour in the night, so my first task of the day is to shovel heavy claggy clay into our wheelbarrow and cart it off somewhere out of harm's way. Once again, I have discovered that if you don't supervise even the most rudimentary task, you're liable to be disappointed.

By the afternoon, though, the sun is out and it's unnaturally hot for the season. I have a rather frustrating call with someone at Holkham Hall in Norfolk. I can understand why French suppliers may not be interested in my unrepeatable offer of publicity, because the programme won't be aired on their prime-time telly, but when it's just a few tins of paint. What's the problem? Where's the risk? Perhaps they can't be bothered with the paper work. However, they haven't said no. I may still be able to sway them. Linseed oil paint would like nice on our external beams and reputedly it lasts 15 years or so without the need for a touch-up.

I drive over to Curemonte to pick up Bret and head for the hills on the other side of the valley. Our mutual friends, Lee and Claire, have moved over from the U.K. to work Claire's family's farm here organically. Apparently, they have some bamboo to spare. Unlimited rods with which to pin together our bales. We find Lee in their typically Corrézian farmhouse, busy turning a gloomy lounge into something light and white and clean. Lee, I discover, has also studied English & American Studies (at Lancaster) and has lived in two of my old stamping grounds, Bath and Brighton. And here we are, graduates both with degrees in something fairly impractical, trying in our different ways to make a living in the same little corner of a big foreign country. *A small world, my masters.*

He takes us to a nearby pond on the back of his tractor. There I spy big beautiful branches of bamboo with a rich olive-green lustre. Masses of it and all free. *Ptui!* I can spit on the garden centre's euro per metre and grind it into the dust of capitalist exploitation. We work all afternoon, Bret wielding an axe while I cut the rods with secateurs and bundle them into faggots, which we transport back to Lee and Claire's barn for storage until I can get back up here with a saw to cut it all up into metre lengths and take it back to our site.

After dinner al fresco on our helipad, my diligent wife goes to Brive for a talk on aromatherapy at the Université Populaire. I read *Harry Potter* to our daughter while Alf barks at anything that moves in the woods. Later, the sky starts to flicker and Debs gets back, earlier than expected, just before the electric storm breaks. Two people turned up for her talk, so it was abandoned. She is down, but far from out.

All night long the rain hammers down on the plastic roof of our caravan.

*****

The weather is probably too hot for the season and storms have delivered torrential rain for two nights running. At least it hasn't rained in the daytime, but trying to shift the last of the levees this morning, I'm about ready to weep. Digging sodden clay with a spade coated with a crust of sodden clay, wearing boots with soles of sodden clay that feel like Elton John's platforms in the 'Pinball Wizard' sequence of *Tommy*, seems akin to breaking rocks in a chain gang.

And while on the subject of such exercises in futility, I return from Brive with a boot load of tin sheets, which will constitute my theoretical termite barriers. We had to fold them to get them in the car and I can't unfold the crease. It could be another expensive mistake. After storing them down below in the *cave*, I wonder how on earth I am going to turn theory into practice.

Meanwhile, back in Brive, Debs has been plagued by calls from men enquiring about a good time ever since her details appeared in the Yellow Pages. Clearly, the category *massage* requires elaboration.

Later, just before I have to go out to pick up our daughter at the bus stop, the phone rings. Thinking the fruity voice at the other end of the phone is our friend Pierre-Jean's, I reply in kind with a protracted seductive *helllllo*? But it's actually the marketing director of one of the biggest corporations in France, who is ringing me up to lay out the terms of their sponsorship. I am so flummoxed that I completely miss the size of the discount they are offering us. Fortunately, he will send me an e-mail to confirm our conversation.

In the evening, we all go to an Italian restaurant in Brive to partake in Pierre-Jean's 50th birthday celebrations. We meet a car coming in the opposite direction down a one-way street. The driver looks as shocked as I feel. The fault is mine. I'm driving under the influence of accumulated stress.

We have a lovely meal in the company of a group of friends from the Corrèze. Pierre-Jean seems to like his presents, though he never gives much away: a beautifully illustrated book of Algerian poetry translated into French and a double CD of jazz singer Anita O'Day's early big band numbers. I'm not sure whether he knows who she is even after I try to describe her legendary appearance in *Jazz On A Summer's Day*, singing a deconstructed version of 'Sweet Georgia Brown' dressed in elbow-length black gloves and a picture hat that would have graced the royal enclosure at Ascot.

*****

It's my birthday and I'll cry if I want to.

49 years young. One more year until I doff my cap to acknowledge my half-century. Realistically speaking, I've used up over half of my credit now and the years are racing by faster than ever.

At 7.45, Tilley the Kid is so excited that she can barely contain herself. Her present is a framed watercolour painting she's done of a stripy cat playing a jazz piano. It's enough to move a grown man to tears. Unfortunately, I spoil the occasion because I cannot hide my concern about my wife's present. A surprise weekend in Paris. Bless her, she's wonderful at surprise presents for her husband. My own attempts to reciprocate generally fall short of the mark. I once took her to Robin Hood's Bay for a weekend when we lived in Sheffield. Unfortunately, I couldn't drive at the time, so we got in her car and I directed her, which kind of dissipated the impact.

Her largesse at a time when the budget is shrinking rapidly and I am unable to contribute income concerns me. My attempt yesterday to fashion my first termite shield ended with the knowledge that I have squandered 100 euros on those sheets of tin. The result looked so naff that I'm more inclined now to take our chances with the natural world. So, although I don't dance a jig and Debs is understandably disappointed and my attempts to reassure her that I *am* delighted, honest, probably make things worse, I resign myself to a nice relaxing weekend in the capital, where I won't have to fret about how we are going to survive the next phase of the build.

Until then, birthday or not, work must go on. The wood I have ordered from the sawmill turns up at midday, a most extraordinary time for a French delivery, but then maybe the two hefty men are en route for a restaurant in the vicinity. They unload the huge pink sections of Douglas Fir and I pay them the 300 or so euros I have withdrawn from the bank. Monsieur Fromage warned me the other day that banks here have the right to ask what you are intending to do with the cash. I always thought it was simple nosiness. Large quantities of cash probably suggest food for the black economy – though Bret has a theory that it is indirectly encouraged. Because so many people have to contravene the law in order to avoid the swingeing taxes and charges, it keeps you compliant. There's too much to hide and too much to lose to go rebelling against the government. He may well have a point.

Fortuitously, I have a visitor during the afternoon. I am

wondering how on earth I am going to shift these lengths of wood, which aren't far off whole trees, when a guy called Mick and his wife turn up. We met them and another couple in our village in the Corrèze when they were lost and looking for their holiday house nearby. We were out in our courtyard stacking wood for the winter in the barn and we heard these obvious northerners trying to make themselves understood to the dumpy woman next door. So we took them in hand and they ended up coming to the house to watch the funeral of Lady Di – or *La Dee-Dee*, as the French called her.

And here, like some benign *deus ex machina*, is this big burly man to help me carry these trees to our heliport for treatment. They are staying somewhere near Cahors and had our change of address via e-mail and thought they'd come up for a nose around the north of the department. His business has gone belly-up in the U.K., a victim of all the red tape that is apparently smothering initiative back home, and he now sells replacement windows on a commission basis. Nevertheless, he is on form and, more to the point, in good shape. Afterwards, the three of us take Alfred Lord Sampson out for a walk before they head back.

Running a little late, I try to get the wood treated with a garden sprayer and some noxious chemical before I have to pick up our daughter. I take these jobs seriously and kit myself out in goggles, mask and gloves. In my haste, however, I attempt to open up the sprayer to eradicate a jam when it's under full pressure. Suddenly, like a whale's spout, the toxic spray shoots out and straight through the little slits in my plastic goggles and into my right eye. I rush to the caravan and bathe it copiously with cold water and a drop of lavender, but I'm in a state of shock and alarm – wondering whether I will lose my sight and what I'm going to do without proper health insurance. My eye is still red and angry looking when I fetch *oor kid*, who is also now worried that I might be blinded for life.

*****

Monsieur Fromage has raised the whole insidious issue of

insurance. I know that Tim has not organised indemnity
insurance for his part of the build. We discussed that together
and I agreed that it seemed like a waste of time and money.
The punter has to prove malpractice on the part of the artisan
to get any kind of payout. Mr. F. points out that, if something
did go wrong, my option would be to sue him. Besides, if by
any horrible stretch of the imagination we wanted to sell up
within the ten years covered by the indemnity insurance,
would we manage to find someone willing to buy it without
the customary guarantees? As yet, he hasn't been able to
organise insurance for the carpentry. Apparently, the
insurance companies consider *ossatures en bois*, or wooden
frameworks, too high a risk (for some curious reason).
Clearly, they are geared up for the bog-standard house in
concrete blocks, the *parpaing pavillons* that you see dotted
all over the place.

At least my eye is better. It smarts from time to time
and occasionally I'm aware of (or imagine) a dull ache, but I
can see clearly now after applying my wife's compresses of
cold camomile tea. Living precariously, as I do, without
health insurance, is tempered by having an in-house
therapist. So far our daughter has been precisely once to the
doctor since we moved here – for measles. In any case, I take
extra special care today with the second coat of noxious
chemicals. I feel guilty as charged using it, but the eco-
alternative cost about five times as much and cost, alas, must
come into the equation.

There's a letter for me today in our green metal box at
the top of our track. It's from an old friend in the Civil
Surface. We were training officers together at one time and
we used to laugh a lot. But all the humour's gone out of it
now, apparently. Her senior managers are *just a load of arse-
licking twats*. It's all targets, targets, targets linked to stats
and more stats. The Daily Grind. When Debs went off to
work this morning, she told me that even her life sometimes
seems to be just an endless merry-go-round of getting up,
going out, working all day, coming back and going back to

bed. It's the treadmill that we try in vain to escape all our working lives. And yet, when we don't have any work, we become introverted and depressed and start pining once more for the treadmill. As a Scouse friend of mine says, *It's a life!*

Later in the day, I pick up the Berlingo at last from the *carosserie*. It's gleaming with its new spray-painted panel and it's a pleasure to drive it back to the bus stop, just in time to pick up Tilley from the minibus.

We parents have a mini-crisis on our hands. Apart from the problems of being a vegetarian in a land of carnivores, apart from hiding the unvaccinated truth from the medical mafia, we've never had any kind of social issues to sort out. She's low maintenance: a good girl who just gets on with her work. Just recently, though, the Martel Marbles have threatened the entente cordiale. Having won a whole heap of them in the playground, she accidentally-on-purpose forgets to take them in with her when she goes off to school each morning. Presumably, she doesn't want to risk losing them in another contest. Maybe it's something to do with being an only child, but she doesn't like to share with friends. We're concerned that she'll get herself a reputation and risk losing more than a bowl of marbles.

*****

I love Paris in the springtime, I love Paris in the fall...

There is method in my wife's madness. It *is* good to get away. Once removed from the scene of the crime, there's no alternative but to get on and enjoy the moment for all it's worth.

We wake up in a hotel room that is effectively our own apartment, which we're sharing with the mystery friends from London whose identity I tried to guess the evening before on the train. There was a delay at Vierzon, so we arrived late and joined them at the tail-end of their meal in a Vietnamese restaurant. By then I had guessed that it would be Helen and Gary from Crystal Palace. *Time Out* recommended the restaurant. I would highly recommend the very attractive waitress in a strapless dress held up miraculously by her shoulders alone.

The hotel room overlooks the northern suburbs of the city, spread out below the mound on which Montmartre grew up. The hotel is a quirky artistic establishment that Helen has used before. I doubt that it's quite as reasonable as my wife maintains, however – for all its slightly dilapidated charm. It's run by a friendly if somewhat officious woman who qualifies for the French adjective *spécial*. Gary thinks she's a dragon. This morning, for example, she flushes us out of our room for a breakfast of coffee and croissants. We fail to see what the urgency is, but humour her nonetheless. In learning of our current situation, she gives me advice about building sites. 'Take your time with the construction. Let the *maître d'oeuvre* oversee everything to ensure that it's done correctly, otherwise the artisans will do it any old way.' Hmmm.

I am already only too aware that the artisans want to do it any old way, and because of the abbreviated schedule, I've had to accept certain things – reluctantly – which may not have been done correctly. Just before leaving for Paris, in between making arrangements for cat feeding, driving Alf over to Thompson & Thompson's for his weekend away and dealing with a confusing call from a Director of Marketing, I had to come to some kind of agreement with Tim and his team about this raised wooden perimeter 'fillet'. I let them persuade me that the best way of fixing them to the helipad was to set them on a bed of concrete. What can you do? I can't lay down the law and make them do it my way, because I haven't a clue what I'm doing. And I can't risk them going off to get on with another job while I do my research, because they may not come back when I need them. Sometimes you just have to grin and bear it in the face of your misgivings.

We agreed that we would lay the bed of concrete on the Monday when I got back from Paris. This meant a frantic few hours with Bret up at Lee and Claire's barn, cutting sufficient bamboo stakes of 50 cm length to set in the concrete on Monday morning for pinning the first row of bales. Bret must have been a time-and-motion man in another life. He thinks things through and works out the most economical way to do the job. So we got it done in just over an hour – to my satisfaction. Perhaps I should sack everyone else and hand everything over to my man from Canada.

Here, briefly, in Paris, I can forget all about my the equations and calculations that tormented me on the train. *If a bale wall is configured as per the diagram given, indicate at which points to plant the bamboo stakes needed to support the wall...* While we wait for Helen and Gary to get ready after breakfast, Debs and I go out for a stroll around Montmartre. I don't know Paris well, but I've always liked what I've seen. I'm a Londoner by birth, but I feel safer in Paris than I do in London: less aggression in the air, less potential for that sudden terrifying eruption of violence. We find a little park just by the Sacré Coeur where – just to confound my sense of comfort – we are hassled by a Senegalese man. Before we know it, he is winding some threads around Deborah's finger and giving us some spiel about *English people, very nice peoples.* Then the milk of human kindness turns sour when he presents us with two plaited wristbands that we don't want and demands 5 euros each for them! I offer him 2 euros for the two and end up paying four just to get him off our backs. We feel suckered and totally ashamed of ourselves. Johnny Country Mouse screwed by Johnny Town Mouse.

After this, it's plain sailing – other than a rendezvous that goes awry in the Musée d'Orsay. Both couples head off to view their favourite artists and epochs and we arrange to meet under the big round window at 4.00pm. It's my second visit to this wonderful museum, but the first *à deux*. I've always loved railway stations and always loved art galleries. The idea of combining the two was sheer genius on some committee's part. This is the same great abandoned cathedral of rusting iron that featured in Orson Welles's version of *The Trial*. Now it is one of the best appointed museums in the world. French art ruled the art world in the 19th and early 20th century and the Musée d'Orsay has got the lot. This time around we can show each other some of our favourites, so I take Debs to show-off the pastels of Odilon Redon and the paintings of *Les Intimistes*, Vuillard and Bonnard. In a place like this, there's never enough time to see everything properly and we waste half a frustrating hour by waiting at the wrong big window. There are two apparently and both couples were waiting in vain at the wrong window.

Later we walk what seems like miles to find a minute vegetarian restaurant recommended in *Time Out*. It's OK and it doesn't break the bank, but it's hardly worth the trek.

The next day, we negotiate with the dragon to leave our bags at the hotel behind the desk until late in the afternoon when we go our separate ways: north to London and south to St. Denis lès Martel. She proves to be remarkably accommodating. So we are able to tour the teeming 'village' that is Montmartre and wander down to a flea market near the Place Pigalle. We resist any temptation to buy clobber that cannot be housed for the moment, but spend our *sous* on delicacies for a picnic that we eat by the open window of our hotel apartment. A quick snooze after our long matutinal march and then back out, this time to explore the Isle de la Cité, where we sample what is reputedly the best (and probably the most expensive) ice creams at an establishment called Bertillon's. Any relations, I wonder, of the Bertillon family that featured in *Français D'Aujourd Hui*, our French textbook at school? Monsieur Bertillon was a customs official at Orly airport and his wife pottered around their suburb on a *mobilette*. Probably wouldn't have had the vision to open an ice-cream emporium in such an up-market location.

And then it's back to the hotel for one last time to pick up our bags, say our goodbyes and head off for our respective stations. The Gare d'Austerlitz is our gateway to the south. A snack supper of slightly undercooked chips kind of sums up the anti-climax we feel about going home to face reality again.

*****

Water, water everywhere…

Someone didn't turn the tap off in the caravan properly and we get back in the early hours of Monday morning to find Harvey waiting for us outside the awning, the pump running in the plastic tank in the wardrobe and a wet floor. Dog-tired, we climb into bed. Thanks to our faux Siamese, Harvey – the little sod – we have a very disturbed night and discover in the morning that he has pissed on the carpet. Presumably an act of defiance to underline that we should never presume to leave him again.

While I'm in the thick of more concrete, Debs learns that our cat-feeder and child-harbourer, Jessica, caught her finger in the car door and had to be taken to hospital with a broken finger. *That's what you get for all your trouble; I'll never help a friend again…* We both feel wracked by guilt.

The morning of frantic activity ends in a downpour of biblical proportions, which threatens to negate all our hard work. We have laid the beams on their bed of concrete and I have implanted my stakes in the concrete we pour into the void between the outer and inner ring-beams after some hasty last-minute re-calculations to locate all the door openings, but the rain has surely washed away all the primer just laid on the east terrace and filled the helipad with water up to the level of the new raised perimeter, so it looks like some weird kind of municipal swimming pool.

I'm in a foul mood at the end of the day, our land transformed into a Passchendaele battlefield. Harvey manages to trip me up on the steps down from our 'front door' as I carry out a bowl full of water to empty outside the awning. All over me, my clothes, my shoes, the awning floor. The curses I direct at her cat bring Tilley to tears. Which makes me feel doubly great.

*****

The men are rendering the walls of the *cave*. Because of the gallons of water trapped inside our swimming pool, there must be a leak somewhere in the roof: there is a patch to which the render won't cling. It keeps falling off, leaving a blister in the light-grey plaster. They keep at it, though, applying more and more in the hope that sheer willpower will make it stick.

I have an article to write for *Caravan* magazine. It's difficult to see how I can get it done with all the constant interruptions: tea for the men, walks for the dog, snacks for the daughter; calls to the plumber and electrician to get them to lay their plastic sheaths for the eventual wiring and pipe-work before the return of the Digger Man to fill in the trenches; calculations to see whether there's any profit to realise on a few PEPs and ISAs as a budgetary fall-back. Then a man from the propane gas company turns up to discuss where the tank should be buried and how much gas we will need to order.

With the pressure building up in my head to at least four or five bars, inevitably I choose to prevaricate. I drive to Bretenoux to record my first radio show in half an age down in the basement of the abandoned hotel on the roundabout. Probably because it's my first show in an eternity, I make all kinds of basic errors and it takes half as long again as it should do. At one point, I glimpse a reflection of a face at the door and jump out of my skin. It's only Christian and not an axe-murderer. He hasn't slept apparently and it shows. He's in the middle of a domestic war with the peculiar woman who runs this peculiar outfit. We go for a tea and I hear all about it. I agree to write him an *attestation* to say that his dismissal from his post at the radio is unjustified. It seems that the charges of incompetence have been trumped up as a pretext to get rid of him. The real reason is that both of them are ready to kill the other. When we leave, he flashes me a V for victory sign. I return the gesture, convinced now that it's time to jump this particular groggy ship. Radio Caroline, pop-pickers, it is not.

*****

All the bamboo stakes are now capped with plastic cups. No

one now will come running, trip and impale themselves. There is even a gentle, restful tintinnabulation when agitated by a breeze – until I decide to secure them with gaffer tape to prevent a friskier wind from carrying them off.

The walls and the *cave* are now covered with two coats of light-grey render. In the end I agreed that we should drain the pool by knocking a hole in the *hordis*. It looks unsightly, but it means that the stubborn patch that wouldn't take any render is now also safely covered.

The men are working on the eastern terrace to create a nice smooth level finish. The roof will eventually extend out over it, so we'll be able to set up an outdoor table and chairs for breakfasts on balmy days. It's all still rather hard to visualise at this point, but there is discernible progress.

The Carpenters will start work in earnest next week, so there's a lot to organise: Paul the electrician is always obliging and helpful; Francis the plumber is hard to pin down; the Digger Man is a rogue cipher in the equation. Ensuring that the various components of the jigsaw will slot together is the most wearisome task of all.

At least there has been a bit of *social living* of late. The rugby world cup has kicked off and I have been round to watch one of England's preliminary matches with Tim, a rugby fanatic in his spare time. This evening, we go *en famille* to our neighbours' house for drinks. It's an opportunity to discuss arrangements for their *petite maison* and to meet their neighbours on the other side. Before they arrive, I get my first glimpse of our home-to-be for the next six weeks. It's small, but perfectly formed. A corridor leads from the front door to the living area with a little kitchen and shower room to one side and stairs up to a mezzanine area where our daughter will sleep. Our bedroom is a kind of ante-room off the corridor. It's going to be a little cold, but it knocks the caravan into a cocked hat. I am no longer dreading the onset of winter.

Our neighbours' neighbours prove a rum pair: a long lean interior decorator with a strong masculine physique and her 'live-in companion', an extraordinary woman in a double-breasted blazer, hair parted to one side like the woman with the monocle in the famous painting by Otto Dix, and a rich fruity Caribbean accent that goes with her slightly dusky skin tone. She drinks like a fish and laughs like a fisherman's wife. The interior decorator used to be married to a German man, who owned and renovated our neighbours' beautiful house. She sold it to them when he committed suicide under slightly mysterious circumstances. But not before she and her German husband had built the house in the next field down.

Both feeling a little like actors in some strange social comedy written perhaps by Alan Ayckbourn after one too many brandies in the theatre bar at Scarborough, Debs and I cast knowing glances at each other throughout the evening. The English couple's command of French is tenuous and the surrealism of the occasion is accentuated by the stilted conversation. Derek, at least, speaks correctly in a v-e-r-y deliberate manner that sounds like a 45rpm single played at $33^1/_3$ befitting, I suppose, a retired chartered accountant. The raucous belly laughs of the woman with the German Expressionist haircut suggest that it's all quite hilarious.

When the guests go off for dinner at a restaurant run by a Croatian ex-pat in the hills above Meyssac, we are asked for our considered opinion whether the *companions* are gay or not. It speaks volumes for their charming middle-English naivety that there should be any doubt whatsoever.

*****

How the *friggin' 'eck* did anyone survive the trenches? The weather has turned filthy, which means that every sortie from the caravan to our boggy terrain becomes a hazardous obstacle course. We do at least have the luxury of being able to change footwear before getting back into the caravan. In my grandfather's time, they kept their sodden boots on for days at a stretch. No wonder he developed trench-foot.

It could well be the weather, but I am irritable with both wife and daughter. Tilley is indignant because I have threatened Harvey, her beloved cat, with expulsion now that we have discovered the ingrate has been peeing regularly inside the caravan. *It's the awning for you, my son!* Alf, for his part, is indignant because we expect him to sleep in his basket in the aforesaid awning. He doesn't understand that it is not Punishment Park; it's just that there is no room for a big damp dog in our cramped quarters. However, we relent when we find him shivering in his basket – even though we suspect him of turning it on for our benefit.

The girls are preoccupied with the task of cooking up a whole pile of flapjacks for the *journée des gouts* at Tilley's school. Tomorrow is the last day before the Toussaint holidays, already, and the headmistress has arranged this international taste-in. No doubt the French children will be bringing little chunks of baguette spread with *fois gras*. Our daughter will be representing the United Kingdom with a tin full of brittle flapjacks.

While they are attempting this improbable feat, I address a query from the company that **had** offered us (or so I thought) a gas boiler in return for the TV publicity. A typical French trait this: reneging on a promise. Right at the beginning of her career here as a backstreet aromatherapist, my wife received a phone call from a big cheese in the Ministry of Health to give her the go-ahead to practise, legally. When she asked for written confirmation, he laughed and said that the word of a fellow Corrézian would surely be good enough. *Ha ha ha.* Sure enough, when she directed some local functionary to phone laughing boy at the Ministry, he denied all knowledge of the conversation. So I have little inclination to address all the prerequisites demanded by the marketing manager of the boiler company. Instead, I substitute the customary sign-off of assuring him, dear Monsieur, of my distinguished salutations blah-blah-blah, with an approximate translation of the Australian invitation to go and bite yer bum.

Francis the plumber turns up at the very end of the afternoon to attempt to drill through the foundations with his massive drill bit. While he pants and struggles, I fail miserably to locate the posts for the rear balcony. Either my calculations are cock-eyed or, as Geordie Mark has suggested, our architect's measurements are *pants, man.* Finally, Francis has to thread the plastic piping through the conduit that was set, somewhat askew, into the cellar floor. It means that the principal stop cock will be a foot or so proud of the walls rather than flush and neat. Earlier, Paul laid the trunking for the electrics and, in the process, straightened our leaning EDF box. You would never know that the 'incident' had happened all those weeks ago. Win some, lose some.

Today, too, I confront Tim about an apparent discrepancy in the final bill. We fail to see eye-to-eye about some planks that he wants to take away from site to use on his next *chantier*. It's good that phase one of the build is effectively over. With hindsight, the elixir of wisdom, I realise that there were elements I could have done myself, and I'm still not entirely happy about the wooden ring-beam, which could prove to be our house's Achilles' heel. But now at least we can get back to the business of being friends again.

*****

After all the incessant and often torrential rain, the sudden cold comes as a shock. All night long I wriggle about in my sleeping bag, trying to get warm and claim some space from Harvey and Alfie. My wife has resorted to socks and hat. When we wake up, we both urge the other to get out of bed and put the gas fire on. It's a quirky kind of ignition and I've never discovered the knack. This time is no exception.

'Oh come here; I'll do it,' Debs says – but she, too, fails to light it.

When I brave the cold outside, I find that both the standpipe and the gas bottle have frozen. It's extraordinary how the temperature can take such sudden nose-dives. As we drive past the pharmacy in Martel in our Berlingo, en route for Pierre-Jean's weekend party at the Atlantic coast, the temperature on the electronic sign says -5°C.

We take the route that follows the Dordogne this time: past Sarlat and thence to Bergerac and beyond. It's long and tedious, but our daughter is, as always, as good as gold. She moans occasionally at Alf, who sits with his head resting on her legs, but likes the attention really. Even when she was a two-year old, travelling with us on an epic journey across the Massif Central to the Alps, she spent much of the journey contentedly learning to tie her shoelaces.

After some surprisingly plain sailing along the *Rocade* around Bordeaux, we make good time down the incredibly straight roads that cut through the pine forests of the Médoc. Were it not for the occasional sudden 45-degree turn for no apparent reason, you could drive them almost with your eyes closed. We arrive around the same time as all the other guests at our friends' summer house – a converted school house in a settlement just a few kilometres from the vast expanse of sand that extends virtually unbroken from the Bay of Arcachon to the Spanish frontier. One o'clock. *C'est l'heure des aperitifs!*

It's Part 2 of Pierre-Jean's 50th birthday celebrations. His lovely wife, Isa, Tilley's first teacher and Deborah's first French client, is surrounded by her sisters, who look noticeably older in the few short years since their brief stay in our old *gîte*. Since the last get-together in the schoolhouse, the girls have got bustier and the boys taller and spottier. Pierre-Jean's lovely daughter, Fanny, arrives after the festivities have started and there's a touching moment of devoted father and child reunion.

It's lovely – and an honour – to be part of the festivities. As always, though, we're conscious of being the only non-French individuals and certainly the only vegetarians. Inevitably, we have to pick the bits of bacon out of the polenta dish and have to shun the sheep roasting on a spit. When we sit down to eat (outside as planned), I find myself in the company of people I haven't met before: an older man in a black polo-neck and an adoring younger girlfriend, who seems to hang on his every word of wit and wisdom.

'*C'est un bon vin, ça,*' I suggest for want of anything to say.

'*C'est toujours un bon vin ici,*' comes the witty riposte.

'Ha ha ha,' titters the girlfriend.

I fail to warm to them.

After lunch, while most of the men sleep or watch the rugby world cup in the sitting room that was once a classroom full of obedient little girls, I join the women folk in an exodus on foot, by bicycle or in cars to the beach. In the summer, you'd have to pick your way around all the people pegged out in sun. But this is the time of year to enjoy it at its best. Just about the last of the autumn sun, a blue cloudy sky painted by an Impressionist, a slight chill in the breeze, an endless expanse of soft squeaky sand and the distant waves, crashing against the shore. Alf does his excitable running around in ever decreasing circles, trying to drum up a game of chase. Debs and I do our best, but the alcohol over lunch has sapped our energy.

Then it's back to the schoolhouse to help prepare the old canteen for the evening's party, fortified by another round of aperitifs. The party, as always, centres on another *bouffe*. It takes so long that everyone's too tired and too full to dance with any enthusiasm. I have brought with me some Tamla from the Motor City, but it's never going to oust all those toe-tapping faves from the Golden Age of French Pop. So we resign ourselves to sitting back and watching people dance that watered-down version of the jitterbug, *Le Rock*, as I think it's called, whose steps are probably outlined in Chapter 7 of *How To Be French*. The gulf between it and the kind of lindy-hopping you see in *Hellzapoppin'*, say, suggests all you need to know about the national inability to let go and *partaaaay*. Fun here seems synonymous with dining tables.

*****

We slip away after lunch on Sunday, when everyone is either watching the England v Samoa rugby match or getting ready for the next round of drinks and nibbles. I watch the group of friends together with affection and a certain amount of envy. We have no real sense of continuity here, no links with our pasts. My best friend, for instance, my sole surviving contact with schooldays in Belfast, lives on the other side of the Atlantic Ocean. We are on the outside looking in: belonging without ever quite belonging.

Never mind! We have the untrammelled joy of moving our affairs from the caravan to the *petite maison* of our dearly departed neighbours. Ready to drive off to the caravan for the next load of boxes, there is a cry of distress. My enthusiastic wife, who sometimes doesn't think clearly about these matters, has fired up every appliance in the place to warm up the house – and blown the main fuse. With no handy torch, I have to hunt around in the dark for the means of reuniting us with the national grid.

We sleep cosily and blissfully together that night. Tilley the Kid is happy with her space on the mezzanine and can sleep with Harvey on her bed and Alfred Lord Sampson on the floor in his basket.

At breakfast, we can eat at a proper table again and, what's more, enjoy the view from the big window. The realisation that we will certainly be happy here removes a huge weight from the family's shoulders.

In the afternoon, I drive over to Christophe and Chantal's, the farmer and his radiant wife. Bret is there and, helped or hindered by their two boys according to your outlook on small boys, we go up to one of their fields to gather walnuts. This is my way of thanking them for storing our bales for the winter in their hangar. While Christophe drives up and down on a kind of tractor-vacuum sucking up walnuts, the rest of us rootle for stragglers through the fallen leaves, now blackened by the rain and frost. It's hard going on the back, but fun to work with a group of people. And it's the kind of work that is of no consequence if you get it wrong.

When I get back, I find Debs entertaining Tom and

Sasha from the programme in our new sitting room. In reversing up our drive, Dishy Tom has managed to drive the hire-car into the ditch. Having had to sit on the bonnet to stop it tipping over the edge till they got out, my eternally good-humoured wife has spent her afternoon off sorting out its extrication. Never a dull moment here.

They're here to shoot me at work, alone, on site, painting the contentious perimeter beams with bitumen. It's going to take longer than I bargained for, because the surface of the wood is not smooth. So I am not in the best of humour when I have to answer Sasha's prompts to camera. She has noticed that I don't sound too enthusiastic when describing developments. I'm not sure whether this is what they want. Perhaps they're hoping that I am more of a gung-ho idealist, oblivious to the pitfalls and soon to be hoist by his own petard. Then there would be plenty of scope for Kevin's pensive ruminations. *I wonder whether he has thought this through...* Sasha asks me if there's any aspect of the build so far that I've really enjoyed and I can't think of a single thing. The move into our neighbours' Wendy house?

After a speedy lunch, I take our daughter over to play with her friend Phoebe, then drive Tom and Sasha over to a distant field to continue the gathering of nuts. While Alf races around with Christophe and Chantal's shaggy dog, Poof, Bret and I get wired for sound so they can eavesdrop on our ludicrous conversation. Working with Bret increasingly resembles the work I've done with my brother in the past – in terms of the nonsense talked. I'm not sure, though, that it will make the most riveting of viewing.

That evening, Tom and Sasha take the three of us out to dinner at a local restaurant. Considering the alarm we customarily cause as a result of our vegetarian ways, they manage something rather good: dolmades and an interesting salad to start with, followed by a mild vegetable curry with saffron rice, lentils and satay sauce, and rounded off with a not-too-sweet chocolate gateau. We are, however, the only ones there. It's a little like being exhibits at the zoo. The veggies' tea party.

During this innocuous meal, I somehow manage to lose a filling: a great chunk of mercury or whatever toxic metal the butcher of Belfast put in my mouth. It has probably been slowly poisoning me for years. Maybe it's the root cause of my jaundiced outlook on life. So what next? Should I get them all taken out? My resident health advisor thinks that I might risk opening Pandora's box. It's probably like trying to remove old glass fibre insulation from a roof space. Better to let it lie.

*****

The crew has gone for now. They will return. It's Halloween – and the end of a significant day at the coalface. I've been seeing toy skeletons dangling from trees by the roadside, which is a little macabre. All of our daughter's friends seem to be doing something to mark this Americanised festival. She's not and is a little peeved. To be fair, she's had a pretty good Toussaint holiday and spent last night with her friends, Rosie and Ione, while their parents went with us to see the latest Ken Loach film at the cinema in Vayrac. We had virtually the whole auditorium to ourselves. *Dirty Pretty Things* is a good enough film. It's worthy in the Ken Loach sense of the word: a drama about the trade in organs. Human rather than Hammond C5s.

There won't be any fireworks *chez nous*, but we can watch the explosions in the plain from our new sitting room window for free. They serve to mark the day's special delivery. While checking the letterbox at the top of our drive at the end of my early-morning walk with the hound, to my shock I see a lorry unloading roof trusses at the bottom. The amiable driver must have been working – in the rain – since 7a.m. There is another shipment on the way, apparently, so I call Monsieur Fromage from the caravan.

Together, we cover up the trusses with a tarp. Then an enormous Volvo truck turns up with all our Douglas fir. While I am directing it down the drive, an Australian woman – of all nationalities! – parks her car at the side of the road and starts asking me about the house. She seems quite oblivious to the fact that I am helping to guide this monster truck and clear the road for passers-by like her. Still, she's friendly enough and I keep a pleasant tongue.

The driver unloads the wood with great dexterity and care, but speeds up as the midday scoff beckons. By now, Monsieur Fromage and I are soaked to the skin, but we have worked well and got all the wood covered up without any trace of tension between us. Maybe the next phase will be a little easier and not such a battle of wits. If today is anything to go by, however, there will be plenty of weather to contend with.

November 2003

It's the tail-end of Toussaint and my daughter's 9th birthday. I fret sometimes that we aren't apparently getting on too well of late. Little things like crumpled discarded clothes irritate me and I seem to spend too much of our time together getting cross with her. No doubt I appear distant and distracted. She probably won't appreciate at such a tender age why her papa is so irritable. I have to remind myself that she's only nine and already better behaved and more thoughtful than most children of that age. What's more, she has one very big thing in the credit column: she is incredibly loving and affectionate. Sometimes, it gets like *The Waltons* here:

'Good night, dad.'

'Good night, sweetheart.'

''Night, mummy.'
'Goodnight, Tilley.'
'I love you both.'
'We love you, too.'
'I love you very, very much.'
'We, too, you.'
'See you in the morning.'
'Yes you will; sleep well.'

We are throwing a birthday party for her. Just a little party. The little house will resound with the patter of tiny feet. It'll be Tilley with three close expatriate friends. As a prelude, our friend Michelle from the Corrèze – who used to work in the *Bibliobus*, the mobile library that would travel around the outlying villages to bring a little culture into isolated lives – turns up out of the blue with her daughter. She and our daughter are friends, but their daughter is a year or so older, even though she's several years shorter, and it's one of those uneven friendships that aren't always very healthy. Tilley tends to do what her friends tell her to do, because she feels that she has to earn their friendship and we both worry that she might be prey to bullies.

I leave them to it and slip off to Thompson & Thompson to watch the second half of a gripping rugby match between Ireland and Australia, which the '*Strylians*, God damn them, win by a sole point. From there I drive over to Bretenoux to record what will probably be my final radio show in a cold and deserted basement, before going off for a follow-up meeting with Bob Ze Builder on the wrong side of the railway tracks. I venture up the dingy stairwell to their apartment on the first floor. I tap on a door that's ajar and venture inside. Bob's New Age-ish wife or girlfriend is smoking a joint with a young man who seems devoid of redeeming characteristics. Waiting with them for Bob's return, I feel ludicrously out of place once again. As a student I might have made a better fist of it. Presumably, they feel every bit as awkward as I do: Bob's middle-aged middle-class client, trying to exude a suitable cool.

So it's a relief when Bob arrives with his pineapple of tight dreadlocks on top of his shaven head. No doubt there's a dog-on-a-rope somewhere, too. When we go through the architect's drawings, he gives me the reassuring impression that he knows what he's on about. He confirms his availability. Finding an available roofer is like stumbling on a Land Rover dealership in the desert. I leave them to smoke in peace with an address of a house where I can go to look at Bob's handiwork before making my decision.

The birthday party passes happily, thanks in part to my wife's cake and obvious affinity with children. Knowing that children's entertainment is not my strongest point, she is happy for me to sidle off to the caravan to make a couple of CD compilations for a friend's imminent birthday. When I return, the mothers are there to collect their offspring. Our friend Baladou Sue, who seems to have assumed the role of unofficial godmother, turns up with a thoughtful present for Tilley: two tickets to see *Cinderella On Ice* in Brive.

However, there are tears before bedtime. Our daughter is worried that her friends may not have enjoyed themselves quite as much as she hoped. *Good grief!* I know that both of her parents have their little insecurities, but this is ludicrous. Debs feels – and I reckon she's right – that we haven't fullly credited just how difficult the whole French experience has been for her. You think, *Oh she'll be all right; children are so adaptable.* But she's a deeply sensitive child and who knows what an ordeal it might have been. The Toussaint break ends tomorrow and as usual she doesn't want to go back to school. Further tears flow when I test her on her times-tables and she is found wanting.

It's also back to work for Debs. Worryingly, our bread-winner is feeling rotten. Being self-employed, of course, she can't just take a *sicky*, like privileged functionaries do.

And it's back to the site for him...

*****

After a day of low clammy cloud and impending rain, during which I finished painting bitumen on the perimeter beams, I wake to see the rising sun suspended like a big red balloon above a veil of mist. Before trooping over to the site, I waste almost an hour taking the paraffin heater to bits and putting it all back again – only to discover that the problem is *elementary, my dear Watson*. The reason it wasn't working properly was that the fuel canister I filled up and placed inside it belonged to the spare fire. *Stupid boy...*

I work all day until five with The Carpenters. The wooden ring beam means that they will not be working from an absolutely flat concrete platform, which means in turn that they will need to measure and cut each individual post (rather than simply cutting them all the same length). That's not too grave, but they have also discovered that the house is slightly longer and slightly wider than the architectural drawings. Geordie Mark must have taken the measurements to the outside of the concrete blocks instead of allowing for an additional two centimetres of render. This means that we will lose two precious centimetres of roof eaves – and with them a bit more precious protection from the elements for our bales. Nevertheless, we work in fine good humour until the two men go off in their respective white vans and I drive to Vayrac for an appointment at the osteopath's.

I come away feeling more supple, but he has told me that he has never seen anyone quite so skinny, that I need to carry out some regular exercises in order to learn how to separate my head from my body and that my painful left shoulder does not know how to relax. We have work to do together.

Debs gets back at nine from her protracted day at the clinic, hungry and knackered. She eats the meal I have prepared for her, cleans her teeth and goes straight to bed, still suffering from this heavy cold or whatever she's caught. What is that cliché about France and its quality of life?

*****

We are looking after Baladou Sue's dog, Peluché: a ragamuffin stray she picked up in Spain. He's no higher than a sausage dog and looks a little like the pyjama holder I used to have as a kid – with attitude. His fur is the same sandy colour as our Alf's and the pair of them are very funny together: Little and Large. Little clearly looks up to Large, who's a good boy, the apple of his owners' eyes. But Little also encourages Large to be naughty and do things that he wouldn't normally even contemplate. They play constantly, which means that it's not much harder to look after two than it is to look after one – only I have to check up on them from time to time in case Peluché has persuaded Alf to take a walk and rustle up some mischief.

Sue is off on her travels again, so we have also promised to keep an eye on her house the other side of Martel and even use it for a night or two if we feel the need to stretch out. Tilley has proposed that she give the other ticket for *Cinderella on Ice* to Sue – about which Sue was clearly touched.

Debs seems to think that Alfred Lord Sampson is looking younger and happier again. I wasn't particularly aware of him being miserable, but I guess he takes his cue from us: if we're happier now, the dog's happier, too. Peluché is probably helping to keep him younger and more active at the moment. He must be worn out by the attentions of the short-arsed ragbag.

While The Carpenters go about their reassuringly careful preparations, I go into Brive to do a bit of financial juggling between accounts. On the way out to Lapeyre on the edge of town to check on delivery dates for the windows and *porte-fenêtres*, the sun streams through the windscreen and I am positively hot. I wonder whether it will stream through the windows of our new house from November to February. Mike reckons we should take down a few of the tallest trees in the wood, because they are taking away so much light. By my calculations, at this time of year the sun is disappearing over the yardarm at around 2.30/3.00pm. During the lead-up to the shortest day, it'll be earlier and earlier, so there won't be much passive solar heat on offer. My head is constantly full of such data at present.

In the afternoon, I have a long chat about boilers on the phone with the marketing manager of Wiessmann UK. He tells me about *air-source heat pumps*, which are big in Germany apparently. They extract whatever ambient warmth they can from the air and convert it into energy by way of a refrigerant. Something like that. It would be ideal for the kind of low temperature under-floor heating system that we are planning. No, he couldn't give us one, but could sell us one at cost. That would be around £2,000, but I need to bear in mind how the price of propane gas keeps on rising.

After this, I try to pick up from the previous day and do some more writing. Get on a roll. Alas, it never seems to work like that. Yesterday I felt good. It flowed like water from a spring. Today it's blood from a stone. Like all things creative, I guess: swings and roundabouts, peaks and troughs. One day, self-confidence courses through your veins, the next day it's gone. What a profession I chose for myself when I announced as a young boy that I wanted to be a *bookmaker*. A turf accountant would surely have been an easier career. Debs once worked clandestinely in a bookie's. We could have opened a small family affair together.

In the evening, I spread out my papers on the round table we use for meals and try to reconcile moneys leaving our accounts with moneys spent. There seems to be a discrepancy of around 1,000 euros. It's worrying, of course, but logically speaking it can't have gone far. Can it?

In bed that night we have a little moan about our daughter's attitude – won't shut doors, won't turn off lights, won't pick things up, won't help out, nothing seems to work – but put these current difficulties down to a phase. *It's just a phase she's going through; she'll grow out of it.* She sure is a stubborn child, though. She refuses to wear a hat to school, because no one else does. Debs reminds me of the day when she refused to wear some pink pyjamas that weren't her cup of tea. Her mother didn't stand for such nonsense on that occasion. So Tilley strode out onto the front balcony, took her pyjamas off and proceeded to wee on them. What can you do? At my school, we had prefects to make us wear our caps. We'd promptly remove them outside the gates. There's a joke isn't there? Something about: *What's the definition of a hat, coat and scarf? Answer, things that your parents make you wear when they're feeling cold.*

*****

Amazing how suddenly the weather can change. This weekend was a case in point. On Saturday it was so balmy that I was playing tennis with a friend on our neighbours' private tennis court. In order to have it built when they moved here, the land had to be blasted with dynamite and the resulting chunks of limestone were laid to create the rocky path over which I now walk to our site most days. While we play, Alfie runs about barking at unseen hunting dogs. Peluché tries to follow suit, bustling around on his short legs and yapping bombastically.

We're well enough matched, but my friend is having coaching. Me, I've always relied on a degree of natural talent that used to get me through sports like tennis, football, rugby and cricket. I've never been coached to correct my faults. My hapless serve, for example. All the coaching in the world, however, couldn't cure my head. 5-2 up in the first set of the St. Polycarps' Tennis Club junior championship in Finaghy, Belfast, I lost in straight sets. I am The Choker. As soon as I sniff victory, I go to pieces.

It was still a balmy day when I went to Thompson & Thompson's to watch France annihilate Ireland and England stutter to victory against a surprisingly good Wales. So we will play France in the semi-final. If they beat us and go on to win the world cup, those pesky Frenchies will be insufferable.

Then the rain came without warning. It rained all day Sunday. So the ground is a quagmire once again. Sod the lawmaker decrees that our delivery turns up first thing. The Carpenters and I – with the help of the driver, a sweet gentle-giant of a guy who reminds me of Randy Quaid, the actor – have to move umpteen French windows down the treacherous muddy slope and all the way along the back of the embryonic house to the *cave*, without falling on our backsides. The double doors, which are 1.40m wide, are the heaviest and the worst. We slip and slide, but never quite lose our footing and succeed in a task that could have been devised for *Jeux Sans Frontiers* (with Stuart Hall and Eddie Waring laughing their socks off to see us struggle with our burden). I tip the man as generously as I am able. Mike reckons that, had this occurred in the UK, the driver would have sat tight in his cab and asked: *How are you going to move those, then?* Maybe, maybe not. I reckon you find the occasional diamond back home, too.

After lunch, I learn to use a cement mixer (*putty, putty*) for the first time. It's a new string to my bow, a new 'Special Skill' to add to my c.v. I pour the concrete I mix up in the machine into the holes I have dug so laboriously in the ground behind the house to create the pads on which the posts for the rear balcony will sit. We work until 5.45 in conditions that are thoroughly miserable, but the appalling XX-rated banter of the two old friends keeps me entertained until the bitter end.

*****

Nobody works on Armistice Day. Appropriately, all is quiet bar the spasmodic reports of the hunters' rifles. With each one, I picture some poor animal buckling at the knees as it slumps to the ground.

When I go over to see Jan and Eric to interview them over dinner for an article I'm writing, Dutch Eric tells me that the hunters frequently come onto their land. Once, their dogs chased their cat Snowflake up a tree and Jan threw stones at them in an attempt to see them off. They reckon that the hunters are as unpopular with the French as they are with the ex-pats. I'm a little sceptical, because it sometimes seems that the entire indigenous population indulges in the so-called sport.

Jan and Eric are sheltering our entire video collection, because they've got the space and because they appreciate a good film. They're working their way through some of the cinematic treasures I recorded so diligently during our years in Sheffield, probably with half a mind to our self-imposed cultural exile in France. I'd like nothing more than to discuss what they've watched so far, but there's an article to prepare for *Country Smallholding* magazine. As friends re-united by e-mail, the editor and I have been exchanging news ever since my initial enquiry. We lived in the same house in Topsham one summer and used to play epic tennis matches together. The only shame of such a serendipitous reunion is that her magazine pays so little.

Dutch Eric and English Jan are a fascinating couple. They met on the Indonesian island of Flores while on Voluntary Service Overseas. Jan used to ride around the island on a motorbike as a mobile radiographer, travelling from one outlying hospital to another. Grateful patients would pay her sometimes with, say, a sack of avocados. Eric, with a degree in tropical agriculture, was helping the islanders with things like animal husbandry. They met and got married in the U.K. when their tenures ran out. Eric wanted to be a farmer and they went looking for land in Spain and Portugal before settling on France. So here they are in the Corrèze, happy together and working their fingers to the bone, growing organic produce for market.

We all agree that, of the many inexplicable public holidays here in France, Armistice Day is one of the most worthwhile. We should never forget what it represents. And yet we do, constantly. All over the world, humanity is at war. Their island of Flores was paradise when they were there. Paradise is already being lost – not through armed conflict, but another kind of war: the fight for natural resources. The loggers are razing the forests and it's too depressing to talk about. We give thanks for our situation here. Not exactly paradise – far too much red tape for that – but not too far removed. For the moment.

*****

It's raining, it's pouring; the two dogs are running about and getting horribly wet and smelly. I'm waiting for my men. They have started erecting the wooden framework – which is exciting, because you can start to visualise what the house might look like.

My left ear is blocked up; my stress level must be high. In times of extreme duress, my toes twitch, my eyelids flutter and my ear closes up. When it happened that last time, half way through a particularly difficult project in the Channel Islands, working with an upper-class twit whose supreme self-confidence, we discovered after he had wreaked unspeakable chaos, masked the vacuum inside his skull, my ear remained blocked for several weeks. One fine morning in the Corrèze, I was cycling to Espagnac to pick up our daughter and bring her back home on the child's seat behind my saddle, when suddenly... *whoosh*! I felt this rush of air and with it a babble of noise. All the natural sounds of the wood through which I was cycling seemed amplified. As if a celestial deity had turned the volume up to '11'.

It's partly all the decisions I'm being asked to make. Do I not like decisions? Yesterday, for example, Mike pointed out that all my carefully designed window levels were too high. So now I have to decide where to site them so that they are harmonious with all the French windows *and* in line with a row of bales. One can reduce the width and thickness of a straw bale, but can one reduce the height? Looking at the wooden framework and all the detailing of the bales it will require makes me wonder whether this could turn into the most complicated straw house in history.

You have to be so careful in this role of project manager. Take your eye off the ball for a moment and you're in danger of losing the plot. Monsieur Fromage, for example, has put in an extra post. Thoughtfully, he has sited it a metre from the corner to allow for the width of a complete bale. However, re-reading my textbook has filled me with alarm. Apparently, there should be a good bale-and-a-half between the corner post and one framing a door or a window to allow for a proper running bond to be created. Otherwise, the corner verticals can bow outwards.

Meanwhile, I still need to find some time for writing, cooking, dog-walking, child-rearing and calls. Today, for example, I try to liaise between Bob Ze Builder, the TV programme and the marketing manager of the roof-tile manufacturer, who wants the programme to include some kind of staged technical demonstration to show off the Roman tiles the architect has picked for the roof. It must be getting to me. Mike handed me three of my CDs that I'd been listening to while digging holes for the balcony posts. *Someone left the discs out in the rain.* The covers are damp and wrinkled, but the CDs themselves seem to have survived the ordeal. What's happening to me?

It's a big, comforting bonus that my wife's work is going so well. She's averaging 14 or 15 clients per week now, having made her initial goal of ten some time ago. New people are phoning up as word gets out about the results she achieves. *Deborah Sampson, curing the untouchables since...* What gratifies her most these days is that doctors and psychiatrists – representatives of the very medical mafia that tried initially to close her down – are starting to refer their most perplexing clients to her last chance saloon.

As for me, there's an e-mail from a contact of mine back home asking me if I can come over for a meeting... tomorrow. I phone him to plead child-sitting duties. The upshot is that he offers me a role on an interesting project that involves a bit of video scripting – but not a trip to the U.K.

At the end of the day, I have my second appointment with the osteopath. He tells me that there's a connection between my ear, my shoulder and my teeth. It could all stem from my teeth being out of alignment. Perhaps I could knock off a film script in which the principal protagonist is a man troubled by teeth that are out of alignment. **He** *was a man whose teeth were misaligned.* **She** *was his long-suffering wife who tried to convince him to go to the dentist. And then, one day...*

Feeling roughly three stone lighter on my feet after some gentle manipulation of my bones, I drive off to pick up the daughter from school and take her and the two dogs over to Baladou Sue's temporarily empty house for a change of scenery. I find her sheltering from the pouring rain with some colleagues under a lean-to. She's happy to see me and doesn't disown me, even though I insist on seeing the headmistress to ask for our tin back. The flapjacks had been appreciated, I am told, but there's no sign of the tin.

Peluché is excited to be home and scampers about the familiar little bungalow, maybe in search of his mistress. All is unfamiliar to me, however. I can't seem to work the gas, so I can't cook the curries I'd planned. I rustle up an egg-fried rice on the one electric ring that I manage to operate and make a savoury flan in the oven for our visitors next day. The evening wears on and on and there's still no sign of Debs. Our daughter probably picks up on my anxiety, because I find her curled up on her bed, sobbing pitifully. As I cuddle her and try to reassure her, we hear the engine of the Peugeot ticking outside. Instantaneously, her tears are staunched.

*****

Weekends bring a little respite. The Carpenters don't work and there's nothing very practical that I can do without them. So, after walking the dogs along the old railway line that used to run from Martel to Souillac, I can watch the first of the two semi-finals of the rugby World Cup on Sue's telly before de-camping to the *petite maison* for the visit of Fi and Giles. They are spending the night with Thompson & Thompson, where we will all gather on Sunday for the showdown between France and England.

Fi is particularly taken with the tennis court. Giles explains proudly that she is a qualified tennis coach, who once beat Annabelle Croft in a competition. This ex-pat community is full of dark horses. If you pooled all our separate strengths and resources, we could put together a self-sufficient principality along the lines of Liechtenstein or

San Marino.

There is high drama before Sunday's match. Dutch Eric turns up on his bike – to be bitten badly by Fi and Giles's dog, Caspar. Apparently, the dog has this thing about bicyclists. Eric never makes a fuss about anything, but he is clearly in distress and Sophie, being a sacrificial woman, drives him to the doctor's. By the time they get back, the English team has almost finished its demolition of the fancied French in the wind and the rain of Sidney. We will play the host nation in the final. The Australians, curse 'em again, beat the All Blacks, who have been by far the most exciting and creative team on view throughout the competition. There is no natural justice.

That evening I sit at our round table, deep in thought about this new work project. I'm always scared before each new one begins that this time, this time I just won't be able to hack it. Unmasked as a fraud.

While the three animals sleep happily around me, Debs reads *Harry Potter And the Deadly Something-Or-Others* to our daughter upstairs. When our child drifts off to sleep, we take my laptop to bed and watch *The Shipping News* on DVD. It's nicely low-key and faithful to the book and offers fascinating glimpses of Newfoundland. I remember looking down on its bleak landscape once from an airplane en route for New York and seeing icebergs adrift in the sea. Not my kind of island.

*****

It's cold in the caravan. Legs swaddled in a sleeping bag, I work on the video script with fingers sheathed in filigree fake silk gloves from Decathlon. When my wife used to travel around Europe with a theatrical troupe, using drama to teach English to the likes of Scandinavian and Italian schoolchildren, she would wrap up in a sleeping bag with holes cut for her feet when it was her turn to drive their old draughty bakery van. My *office* suggests what winter in a caravan might have been like had we not been granted our house.

I've had to develop a way of holding the phone with my left hand to my right ear in order to scribble notes with my right hand. The osteopath would not approve. A whole body, let alone teeth, out of alignment. Nothing good can come of it. I've had the marketing manager of the roof-tile manufacturer on the blower to complain that he can't to get hold of Bob Ze Builder. I bluff about a family holiday for fear that he might pull out of the deal. Meanwhile I have a week in which to finish the script before the return of the TV crew.

At least I can leave the men to get on with things. The Carpenters are now two men and a youth. Oliver, Monsieur Fromage's nephew, is labouring for them for the next fortnight. Thanks to some beautiful crisp weather, recent progress has been swift. The framework plus temporary bracing is finished and the first roof trusses are in position. I can see that these eaves are going to afford limited protection from the elements, but it's too late to stop now.

When I trudge back past the tennis court at the end of each day, I can now turn to see a proper embryonic house rise above the undergrowth that separates us from our neighbours.

As evening closes in, Tilley and I entertain Baladou Sue at the round table with tales of the dogs. She's back in France now and here to claim her pooch. I'll miss the little mutt. He and Alf are such firm friends now that they wear each other out and thereby reduce my allocated dog-walking time.

*****

On a windy Saturday morning, I make my way over to Tim and Gilly's for the rugby World Cup Final. England against the old enemy, Australia.

Throughout the previous afternoon, I was spraying the wood destined for the interior of the house with an indecently expensive 'natural' product. While Mr. F. was in the *cave* with pencil and paper, trying to figure out the complexities of the mezzanine construction, Mike and Oliver were up among the trusses fixing the lateral bracing. Emerging from the caravan in the darkness of early evening, I was suddenly aware of the looming presence of our future home. It's really starting to take on the shape of a house.

When Debs got back from work, she was cock-a-hoop because her business is really starting to take off. She's already approaching a new target she's set herself of 24 clients per week. I'm very proud. Tilley, too, was in a good mood. She and her class went to the *mairie* in Martel to see a film about the human body and then, during the afternoon, the entire primary school de-camped to Souillac for a musical comedy about Christmas. Cripes! Only just over a month to go...

There's a whole crowd of us in Tim and Gilly's sitting room gathered around the wide-screen telly for the final: partisan English ex-pats, local French friends apparently rooting for us (but maybe secretly hoping that the Australians win it, due to our emphatic semi-final victory against *les Bleues*) and an American friend, who's over here from Madison, Wisconsin. We chat quietly about our team, the Green Bay Packers, during the pre-match analysis and, throughout the match itself, I try to help John with the opaque rules of rugby. American Football is a piece of cake in comparison.

The climax to the match is one of the most tense and gripping that I've ever had to endure. We hold on to a precious three-point lead, but then the Australians – as Australians tend to do – land a penalty in the last minute to tie the score. Ten more cruel minutes of extra time to go. Wilkinson slots a penalty to put England back in the lead. They keep it till three minutes from time, when a pained cry reverberates around the room. Another penalty to Australia. The score is level again. Then England drive into Australian territory, win the ball back at the lineout, move it down the centre of the field. Someone ferrets the ball out from a ruck, gets it back to Wilkinson, who takes aim and drops a goal with his wrong foot. Pandemonium erupts. Even John, the

American friend, is delirious. We leap around and embrace each other and yell our heads off like the possessed at a voodoo gathering.

I've done so much yelling, in fact, that I've just about lost my voice by the time it comes to returning with Debs for Tim's annual birthday party. Tilley has gone with Sue to see Cinderella On Ice, have a pizza together afterwards and then stay overnight with her benefactress. It's the fourth or fifth November party we have been to here, ever since that first wonderful occasion when we were welcomed into the fold as outsiders from the Corrèze. We had foolishly believed that we could do without the company of people who understood our own culture and humour. Debs is deep in conversation with Evelyne, whom she met that night. You could imagine Evelyne in a painting by Delacroix, brandishing a *Tricoleur* as she urges a revolutionary crowd over the barricades. Together they're lamenting the fact that time passes so rapidly. Every year we spend a few hours together, but nothing much happens in between and no one knows what to say when we meet up.

Our new German friends, Achim and Martina, have turned up and I spend an interesting half hour or so, chatting in broken English and limited French with Martina. This time is the first time that they have brought some of their furniture from Heidelberg with them. The move is on and she is feeling very positive about the change. Her *head feels a lot more open here* and she wants to do it now rather than in four or five years' time, when it will be harder still.

Achim once co-owned a house with a friend in the Auvergne, so this is his second try at it. Life was hard there, somewhere south of Clermont-Ferrand. The weather would ricochet from warm sunshine to snow in a matter of days and the prevalent mentality was equally tough. But the experience didn't deter him. The house in Heidelberg is on the market and I always get a sense of confirmation that we have done the right thing when I hear other people talking like this.

*****

Around this time of year, one usually starts counting off the days until Christmas. This year, there's nothing further from my mind, although the respite from the daily grind will be most welcome.

Tom, Sasha, Kevin and the whole crew are back in town. As requested, they've all brought newspapers they picked up on the plane, so I can devour countless articles on the World Cup final. Scott, the Australian cameraman, gets a ribbing from the men about the result. Apparently, his cousin is Matt Rogers, who played a notable role in the match.

They are too late to film the summit meeting between Gilles the architect and Monsieur Fromage (who was apparently expecting someone rather younger and without a beaded beard). As Gilles explained the roof structure, Mr. F. had the look of someone dazed and confused. I checked, though, once Gilles had driven off on his scooter, and he did just about understand what the great man was on about. Which was more than you could say for me.

With the first draft of the script finished and sent off for comments, I can concentrate on the filming. It's cold and damp and more rain seems imminent. Kevin puts us through our paces in the morning, when the marketing manager from the roof-tile manufacturer turns up with a young assistant in a suit and pointy shoes, who speaks excellent English with a charming accent. Kevin earns his fee by taking charge of the situation and curtailing what could have been a long, redundant presentation about the benefits of these roof tiles. Despite my fears, Bob turns up – with Christian from the radio. It seems that they have gone into partnership, which may or may not prove to be a good thing.

The rain holds off until Kevin has done his bit and is ready to be whisked away to Toulouse airport to catch a plane to Edinburgh and the next programme on the schedule. I eavesdrop on his spiel to camera in which he suggests that we should cover up everything and start again in the spring. He's a nice guy for a big star, but clearly knows little about real life.

*****

Work demands a trip back to the U.K. I always have a heavy heart when it comes to organising trips back home. Going through all the permutations on the internet, trying to work out a schedule that will get me there without causing my hard-pressed wife undue extra hardship. I opt for a flight from Toulouse to East Midlands, which will involve catching a train that leaves from the little station here at some unearthly hour.

Once this is done, while the men fill the air with their curses, some genuine and others playful, I get on with the business of wintering the caravan: draining all the water from the system, cleaning the inside walls and, gulp, cleaning out the canister underneath the loo.

By the time I've done that, I feel virtuous and fully deserving of my trip at the end of the day to see the osteopath again. He's pleased with progress, but still a little concerned by my ear. He talks about a possible visit to an ear, nose and throat specialist. I'm rather keener to try some Hopi Indian ear candles if I can get hold of some in the U.K. The idea of flying with a blocked ear fills me with dread. You read of ear drums popping under pressure – and that would really put the old tin lid on everything.

December 2003

It's the moon, apparently, that's to blame for all this rain. The south of the country is on orange alert, presumably for flooding. As if I weren't already feeling uneasy enough about my impending journey to the U.K.

It's so wet today that there's no sign of the white vans, but I rustle up Bob Ze Builder and we go to the builder's merchant in St. Céré to order some accessories for the roof. Sometimes I can understand why my daughter doesn't like me to open my mouth in the company of her classmates. It can be so embarrassing to hear stilted French. My own is no great shakes, but I'm positively fluent compared to the type in a South African rugby shirt under his jacket, who keeps roaring *Weh, weh!* in a faux-*Lotois* twang whenever he recognises something that the patient assistant explains. His wife is either red-faced with embarrassment or she drinks too much *vino*. Earnest husband continues to nod desperately like one of those dogs that used to sit at the rear windows of cars. Thank God I'm past that stage now.

On the way home, I can't help but notice the skeleton of the house sitting on the hillside. Jan and Eric came over yesterday for a walk with their dogs and liked what they saw of our future home. From the flood plain of the Tourmente, it looks very grand. Perhaps rather too grand for someone who craves a certain anonymity in a foreign country.

After dinner, I nip over to Baladou Sue's house to look out some semi-smart clothes for the trip. I'm hoping the customers will understand if I don't turn up in a suit.

*****

It's the first time I've taken the early morning train that winds its way once each day through the glorious landscape of the Lot and the Aveyron to the Lot et Garonne and, finally, Toulouse. It was raining when I left before six and too dark to see much of our department.

As we merge into daylight, the rain has stopped but the sky is a sickly shade of grey and the Aveyron's beautiful countryside looks like it has been doused after a fire. I discover at Najac that, if you're sitting by a window on the appropriate side of the train, you can look up and catch a glimpse of the castle walls high above the track. It's *l'un des plus beaux villages de France*. The Aveyron has, I think, more classified villages than any other department. Further down the line we stop at the exquisite Cordes sur Ciel and I see the old village perched on top of its outcrop. You walk up a steep cobbled street and you think, *Oh this is rather nice*, and then you emerge at the top to find a kind of Tibetan-like kingdom. It's a Shangri-La that ignores the ravages of time below.

We stop, too, at Gaillac – where the wine comes from – a town like Albi, further up the river Tarn, built of sandstone the colour of spilled blood. A blonde woman of around 60 gets on and stinks out the carriage with a perfume that smells of some intense artificial blend of pear and vanilla. Her foolish hair is lacquered into a perfect perm and she sports a jumper that involves a combination of pink and black shapes reminiscent of that basic psychological exercise on perception. *Bearded man or naked lady?* I see humanity in all its folly, unthinkingly pursuing its daily routine in the face of impending disaster.

Despite all the familiar *what-if* scenarios that make travel such a misery for me, the train is not uncommonly late. There is no mad dash to get the bus to the airport. No last-minute vaulting of barriers and breathless race across the tarmac in pursuit of a plane that's already started to taxi towards the runway. The plane leaves on time – with me comfortably on board – and arrives on time at East Midlands, where I pick up a National Express coach bound for Sheffield.

Increasingly these days, I get the feeling that shopping is all we Brits are fit for. Certainly, I get the bug as soon as I set foot in the old country. Perhaps it's the deprivation that comes with living in *France profonde*, or maybe I'm just particularly susceptible to ubiquitous images of consumption. In fact, my short stay is a hectic schedule of journeys by public transport and business meetings. Right at the end, I am able to nip into Fopp in Division Street and buy a few cheap books and CDs: some for me and others for friends. Maddeningly, the bus doesn't turn up and I have to take a taxi out to my friends' hostelry in Fulwood. I could have bought a couple more discs with the money spent on the fare.

All goes remarkably well on the way home, too. No need to vault a safety barrier and chase the plane down the runway, pursued by airport security staff armed with sten guns. Somewhere just south of the Loire, the cloud cover suddenly lifts to reveal the topography of our region, all laid out like one of those 3-D maps. There in the distance, the snow-capped mountains of the Cantal. And there, flowing from them, our great rivers cutting deep channels through the rumpled landscape of velvet greens and browns on their way west to the Atlantic. The rain has clearly continued to fall. The signs of flooding are everywhere to see.

The descent is very painful, but my eardrums don't burst. The Werther's Originals have done their trick. My grandma always advocated barley sugars, but they're not easy to find these days. Balladou Sue is there to greet me, bless her. She has taken her neighbour to see her husband in the hospital in Toulouse and has assured me that it would be no problem to pick me up from the airport. No need to run down a platform in pursuit of a departing train. She is kindness itself and absolutely refuses to take my money for the motorway tolls. Knowing her, she probably hasn't even asked her neighbour to share the petrol costs.

She gets me to the bus stop just in time to pick up my daughter, too. So there is no need for the contingency plan of her waiting at the farm with their daughter, Aurore (which she would have hated). There's even time and just enough daylight once Sue drops us off at the dolls' house to take Alf out for a walk after a whole day's incarceration. We go via the site and I can see that The Carpenters have decked the back balcony. It's good to be back home.

*****

We seem to have settled after all the rain into a period of clear, crisp winter weather. A perfect time, in fact, to start putting the roof on – only there's no sign of the tiles. Terrific! I find a sponsor that doesn't deliver. I phone the rep and leave a message, but he doesn't get back to me. Well of course he wouldn't, he's French. They don't return calls.

Bob Ze Builder and Christian turn up nevertheless, ready for action. Yesterday, Sunday, I spent the entire day finishing spraying the interior wood for Monsieur F. when I should have been hard at work on what I've brought back from the U.K. With the gas bottle swaddled in roof insulation and black plastic to protect it from the elements, I can have heating inside the caravan and I'm hoping to make progress today. However, it's becoming clear that I can't leave my cowboy roofers to get on with things unsupervised. There's a drama first thing, which doesn't inspire me with confidence. I suggest they park the van by the electricity post half way up our drive. Next thing I know, the van has slipped down into the field below from which there is no return. Christian is muttering about his useless new partner. Apparently, he called for help when he realised that the van was slipping, but Bob hadn't come to his aid – because, according to Bob, he hadn't heard.

So I suggest that Christian drives down to the bottom and tries the *chemin rural* that runs down beside our land. His (probably balding) tyres find no traction, so he gets stuck a third of the way up. Meanwhile, without any apparent reflection, Bob launches into the work of fixing to the roof trusses the poplar battens, which I've been bringing back in the Berlingo from a local sawmill. (I chose it because it's run by a friendly woman, whose husband died in a work-related accident. Every time I see her, I have this awful mental picture of her old man being sliced in two by a saw wheel.) So I tell him to slow down while I go off to the farm to seek help.

It comes in the shape of Jean-Louis' glaucomatous-looking older brother and a green John Deere. I propose to the Crazy Gang that we buy him a decent bottle of something to thank him for his time.

Later, just as I'm finally getting stuck into my work, there's a knock at the caravan door. Christian steps inside and bends my ear about Bob. He doesn't like the way that he's going about his work. A bit like a bull in a china shop, it would appear. It seems a shame that he didn't check his modus operandi before going into partnership with him. I reassure him that I will be checking the quality of work. This doesn't bode well. I've been to see the house that Bob built and talked to its proprietor and had a verbal reference, but perhaps they have contrived to pull the wool over my eyes.

No wonder that I'm getting up twice in the night these days and making my way by torchlight to the little bathroom by the stairs.

*****

We are a troubled family at present. Judging by all the disturbed nights, our daughter is clearly perturbed by the disruption to the reasonably cosy domestic life she has known. What's more, she has the scary prospect of playing the piano at a concert in a church on Saturday night. It's connected to her Saturday-morning music class and not something that pushy parents have arranged. We worry sometimes that the relentless education system in France – lauded back home, where the grass is always greener – snuffs out the joy of childhood. The French seem to expect their children to be superhuman.

My wife, who has been plagued of late by last-minute cancellations at work, is troubled by an apparent demand for back payment of U.K. National Insurance contributions in the region of £2,000. Me, I'm still troubled by my ear, which seems to be both blocked and buzzing now full-time. It's probably exacerbated by the saga of the roof tiles. I've been ringing up the rep, the marketing manager and the builder's merchant with no satisfaction. No one seems to know anything or give a monkey's. Ironically, if I had ordered them direct from the builder's merchant, I might have had them by now.

The day on site is characterised by frustrations. The Crazy Gang go off to a nearby family-run restaurant and take about two and a half hours over lunch. I'm paying them only for the hours of work they put in, but tell them nevertheless that *ça ne va pas aller*. What's more, when Bob explains to me the technicalities of boarding up the eaves, I can smell alcohol on his breath. This is deeply concerning. If Bob were to fall off the roof, inebriated or not, no doubt I will find myself liable. I sense an imminent major decision.

Towards the end of the day, the first drops of rain began to fall as I am helping The Carpenters put up the huge vertical posts for the mezzanine. With the architect's trademark big wooden X between them, they look like some ancient civilisation's totem poles.

It's tough sometimes to keep the mask of good humour from slipping. The last thing I want is for our daughter to witness the beast within. However, I come close to a Captain Hurricane-style *raging fury* when I pick up Tilley the Kid from school and take her to Sue's for her piano practice. Sue is away again and has left us the keys to her house. But I must have picked up the wrong keys in my haste to leave on time. They're the keys to the *cave* and not the house. I blame Maggott Malone, the Captain's long-suffering batman.

I mean to work on my paid project that evening, but am too knackered. Debs and I go to bed with the Coens' *Oh Brother, Where Art Thou?* It's marvellous. George Clooney's Clark Gable routine is a revelation. Just what the doctor ordered, I nevertheless dream of roof tiles that night.

*****

The piano recital is hardly Herbie Hancock at Carnegie Hall. Our girl, bless her, is no child prodigy on the eighty-eights. In fact, the whole caboodle proves to be a complete waste of time. When we get there, no one makes any attempt to meet and greet or introduce people. We are left to feel like plain-clothes guests at a fancy dress party. Tilley's teacher, who lives with a cork permanently up her bottom, eventually gets round to informing us that she has decided to take Tilley's part. Our poor child, who has worked hard for this in spite of her misgivings, cannot apparently keep up with the orchestra. In all honesty, she's probably more relieved than disappointed, but what a great way to build your pupil's confidence. We should really have slapped the woman or at least have made some kind of stand, but don't want to compound the situation by embarrassing our daughter. So we let it lie, as we often do as outsiders in a country whose customs we still don't comprehend, and we take our seats meekly among the other proud parents in the church with its garish wall paintings and electric bar heaters on tripods.

The piece lasts about 30 seconds and you can't even hear the piano. So what's the big deal here? Note-perfect accuracy or a chance for the kids to show an audience what they've been learning?

Our friends, the Jacksons, are here and Steve has brought his new hand-held JVC camera to film Rosie perform her piece – beautifully – and Ione to sing with her friends a rousing chorus of 'We wish you a Merry Christmas'. Their school, with their groovy long-haired teacher, are the stars of the show with a varied performance of baroque, Irish, classical and pop pieces, which at least suggest that the kids are really involved and enjoying it.

Afterwards, we hang around for a few minutes for the obligatory drink and finger food and meet an American guy who chats to Steve about the old country. He and his wife and their five-year old son have moved from Oakland, Ca. to Martel for *l'aventure*. An architect who can't practise over here, he's busy renovating a house in the old town to sell, so they can move on to their next port-of-call. The peripatetic life doesn't appeal to me.

*****

Christmas! You take your eye off the ball and turn around to discover that it's less than a fortnight away. It's a mixed blessing, of course: on the one hand, I can't wait for the enforced rest; on the other, there's much to do before the shutdown.

So it's worrying that the momentum, which had picked up nicely only a couple of short weeks ago, has been slowed by peripherals. Monsieur Fromage has presented me with a quote for the 10-year structural guarantee for the wooden frame. The only company prepared to provide one has quoted nearly 3,000 euros for the privilege. This, of course, will be passed on to me, because the kind of interior work that The Carpenters do is covered by a standard *responsibilité civile* and does not require this *décinel* insurance. Even if I pay it, the guarantee covers only the wooden framework. Gilles is horrified that I have even considered employing someone without this insurance. I have to remind myself that the French are insurance-crazy – accidents, death, teeth, health, frozen pipes, civic responsibility, probably loss of libido for all I know – and it only covers you for ten years maximum. If I pay it, it means an extra 3,000 euros to add to a budget that's expanding like a pair of elasticated trousers.

That's one peripheral. Then there are the flaming roof tiles. They're substituting for rivets in my own version of Conrad's *Heart of Darkness*. They'll find me one day, slumped at my laptop in the caravan, muttering *The horror, the horror*. The regional director has at least taken the trouble to phone me back and has told me how (and this is quite extraordinary coming from a Frenchman; I can only assume he has a British grandparent) **sorry** he is to hear of my problems. He will look into the matter, he assures me.

And finally… there's the Crazy Gang. Those loveable knock-about comedians, who just love to hate each other. Neither has reported for work today. Christian has offered to undertake the work with a friend who is a *trompe-l'œil* artist (can he simulate a roof?). Observation suggests that what he says about Bob is probably true, but I don't like the way that he has usurped the guy to whom I offered this work in the first place. I want at least to talk to Bob and give him a stern warning and some kind of second chance.

Fortunately, my circumspect wife's potentially dodgy morning client proves to be just a decent if diffident man and not a rapist, so there's no need to answer her anticipated call by jumping into the Berlingo and driving like the clappers to Brive, armed with a hammer and a length of rebar.

*****

If it doesn't rain, it pours… Just as I am beginning to make good progress with my work project, my little antiquated laptop develops a problem. Staring stoically at the screen doesn't help. I phone Bret and do what he suggests, but this seems to open up a can of worms. Finally, I bite the bullet and phone the technical support line at Wanadoo. It costs something daunting per minute and then I struggle to understand what the guy on the other end of the line tells me. His advice seems to be about reinstalling Windows, but since my discs are all in a box in Debs' *cabinet* in Brive, I override it and try to sort things out myself. I try ticking a check-box and... *waddayaknow*? It works. If only this construction could be resolved by ticking a box.

Outside my window, the engine of a huge crane is throbbing away. This monster is costing 100 euros per hour and the men are labouring under evident stress in a steady drizzle. Mike and Oliver tie up the huge beams for the crane driver, who lifts them high into the air to be manoeuvred and bashed and engineered into position. The foul language suggests intransigence, and Monsieur F. has to do some emergency chiselling before the tenon will slot into its intended mortise. As the drizzle turns into rain, I can almost smell the stress levels. The man in the cab, by contrast, is implacable. He sits serenely at the controls, inviolate behind his windscreen.

A lorry turns up and my little heart skips a beat, thinking momentarily: *Aha! The roof tiles*. Who am I kidding? It's a pallet full of larch cladding for the mezzanine walls and the ceiling of the covered terrace.

With a head splitting from too much screen and the vicarious tension of this construction work, I leave early to go and see the osteopath. As I lie on the couch like a stiff in a morgue, his gentle manipulation of my neck makes me feel inconceivably relaxed. He seems to have found the source of the problem: an interior muscle just where the chest and shoulders merge, which is as tight as a high-tensile wire. He gives me some stretching exercises as homework – and hope that my ear could be unblocked for Christmas.

On the way back, I pick up our daughter who is deliriously happy that she has finished her first term at Martel primary school. Two whole weeks of Christmas to look forward to. Despite her new friend, Lucille, she dislikes school even more than I used to. I drive her to the land to see what has happened while I've been away. Through the bare trees, we can see flashing lights. We park the car by the roadside just as Debs turns up, early for once, from the opposite direction. We walk down the drive together – to discover that the crane has got stuck in the mud and that another huge vehicle has turned up to try to extricate it. The devastation to the terrain is terrible to behold. The thought of the expense involved is even worse. Monsieur Fromage informs us that they have decided to knock off now, because the rain has made the work too hard and too dangerous. They will have to get the crane back on Monday – if, and it's a big if, it doesn't rain any more – and finish the job. All he wants now is a nice deep hot bath.

Later, after dinner, the three of us play Cludo to celebrate the end of Tilley's term. *Madame Pervanche avec le pistolet dans la bibliothèque...*

*****

The day of our family trip to the Corrèze starts badly. At the caravan, in search of a bucket for the Christmas tree I bought in Bretenoux over the weekend, I find the white van of Monsieur Fromage. He is not a happy man. The forecast for the week is as bad as it can get. Snow. So no crane for tomorrow. No time to finish the framework for the mezzanine and get a temporary plastic covering over the middle section of the house before the holidays begin. This jeopardises all my plans and schedules. Dutch Eric is off to India in mid January, so I was hoping to get him to bring the bales over in his tractor before he leaves. But that depends on having a dry shelter in which to store them. The rain has been hammering down over the weekend and collecting in the concrete platform, so the posts are sitting in two inches of water. Which means that I'm going to have to vacuum up the water each day or risk the wood rotting. There's nothing we can do about it. The weather is beyond our control. If only the crane had been available on Thursday. If only it hadn't pissed down all day Friday. If only, if only...

My grey mood is not brightened in the car by the sight of hunters everywhere in their fluorescent hard hats. They've started wearing these quasi-military helmets to go with their quasi-military combat fatigues just in case they shoot each other (which they tend to do: *a consummation devoutly to be wished*). My daughter, bless her, flips them the bird. Something she probably picked up on *The Simpsons*. She's a chip off the old block, but at that moment I realise how easy it must be to preach hatred to your children. Can one, however, learn to be open-minded about these ignorant antediluvian specimens who shoot living, breathing creatures for sport? It's like the brothers at the farm. They seem decent individuals with nice families. Yet they make their living by keeping calves cooped up in the dark, grizzly sheds they built themselves and selling them for veal. What a way to earn a living.

When we reach our old village, the mayor's poisonous wife is going from door to door with a compliant kid, collecting money for some poxy calendar. Ron and Ingrid have already transformed our old house into something that bears their own stamp, but Ingrid tells me that if she has to pay for another bloody calendar, she'll scream. The firemen, the bin men, the post woman, the mayor's wife and so on.

Lean and lanky Thierry with the funny piping voice is still there in the house opposite. He's looking and feeling pretty miserable. He tells me that he'll be glad when the year's over. Popeye turns up in his Citroën BX and releases his two dogs from the back of the car. They immediately collar our poor submissive Alf, who rolls onto his back with his paws in the air as if to say, *I'm neutered and docile*. Then two bone-thin hunting dogs turn up and cause mayhem. Thierry checks their collars and phones their owner.

I fill up some water bottles at our old fountain and Mireille, the bitter retired teacher, emerges from her house opposite. Fortunately, she's off to the hospital and in a hurry, so there's no need for the routine hypocrisy of the kissing ritual. Then I pop into Mad Sad's old house, which has been lightened and brightened and generally transformed by the young couple who have bought the place. Victor takes me up to the cavernous roof space, so I can retrieve my CD and cassette players. This was the house where I watched France beat Brazil in the world cup final with the old dear a few years back. Outside, under their perfectly manicured tree that served as a parasol for the *heure des apéritifs*, we would drink and nibble and chat with the old couple before heading back to Sheffield at the end of another stay. I must have made significant progress since June: for the first time, I feel that I no longer want a piece of what we have left behind. It's over. Our house belongs to the Squirrells now and I hope that they will make a happy life for themselves.

We take Alf over to our old lake – the one aspect of life here that we do agree to miss – so he can have a walk and a quick plunge. In the summer, it resounds with happy human activity, but it's deserted at this time of year and there is a great sense of peace and timelessness. It was here I watched a heron one misty morning, skirting the static water of the lake.

Afterwards, we meet up with Ron and Ingrid again for lunch with some mutual friends in the nearby village of Espagnac. Both deeply religious schoolteachers, they are throwbacks to the kind of Catholic France that probably existed between the wars. In their elegant and austere dining room, we enjoy a delicious lunch. God knows, though, what Ron must think of it all. Ever since his stroke, he has effectively led the life of a prisoner trapped by his immobility and an inability to express himself. He can still talk, but it's difficult to understand what he is trying to say and Ingrid often has to act as an interpreter. With his white hair and white beard, however, he seems to be treated as some kind of mysterious dignitary from the planet Addi-Skizm.

Debs and I excuse ourselves for half an hour to nip down to the restaurant and check on our friends, Régine and Bernard. The latter has gone back home already, but Régine is sitting at a table surrounded by the last of the Sunday stragglers, totting up her lunchtime receipts. She has shed a ton of weight and looks shockingly thin since the last time we saw her. She has this mysterious and apparently life-threatening eating disorder – kind of ironic for someone who runs a restaurant – and so we are keenly aware that whenever we see her now, *this could be the last time* (but you never know with Régine). Her nose looks bruised from the feeding tube she has to pass down through her nostril to her stomach. Never one for effusive shows of emotion, her eyes nevertheless light up to see us both. She insists that we sit with her and drink one of her celebrated hot chocolates. Apparently, it's traditional at this time of year. Indeed, it is rather extraordinary: like a liquefied *mousse au chocolat*. It defeats even a pig like me.

Back at our friends' just up the road, Michelle drops by with Tilley's undersized friend, Manon. She saw the Berlingo parked at the side of the road with the 46 on the number plate to denote the department of the Lot and put two and two together. The girls play grandmother's footsteps in the garden with the religious friends' little boy and we chat about old times at the lake and new times at the building site.

Finally it's off to Puy Chamant for a quick tisane with Didier and Nadine, with whom we deposit our little girl, so she can spend a few days of the holiday with Juliette, her best friend from her school days here.

*****

I am not normally the type of person to leave Christmas shopping till the last moment. Unlike my brother, say. One year, I remember, he bought all his presents in a motorway service station en route for a family Christmas in Bath. But on the morning of Christmas Eve, my favourite day of the year, I go to Brive to take part in the seasonal madness. Shopping-till-dropping. A mad trolley dash to ensure that everyone has much more than enough for the festivities ahead. I drive back with a throbbing head (and an ear that's still blocked) to find Debs wrapping presents. Tilley is upstairs on the mezzanine, still in her nightie and feeling inexplicably melancholic. She's had a good cry already, it would seem. Debs reckons it's part tiredness and part reaction to having left Juliette's, where she has been playing happily with children her own age (as opposed to these two crusty, distracted parents).

Everyone's very tired. My wife, the renowned aromatherapist, has almost too many clients now to cope with. And, under pressure to get the initial draft of this work project off to the clients, I've just spent two freezing days in the caravan at the laptop with an icy wind snapping at the awning. France is on a meteorological orange alert and snow has fallen in many parts. We're waiting for the first flakes to fall.

The site hasn't quite gone away. Yesterday, I was struggling manfully to try to tame the flapping tarps that are covering the Douglas fir. Because the mezzanine is unfinished, the posts are still sitting in water and trying to evacuate the concrete platform with an Aqua Vac and freezing fingers proved fruitless. So I gave up and drove up river to Bretenoux to buy more groceries for Christmas and drop some money off at Bob's place.

I find his rusting red Peugeot up on blocks outside the tawdry house and hope to find him working on his car, so I can *talk* to him about drinking on the job. Alas, he is inside with his woman and their feckless friend and everyone is smoking and stoned again. As for the poor baby, noises off suggest that he or she is shut away in some room. It's a squalid scene and I'm wondering what the hell I'm doing even contemplating giving him work. And yet... there is something very engaging about him and I just can't help liking the guy – for all that I want to give him a damn good shake. *Look at your life, man! You only get one. Think of that poor child!*

On the way back, I drop in to see Bret and spend a couple of sociably warm hours in their cold, draughty house with him, his wife, her two daughters and their father. I manage to talk a bit of shop with Bret and get an almost definite offer of help with the walls themselves and the ensuing stages of the build. On taking my leave, I laugh at one of his quips and fart loudly and involuntarily. It cracks everyone up and I laugh to hide my deep embarrassment.

The next day, an e-mail arrives from *France Magazine* with not one but two commissions for articles. *Happy Christmas, one and all!*

*****

Maybe, I realise now, my daughter's tears were born of frustration with her irredeemably daft parents. No doubt she fancied a quiet Christmas *à trois*. So what do they do? They invite the Squirrells plus Jan and Dutch Eric to join us on Christmas Day.

Still, Christmas is a time to share, so it might do our daughter some good. Being an only child, she can find it difficult to share – the marbles at school being a case in point. Besides, they don't arrive till just before lunchtime, so there's plenty of time for all our Waltons' stuff. *Love you, too, granmaw...*

For once, I sleep through the night without having to creep to the loo, so I fail to perform my Father Christmas routine until I wake up on Christmas morning at around 6.30. I tiptoe up to the mezzanine with a sock stuffed with frivolous goodies and deposit it at the foot of Tilley's bed, but I sense that she is simulating sleep. Sure enough, she joins us a few minutes later, clutching her bulging sock, which resembles a war veteran's artificial leg. Opening stockings in bed together is maybe my favourite facet of Christmas Day.

When we draw the curtains, we see that our little house is swaddled in a cold, clammy fog. And yet, when Debs takes Alf out for his morning constitutional, she reports back that – just a little higher up, by the farm behind us – the landscape is bathed in glorious wintry sunlight and you can see right across the thick duvet of fog to the mountains of the Cantal.

We revel in our quiet time together: breakfast at the round table with a pot of good strong coffee accompanied by Phil Spector's *Christmas Album*, then presents around the smallest tree I could find, decorated with anything we can find and make. Afterwards, I step outside into the fog and phone my parents to chat about the festivities in Southampton. There is still an element of me that hankers to be part of it all, even though I remember only too well the reality of extended family Christmases. I'm sure we're better off here, making our own entertainment, and yet... where are the Queen's speech and the Morecambe and Wise Christmas Show?

The Squirrells arrive first, bearing countless gifts. There are mince pies that Ingrid has made in our old *cuisinière*, art materials for our girl, and sculptures she has made in our old basement apartment, now converted into her studio: a beautiful reclining lady for Debs and the crazy toucan that I have always secretly coveted for me. Her generosity brings tears to my eyes.

It's a squash, but there is just enough room at the round table for the seven we have become with the arrival of Jan and Eric. A vegetarian Christmas lunch, supplemented by a little pre-prepared meat for Ron and Eric.

After lunch, we take everyone to see the embryonic house, which looks decidedly spectral in the mist. I try not to think too much of the posts sitting in their big puddle of water and take heart instead from the positive comments of our guests. *Yes, it will be fine. It will be splendid.*

We retire to Jan and Eric's old farmhouse in the valley below for part 2 of our Christmas Day, which involves an evening nut roast with trimmings polished off with one of the videos we have left with them for safe-keeping. I propose *Sweet Charity*. It seems to be a happy choice, even though several of us doze through Bob Fosse's wonderful choreography. Not me. I can never get enough of Shirley MacLaine's long-legged dancing and that captivating, slightly Oriental squinty smile of hers. Poor Charity, always unlucky in love, like her Fran Kubilick character in *The Apartment*. I am delighted and proud that my daughter fights off sleep to take in all the romantic tosh in which her parents revel. Maybe one day a nice young Jack Lemmon will strain spaghetti with a tennis racquet for her. Only it will be made of graphite and not wood.

Ron and Ingrid sleep in our bed that night, while Debs and I camp out on the mezzanine floor, which pleases our daughter no end. The following morning, the fog has lifted and I ask Ron if he would like to join me on my walk with our faithful hound. 'I don't think so,' he replies in a manner that makes me feel stupid for having asked.

By the time they drive back to our old house, I have had my fill of the white-haired dignitary from the planet Addi-Skizm. I know that one shouldn't speak ill of invalids, but he has been bugging me: hovering around like an *éminence grise* who disapproves of everyone and everything, especially his wife's generosity. To top it all, he tries to go off with our pâté dish and saucepan lid, which I rescue when stashing in their boot Ingrid's skip now rather less full of goodies. And when she tries to offload some mince pies on us before departure, he barks *No!* at her. A good slap would be in order.

*****

The worst thing about Christmas is that – as sure as chestnuts is chestnuts roasting on an open fire – Christmas must end. If you try not to think too hard about the homeless and dispossessed, the suffering and the starving, Christmas gives you the illusion that all is right with the world. Happy families, happy faces; Christmas trees and turkey treats; fun and games for everyone. No more work for a whole week; no need to bother yourself with all those troubling things that normally demand your undivided attention.

Our daughter hasn't stopped playing her new CD by Sophie Ellis-Bextor. I am delighted that she has reached a stage when her own music is important to her – like that wonderful moment in the early '60s when I discovered The Beatles and listened to their first two albums over and over on my dad's gramophone – but there comes a time when repetition can drive you mad.

We have spent our holiday walking and discovering our new territory and eating nice meals and watching old films on video, like Tilley's favourite, *The Philadelphia Story*. She now does a very passable Katherine Hepburn, which has us both in fits. But the spectre of her parents' return to work hangs over our child. She is never happier than when the three of us can be together. Soon it will be back to hated school.

Back in the freezing caravan to make some calls. There is another imminent decision looming large: what kind of heating system will we install? The plumber needs to know. But there's no one about to answer my questions. Everyone is *en congé*. It's Holiday City. France has gone to sleep. There's nothing for it but to read yesterday's news in *The Week*. Saddam Hussein has been captured and Michael Vaughan's captain's innings has saved the second test in Sri Lanka.

The night before my wife's return to work is hellish. Tilley the Kid is restless and joins us in our bed, and we all pass *une nuit blanche*. So I suggest that Debs doesn't drive to work and I take her down to the station to catch the early-morning train to Brive. I volunteer to pick her up from her *cabinet* after some food shopping. This necessitates some hasty child-sitting plans. Tilley's nine now and the French seem to look upon that as an age at which their children can be left alone. We don't. So I take her over to Tim and Gilly's to play with Phoebe, then head for Brive with Alf in the back of the car.

While killing some time after my trip to the supermarket, I decide to take Eric's advice and drop in for a look at the central library. The *médiathèque* is on the second floor. I push open the double doors – and it's like stumbling into Aladdin's Cave. Music, music everywhere. Every genre, every artist. I almost find myself hyperventilating as I riffle through the jazz section. It's better than Mole Jazz in London. There's the complete Charlie Christian, several Charlie Hunters, a handful of Pharoah Sanders, more Miles Davis and Thelonious Monk than you could dream of... There is just enough time to drop by the *cabinet*, borrow a gas bill to prove a Brive address, get back to the library and sign up for not just one card, but a card for each of us. I return to Deborah's domain with six CDs and a big smile on my face.

*****

Whose bright idea was it to spend New Year's Eve in the Corrèze? OK. It's no one's fault: we were invited, God damn it. You can't just roll over and let the old year end with a whimper. Besides, we've never before been privy to a French *réveillon*.

So once again, after dropping off the hound, basket, dish, lead and anti-rabies certificate with Baladou Sue and her canine pyjama case, we find ourselves driving up the *Côte de Lostanges*, bound for the deepest Corrèze. It's a beautiful winter's day and the limpid quality of air is such that the view of the mountains at a familiar junction is simply breathtaking. They look huge and surely a mere half-hour's drive away. You can see every contour of the rock faces and the snow on the peaks is like a white chocolate sauce poured over dark chocolate buns.

At Puy Chamant, Tilley and Juliette greet each other like long-lost best friends, which is heartening – particularly as they've only very recently spent a few days together. Juliette's dad, Didier, is outside in the warm sunshine, making a cupboard for the family cheese. We leave him to it and take a stroll with Juliette and her mum, Nadine, to a nearby waterfall. It's so beautiful in among the bare trees with the rays of an oblique sun lighting our way. Four years after the hurricane, there are still flattened trees to be cleared.

Later, I drive over to Beysse to pick up Bernard, who's getting dressed after his shower. He's had to dig up their septic tank to try to locate a blockage. A nice way to spend the last day of the year. He smells sweet enough as we drive to the old school in the lovely, hidden village of La Roche Canillac. His IT *association* uses an old classroom and we're here to pick up an old computer that he's letting me have. On the way from there to the restaurant in Espagnac, we talk about his wife, our friend Régine. Only five people in France, apparently, have her condition. She's lost about 30 kilos in a year. The trouble is that the liquid nourishment that she takes in via her feeding tube is not enough to sustain her. She has to supplement it with her body's reserves – and they're becoming as depleted as the world's oil supplies. And yet, miraculously and probably through the force of her will, she keeps going. At the restaurant, she's busy with a few friends preparing a huge table for the evening's festivities. I say my hellos and kiss my goodbyes and drive back to Puy Chamant for our own humbler celebrations.

Needless to say, they centre on the meal. As usual, I eat too much and, unusually, drink too much. Apart from an incident, though, with a mobile phone when a complete stranger calls Didier by mistake and they end up wishing each other a *bonne année* and all good things, there isn't a lot of laughter. Mother Brown's French equivalent prefers to rest her knees and to sit at table and scoff.

There are two things I find about New Year's Eve. Firstly, they rarely live up to your expectations. No sooner have you kissed and hugged everyone than you feel like a deflated balloon. Secondly, you have to stay up so late. And that includes the children (who will be grumpy the following day). We manage to get Tilley, Juliette and her older sister off to bed when the Chatours turn up: Jean-Claude, Michelle and pint-sized Manon. Of course it's nice to see them – and we drink another obligatory glass of champagne and eat another slice of sickly chocolate cake, despite the fact that I've no more room for either – but Debs and I are both dead on our feet by now and don't manage to retreat to our bed until gone two o'clock.

I realise that we've already consumed our first two hours of 2004. The old year is history. I look forward to a rather calmer and less disruptive new year. In view of the schedule ahead, this seems suspiciously like wishful thinking.

January 2004

This is it, then: the start of the year in which I reach the age of 50. If I'm very lucky, I've already lived half my life. By the law of statistics, it's probably more like five-eighths already gone. When faced with such knowledge, you start asking yourself exactly what you've managed to achieve thus far. But you can't afford to dwell too long on mortality when you've got a house to build. Maybe it will be my monument, my Nelson's column, so to speak.

We start the new year with a drama. A mere quarter of an hour or so after Debs and Didier observe that it looks like it might snow, the white stuff starts to fall. We leave our friends to recover from their late-running party and drive to the restaurant in Espagnac to wish Régine and Bernard a *bonne année*. We chat over a coffee and the lovebirds bicker, as is their party-piece.

Thence to the Chatours' house, hidden away among the woods at the edge of our old commune. It's already a winter wonderland and I'm nervous about the return journey, but we are invited to lunch and we don't see them often now, so lunch it is. And it's a nice simple, cosy lunch at their rustic table, warmed by a roaring *cuisinière*. Every time we see them, we're convinced that they are just about the most unlikely couple ever: Michelle, an attractive and, when she has a mind, rather elegant woman from a *petit bourgeois* background; Jean-Claude, the original Wild Man of Wongo, a woodsman whom one could easily imagine flitting through the shadows in the dense undergrowth, living on nuts and berries and talking to the wild animals, five-foot-almost-nothing in his stockinged feet, with thick Mexicano-style moustache and boyish pudding-bowl hairstyle. We are tempted to imagine that they have fantastic sex.

He has already run a course with my wife (behind closed shutters in the old school house in our commune and threatened with closure by the agents of the medical establishment) and they talk about another one for 2005. This one would combine wild mushrooms and aromatherapy massage. It sounds uncomfortably like our *aroma-donkey* project that never quite got air-born, so I'm mentally tempering my wife's enthusiasm with words of caution – and particularly when he starts proposing an exchange of a massage for some radishes from his garden. Debs and I exchange a look that reassures me that she won't be selling herself too cheap on this particular occasion.

After lunch, their son Robin goes off on his scooter to join his pals in nearby Espagnac. Only a year or so ago, I was attempting to teach the boy English. I think he enjoyed the ordeal even less than I did. Tilley the Kid goes outside to roll in the snow with their daughter, Manon. We move into the sitting room to eat a chocolate *buche* by a roaring fire, then round up our daughter, say our goodbyes and gingerly drive off. It's a winter wonderland that heightens the beauty of this ravishing part of France, but the twisting snow-covered roads are not conducive to relaxed motoring.

And then the drama… We arrive back to discover that we have no electricity. We manage to locate the trip switch for the *petite maison*, but that doesn't appear to be the problem. So I trudge over to the caravan by torchlight and find that the electricity is working there, which is bad news because it means that it's something specific to the house and therefore **not** out of my hands. In other words, it is I who must deal with it. I phone up our neighbour in England, but have to leave a message. And then I phone up the EDF emergency number. The guy at the other end is maybe so impressed by the fact that I read out the reference number in the French fashion (rather than digit by digit) that he promises to send someone out that evening.

On the way back to the house by torchlight, it suddenly dawns on me, ironically, that the blockage in my ear has shifted. I stand stock-still and take in the sounds of a winter's evening. Yes, it's true. I can hear again in that ear. I surmise that the Christmas break and the enforced lay-off from the building site have provided just enough relaxation to do nature's work.

And so, despite the black-out in our quarters, my mood is surprisingly positive – especially when I spy a pair of headlights in the mist a half hour or so later. It's a man with a van (and a little bushy affectation just beneath his bottom lip). He checks our box and the one in our neighbours' *cave*, for which I have a key. No problem with either one. So there has to be something between the post in the garden and these junction boxes. But where? Something underground? Some irreparable problem that will drive us out of our temporary refuge?

The man with the affectation wants to look inside the house, but we don't have a key. Debs offers to go and try the neighbours on the other side. The Odd Couple. She bangs on the shutters and rings the bell, but in vain. But I have seen cars down there, so I offer to try again. Muriel keeps a key to the big house, so I am determined to stay there outside the front door until someone answers my urgent ringing. Eventually, I hear footsteps on the stairs and the door is opened. I am ushered inside by a woman I haven't seen before. I follow her up the steep stairs to their sitting room. There are four women and the room is full of smoke.

Whatever it is that a room full of female *companions* get up to of a winter's evening, Muriel is willing for me to drag her away. We take her car, which seems sacrilegious given the short walk across the fields. But yes, it is dark and it's snowing again now, and I'm anxious to get there before the EDF man tires of waiting and drives off into the night.

Muriel opens up the neighbours' front door, locates a supplementary junction box, trips the switch and... *Hey Presto, It's Rolf!* The lights come on again and Debs comes running out of the *petite maison* with arms aloft in triumph. It's left to me to apologise to the EDF man for a wasted journey. He is very understanding (being, no doubt, on double-time). Muriel drives back to her bacchanalia and I make one more torch-lit trip to the caravan to phone our neighbours and leave a message to the effect that the crisis is over. *Oh, what a night!* – as the Dells once sung on the Chess label.

*****

Languishing in bed this morning – and after several months of very intermittent reading – I finish at long last Don DeLillo's extraordinary *Underworld.* An epic saga in the tradition of John dos Passos' *U.S.A.* and all those rambling Thomas Wolfe novels I read for my masters. The narrative thread is too tangled for a protracted read. Still, it will live in my memory with some of those other convoluted works of American fiction I've read over the years. At least I understand it a little more than I did on reaching the end of William Gaddis' *The Recognitions.* I was young when I read that and hadn't yet worked out that life's too short to bother with something so perversely obtuse. For all DeLillo's often revelatory writing, though, I can't honestly say that I enjoyed it as much as something rather less ambitious like, say, Richard Russo's *Empire Falls.* Given the demands of the build, I think I'll opt for something shorter next time.

Later, I take our daughter out in the interests of research. I drop her off at her friend, Lucille's. Her dad built their house almost entirely by himself. He's a funny little dark-haired guy with a boyish fringe and giggle. He takes me down into the bowels of the house to show me their heat pump that extracts the constant latent 'warmth' of the Dordogne river and converts it into energy to heat the water that circulates around their under-floor heating system. There's a nice ambient warmth about the house, so it appears to work well. Proudly, he shows me around the house. I find its perfection a trifle intimidating and Jean-Luc's modesty slightly forced.

On the other hand, Monsieur Boit, who lives a few kilometres further up the main road that leads from the river to Gramat, the self-styled capital of the limestone *causse*, is modest enough to be retiring. A charming and helpful man, he shows me around his solar installations. During the tour, I learn that he supplies vegetable-based foodstuffs for animals. Among his clients are the couple with the donkey-trekking establishment, with whom we joined up for our ill-fated *aroma-donkey* project. It's a small world here. Whenever I think of that couple, I hear JP's funny piping voice and relive the sheer awfulness of the afternoon when he left me to make some amendments to the website he had created and I hit the wrong key and deleted the whole bloody lot.

I meet the tall man's young daughter, who seems far too young for his apparent years. In the kitchen, his wife pours out cups of fierce coffee. It's late morning and she is still in her dressing gown. There are dark, dark circles around her eyes and she has the air of a sickly addict. Her husband makes some comment about the strength of the coffee. Perhaps she's addicted to caffeine. Coffee provides the strength to face another day of tedium on the edge of this wind-swept plateau, where the only visitors are earnest *ecolos* like myself, come to view her husband's handiwork.

On the way home, I pick up my daughter from Lucille's grandparents' house, just down the lane from her father's auto-construction. Families are as close here as they are in the Corrèze. The progeny don't wander far from the parental seat. Lucille's grandmother is a sweet, slight old woman with a radiant smile. She offers me a slice of the local *Lotois* delicacy, *pastis*. Not in this case the drink, but a kind of enormous communal apple tart, made with layer upon layer of puff-pastry built up on a huge cooking tray. It takes a day or more in preparation and usually involves several people. I'm not sure whether the result quite warrants such labour.

*****

The decorations are down, the *petite maison* feels barer but roomier, the unreality of the holidays is over and it's back to the grindstone. This morning, I plod rather than trudge to the caravan. The reluctant project manager.

The caravan is freezing and I fire up the computer, ready for work. The Carpenters are back and busy securing decking to the back balcony. Alf is disturbed by and barks at the reports of their nail gun, which he mistakes for hunters' rifles. Bob Ze Builder and Christian both phone for news. There's an e-mail from the Sales & Marketing Director of the roofing supplies company, promising to look into my problem with the standard *least delay*. But there are still no tiles, so there's nothing to tell the Crazy Gang.

A conversation with someone at Wiessmann – one of those evidently trained sales types who call you *Monsieur Sampson* every ten seconds to reassure you that you have their absolute attention – leaves me with more questions than answers about air-source heat pumps. He suggests that I could need as much as a 15kw model for the surface area of our house-to-be. This would demand a much bigger (and costlier) annual supply than I had bargained for.

One of my new-year resolutions is to get back to work on a book I have left fallow for the past few months. Reading over what I have written so far, however, only makes me wonder why I bother. Will people want to read my musings? What sets it apart from anything else on the market? If it **has** got something, what suggests that I can persuade some chary publisher to take a chance on a total unknown? *Dear God, couldn't you have equipped me with the talent to be a jazz* *pianist?* I write partly because I am driven to do so, but also partly because it's the only flaming thing I can bloody well do.

Never mind… the crane arrives during the morning. In no time at all – given these cold, sunny and happily dry conditions – the sidekicks assemble the pieces hoisted by the jib into something that clearly resembles our architect's drawings. Monsieur Fromage glows with the relief of it all. He tells me that it's as if the crane has lifted a huge weight from his shoulders. It has been niggling away at the back of his mind since that hot day in August when he voiced his doubts to me in our oak wood.

During the afternoon, I phone the sales rep about the tiles only to get the usual evasive response. He promises to phone me back and, of course, he doesn't. An e-mail reply to one of several I have sent off to propose my book only confirms my doubts and further undermines my self-belief. But, despite such setbacks, I head off to pick up my child from the bus stop, glad all over from a good morning's work. We have a house in outline.

*****

There are times – many times – when we wonder what we're doing here. Debs, being a mystical, spiritual type, has this vague feeling that she's come here for a purpose. She has answered a calling that only people like her can hear. Like a dog, in fact. Frequently, Alf launches himself out of doors to bark hysterically at some unseen, unheard presence. Being a more prosaic sort, I don't tend to pick up on these callings, but am quite ready to believe that she feels this. *Meet my wife; she's answered a calling, you know.*

As I sit cocooned in a sleeping bag in a freezing caravan, her healing hands will be massaging essential oils into a body, prone on the couch at her Last Chance Saloon. Last night, she was sitting at the round table doing her sums. Something to do with her *taxe professionelle*. Only in France would they have the great idea to tax you for having the gumption to set yourself up in business, rather than bothering the state. She came up with a respectable figure for her six-monthly earnings: something like €12,000. Then I calculate her outgoings for the same period and we realise that she is just about breaking even. Some years ago, a fellow therapist suggested that she would have to massage seven clients a day, six days a week, just to keep her head above water. He wasn't wrong. They sure know how to stimulate enterprise and kick-start the economy here.

Dishy Tom calls to quiz me on the current state of the construction. Well, the rep is still refusing to call me back and we still have no roof tiles. Dutch Eric is off to India at the end of next week, so he won't be around to move the bales over here until he gets back. Bret is pruning some farmer's vines for the next month, so he can't start here until well into February. Tom offers to phone the roofing company for me *and I just say good luck.*

With The Carpenters now fixing the rafters to the mezzanine framework, a delegation from St. Astier arrives. They make the lime that will eventually cover our walls. They haven't said yes to my sponsorship letter, but they haven't said no. So I guess that these three men in their silver Mercedes are here on a fact-finding mission. Either that or they're here on a jolly and wasting my time. They take a cursory look at the house and then we move to the *petite maison,* where we sit at the round table and chat. A rather surly man in an anorak, with Bobby Charlton hair, expounds on his pet theories with a characteristic blind confidence in his expertise. I will definitely need a metal mesh if the render is to stick to the walls apparently. And my eaves should be more pronounced.

A fairly unpleasant man, with gold-framed glasses, a navy-blue jacket and hair combed severely to one side, has enough knowledge of England and the English language to be dangerous. Seeking to air that knowledge at every available opportunity, he is determined to talk over the guy in the middle, typically the only one that I like: a burly chap with thick oily black hair and a bushy moustache, whose mobile phone keeps bursting into life with an awful siren-like ring-tone that makes me jump out of my seat.

The conversation beats resolutely about the bush. They comment on the excellence of Peter Mayle's infernal Provencal best-seller and ask questions about why house prices should be so much higher in the U.K. and what the difference is between England, Great Britain and the United Kingdom. I feel, as I often do in such situations, a little like an exhibit at a freak show, and look for an opportunity to get down to business. Their premise seems to be, unremarkably, that straw should be protected from moisture at any cost – and so I should be doing everything that the authorities recommend. Monsieur Moustache does at least offer me some food for thought. Had I considered covering the western elevation in wood panelling? It would harmonise with that of the mezzanine and protect the wall from the prevailing elements. Not a bad idea...

Eventually, and suddenly, they get up as one delegation. It is time to take their leave. Of course it is: both the big and the little hands are pointing straight up towards the number 12. Off they go in their silver Merc, looking for some local hostelry where they can eat and drink copiously for two hours. I am left with a mystifying diagram that supposedly explains the difference between hydraulic and aerated lime, but none the wiser as to whether or not they intend to sponsor *Maison Sampson*.

Later that day, I take Tilley with me to meet up with her mum at nearby Cavagnac, so we can visit our friends the Jacksons' glass-blowing studio. We have decided to spend extra money that we can barely afford on some wall lights. The wife is right. There's no point in building this house only to skimp on the kind of fittings that would transform our living space into something beautiful. And Steve and Jessica do make exceedingly beautiful wall lights. They are effectively functional works of art. We decide on two pairs, but to let them choose the colours to blow. They will set us back €175 each, but they've kindly offered us one as a house-warming present.

It's good to be frivolous once in a while. Good to focus on something like house-warming. Our daughter has entered into the spirit of things by spending some of her Christmas money in the January sales on her second CD: Madonna's *Material Girl*. Nothing if not loyal, though, she announces earnestly that Sophie Ellis Bextor is still her *best singer*.

*****

Suddenly the temperature has leapt 15 degrees. This, of course, brings the rain. It pissed down all day yesterday and filled up the swimming pool, so once more the beams are sitting in a couple of inches of water. It's supposed to rain all week, which will make it very difficult to finish off the roof battens.

It's an ill downpour, however, that brings no one any good. There is a message from the roofing rep on the answer phone in the caravan. Typically, he speaks so rapidly that I fail to grasp what he's on about and, when I phone him back, there's no reply. But... Dishy Tom phones a few minutes later to tell me, *mirabile dictu*, as Cicero might have it, that he has been told that the tiles will be delivered to the builders' merchant's at the beginning of next week. In other words, he has managed more in a couple of days than I have in a couple of months. The power of television. It seems that it can mobilise even the most recalcitrant of Frenchmen.

The rain may be turning meadows into great lakes again in the valley below, but The Carpenters are now fitting the boarding to the two side walls of the mezzanine, the estimate for the aluminium guttering doesn't make me gasp, and the colour chart for Holkham's lovely linseed oil paints arrives in the post. They have offered us a discount decent enough to make them feasible. They go a long way and three coats are apparently good for almost 15 years.

I phone Debs in her lunch break to deliver the good news. She tells me that Baladou Sue, who lives by the stars, has told her that all the frustrations about the tiles and stuff are attributable to Mercury. The planetary imp has been blocking all these companies, but now its bad influence has lifted. So everything's coming up roses, it would seem.

*****

I sit in the caravan watching the rain slide down my plastic window on the outside world. It's not a pretty sight out there: another film set for a drama based on the Somme offensive. Christian has just phoned to tell me that he would have come today, only he bashed his hand with a hammer and then had to dash over to his mother's house near Gramat to deal with a chimney fire. He is excused. However... the battens wait to be finished and I'm beginning to fret quite seriously about what the Crazy Gang have done thus far – and what they might do. Monsieur Fromage has expressed his doubts, too, but hasn't gone into detail because he's reluctant to bad-mouth his fellow professionals. The trouble is: just how professional are they? This whole roof could shape up into one great big false economy.

Waiting for e-mails to come in, the rain drums on the caravan roof. Today is the day I'm hoping to conclude this current work project, but the lack of incoming information suggests that it's going to run on into another week. When a wave of depression washes over you, there's only one thing to do: crawl back into the womb. I phone my mother – and soon regret it. We get onto the subject of dogs. She'd love a dog, she tells me. So I ask her why she doesn't get one, then. Whereupon she reels off a list of excuses so specious that I close my eyes and rock in my chair as if preparing for a stroke.

I cut her off in her prime, however, because I spot a lorry backing down the drive. Surely not... It couldn't be. They haven't informed me, of course, but who cares? If it really is...

'I have to go. I think they might be delivering the roof tiles!'

Who cares if it's *raining dogs*, as Tilley once told our old cat, Dizzy. I feel a Gene Kelly moment coming on; I could twirl my umbrella as I splosh through the muddy puddles. THE ROOF TILES HAVE ARRIVED!

Only… After the *chauffeur* has dexterously deposited 15 or so pallets of terracotta tiles, side by side and on top of each other, it becomes clear that there are no *accessoires*. All the edge and ridge tiles. Where are they? Back, it would seem, to the endless fruitless calls to the sales rep.

That evening, I take time off from my angst to meet Jan in Vayrac after she has deposited Dutch Eric at St. Denis station and waved him off on his trip of a lifetime to the sub-continent. We go together to watch the new Michael Winterbottom film in the empty vault that is our local cinema. While busy filling in the market research questionnaires we have been handed at the box office, someone announces a car registration number that rings a bell. It's mine! The Peugeot 205! I have left the headlights on. Thanks be to the diminishing number of public-spirited citizens left in the world.

Because it's a sub-titled *version originale* copy, there are about six of us and the place feels like a mausoleum. It's a worthy but gruelling film that surely tells the truth about the refugee racket. Two desperate Afghanis make their epic and, for one of them, doomed journey across the bleak Middle East and into Europe and across the Channel to London. There's me fretting about my *accessoires*, when people like this are enduring constant suffering.

On the way back home, it's as if I'm still in a film: the rain lashing the windscreen, the wipers swishing back and forth at double tempo, the forks of lightning briefly illuminating the bluffs of the Dordogne. Debs is due to go and see the film the next evening with Jessica. I might suggest that either she takes a strong anti-depressant or simply stays at home.

*****

We awake on a cold morning in our cold bedroom. Neither of us wants to get up, but Harvey – who has slept all night on our bed – wants his breakfast.

'Harvey, go away please. Not now,' Debs tells him

sleepily.

Whereupon Harvey raises his hind-quarters and pees on her head. She screams with justification. I leap out of bed, grab Harvey and take our wriggling faux Siamese to the front door and lob him onto the lawn. The little bastard. My poor wife, one of the most patient and understanding of souls, is in a state of shock and already in the shower. One way to get us up, I guess.

Later, I'm called back from the caravan for another kind of liquid crisis. Debs has taken our washing into the *cave* to find the floor a couple of inches deep in water. On investigation, it seems that the big plastic tank linked to the pump and their industrial-sized boiler has burst its banks. I phone the plumber and, while waiting for his appearance, I get a call from someone high up in the roofing materials company. He is kindness and courtesy itself. He explains that the dearth of materials at the factory is due to abnormal demand before their prices go up this month. It is the first time in two months or so of frustration that someone has taken the trouble to explain the situation honestly. Knowing that it is neither a conspiracy nor something personal, I feel immediately better as a result. I can accept this. Why couldn't someone have told me this weeks ago? I could have made contingency plans. I feel like writing to his boss to praise his genuine customer service.

On the point of sending my work file to the customer and thereby meeting the new improved deadline, there is a knock at the caravan door. There stands a man of, I would imagine, almost 60, dressed in blue: blue cap, blue bib and braces. It's the plumber, my blue plumber. We chat about the view here and the valley below as I take him over to the big house. It doesn't take him long to diagnose the problem: the ball-cock in the tank is buggered, so the water has risen too high and, as soon as the pump kicks in, it has spilled over the sides. He turns off the pump for now, which will leave us with fairly minimal pressure, but I am happy to phone up our neighbours and report back. It's good to be of service.

Later, in Vayrac, I have an abbreviated session with the osteopath. It's long enough, though, for him to pronounce my shoulder cured. Walking back to the car, I feel like the cripple cured by the Messiah.

With my clean bill of health, I pick up our daughter from school and drive her to Brive, where I buy some rudimentary door handles from Lapeyre. Then, singing along to Sophie Ellis Bextor, we pick up her mum at the clinic and drive home with a takeaway pizza for our supper.

Harvey does not sleep on our bed that night.

*****

Our daughter is fast developing an artistic temperament. As if there weren't enough in our families, what with my mother and Deborah's sister. In the middle of making a beautiful card for my sister, who is in hospital, she tries to write something with a glitter pen on the beautiful dress she has created for this particular fairy. It goes wrong and she cries such bitter tears that it's quite shocking to behold. She cares this deeply about her art. It makes me question my own motivation and underlines my feeling that I grew up to be a dilettante. I hope that she will be able to follow her true path in life and not be deflected by irksome distractions, like building a house.

Being up on the roof with Christian is sheer misery. Not from any fault of his, but because the wind cuts through me like a scalpel. Debs tells me that, because we're both so thin, we feel the cold more than 'better padded' people. Nerves don't help. My body tenses up due to my fear of heights – and only relaxes a little with the confidence of learning how to place my body weight at the intersections of the battens. Logically, it isn't far to fall in any case, now that there's a balcony on the back of the house, but still...

Christian's a nice guy. He seems to know what he's doing – which helps. But I wish he were as reliable as Monsieur Fromage. I've got used to the white vans rolling down our drive in tandem, as regular as clockwork. When Christian says he'll be here some time during the morning, inevitably he turns up sometime during the afternoon. It won't be long now until The Carpenters have finished their work. Then I'll really be on my own. No one to talk to, no one to joke with, no one to ask for advice. I've grown accustomed to their banter and the way they behave like a pair of naughty boys, using bad words and calling each other every name under the sun. In truth, though, a little tension has crept into their relationship. Mike has told me how much he loves working with his partner in grime. He used to earn three times more money in London, but each day was a 12-hour day, full of stress and anger, while working with his old mucker is just plain fun. But… he is going to have to lay off work for eight weeks or risk going over the earnings he is allowed to earn under the *micro-entreprise* scheme, so is having to face the prospect of letting down his best mate. Monsieur F. understands the situation, but a few niggles of late suggest that he is uneasy about the prospect.

Tom and Sasha have arrived to film the closing stages of their work. At least they can point the camera now at an action man, clambering around his climbing frame, as opposed to a standing-around-looking-concerned-man. Poor Sasha huddles in a corner, frozen. She has been in Martinique for a couple of weeks over Christmas, so this must be a shock to the system.

Back in our *petite maison* that evening, my wife is on top form. Her work involves filtering and re-processing people's problems, so inevitably she comes back from a hard day at the couch feeling tired-out and lacklustre. Somehow she manages to preserve a good humour, but there have been times during the last few difficult months when the mask has slipped. This afternoon, though, she has been to Tulle for a session with her mentor, a big man with a charisma and a successful psychiatric practice to match. Together they have been re-visiting some old childhood fears and hang-ups, and she returns full of life, with the old raucous, sexy laugh restored that I remember with such affection. It's good to have the old frisky, carefree model back.

*****

The rain has churned up the mud again, and Monsieur Fromage is complaining of trench foot. A call to the builders' merchant suggests that *normalement* the accessories will be with them next week. Good news, but beware that over-used French word, which carries a multitude of meanings.

Bob's car is still sitting on blocks in his yard, so he has no way of getting here for the moment. Christian has promised to put in an appearance today, but I'm still sitting here, wishing and hoping and twiddling my thumbs, wondering what I should get on with while I wait expectantly. Obviously there are all those tiles to move, but the prospect of pushing a wheelbarrow laden with terracotta through the mud fills me with horror.

By the afternoon, he still hasn't arrived. I try to get on with some writing, but inspiration is just a distant flicker. The phone rings. It's someone from the builders' merchant to tell me that the lorry has been down to the depot in Toulouse to pick up the accessories, but – for some inexplicable reason – wasn't able to load them up and bring them back. What *is* going on? I'm beginning to see myself as some latter-day Joseph K. character, entwined in some conspiratorial web, unable either to extricate himself or make any sense of it. I believe it's turning me into a quivering wreck.

Cometh the hour to walk the dog, cometh the man. Not Christian – I have given up on him for the day – but an old chap in a cap, who introduces himself as *le paysan du coin*. The peasant farmer of this neck of the woods. He tells me about the problems his son had in obtaining planning permission for his family's house. Apparently, he had to turn the house around effectively, so that the narrower rather than the wider elevation was visible from the plain below. It makes me wonder how we got away with ours. Did Gilles *pull some strings*? I doubt if any corruption was involved, not with the modest fee he charged us. The *paysan du coin* also tells me that it's getting harder and harder to obtain a *certificat d'urbanisme* – or outline planning permission –

these days, so land is becoming more expensive. Altogether, it's reassuring to know that we have done the right thing in doing what we are doing when we are doing it.

Back home, I find a Wendy house full of small girls. The Jacksons have brought their two daughters over to play, because they are going out for the evening and couldn't find a babysitter. Debs is trying to entertain them by candlelight. The electricity has gone off again. In the *cave*, I discover that the main fuse has tripped, but when I push it back in, the electricity comes back on briefly before tripping again. For once, I don't panic. I have the bright idea of throwing all the fuses in the *petite maison* and then trying again. This time it holds. With Debs leaning out of our bedroom window, I shout out instructions from our neighbours' cellar. *OK, now try the next one!* In this way, we identify a dodgy circuit and illumination is restored. It's a little thing, but I am filled with pride when I think how far I have come along the path towards manhood. Less than a decade ago, in Sheffield, I would have simply gone round to see our capable neighbour, Kevin. To paraphrase that irritating song by that irritating group, Sweet, I wouldn't have had had *a clue* **what** *to do*.

Moving to France has often seemed like a road of trials, but maybe it'll make a man of me yet.

*****

The forecast for the week to come is not good. Rain, rain and then snow. So I knuckle down to the task of shifting tiles all weekend long. On Saturday, I have moved seven pallets full. That's 180 x 7 = 1,256 terracotta roman tiles, all stacked up neatly against what will be the rear wall of the house, waiting for a day when finally we're able to start hanging them from the roof battens.

The following day, a sweet young couple, sent by Gilles the architect, come to take a look and ask some questions. They're looking for some land and hoping to build something similar, maybe in straw. But land is getting harder to find, apparently. It's only really the under-populated departments, like the Corrèze and the Creuse and the Lozère, where you can still find cheap land for sale. The Lot, they say, is expensive now and even the Aveyron a little further south, the department that provided Paris with so many of its restaurateurs, is no longer cheap.

They give me a hand with the tiles for half an hour and offer to come and help with the plastering when the time comes, but I'm not holding my breath. It's OK; they're nice people and I'm happy to help them on their own particular journeys. No doubt other visitors will follow in time. Perhaps I should start charging for guided tours and describing myself as a consultant.

Half way through Sunday, I have shifted ten pallets in total. *Count 'em*, 1,800 tiles. The girls are out walking the dog with Thompson & Thompson and their skittish dog, Ella. My back is spavined and I'm beginning to shuffle like an infirm octogenarian. It's time to stop.

I wander down to see Muriel, who has invited us to dinner during the week. It's a simple, discreet house down in a dip, hidden from the road. However, it's within spitting distance of a dirty great pylon. All those magnetic force fields; they can't be good for you. From the southern side of the house, you can see the cliffs of the Dordogne valley. Muriel and her dead husband built it over the course of two winters and she added the swimming pool after his death – all by herself.

It's a strange situation: she talks of her ex-husband with evident affection and there is a palpable air of sadness about her. She seems to dote on her *lady companion* as much as she does on her two fat spoilt cats. It's a weird business, going from a heterosexual to a homosexual relationship. I don't profess to understand it, but it certainly doesn't stop me accepting the invitation for a *straightforward and vegetarian* dinner.

Although I could do with a massage, I'd be a cad to ask my hard-pressed wife on her day off. Instead, I find our Scrabble set in a plastic skip on the mezzanine and that evening we play our first game for months. I scrape a close and hard-fought victory.

*****

High up on the roof, the view is very special today: a clear blue sky with the contours of the plain emphasised by the bright winter sunshine and snow draped like rugs over the hills beyond. It's peaceful up here. Only the occasional barking dog and sporadic agricultural activity breaks the silence.

Any self-respecting artisan would no doubt sneer at all the layers I've got on, but it's warm enough in the sun to remove at least my scarf and jumper. The warmth is probably partly due to the internal combustion of my fear of heights. Christian has driven me to this. He turned up yesterday – but only at the beginning of the afternoon. We worked until the moon appeared as the tip of a fingernail in the sky and the light had faded, but – frustratingly – couldn't quite manage to finish battening the mezzanine roof.

Today he hasn't showed. He did at least phone to say that his mother had been taken to hospital, but I'm beginning to wonder whether he's fabricating all these excuses to mask what could be the real problem: that he's bluffed about his capabilities and is now feeling the stress of having to live up to the hyperbole. So finally, after waiting in vain yet again, I thought *sod it! I can do this myself* and boldly went where no *wee timorous beastie* has gone before.

My courage is rewarded. Yesterday, I phoned the sales rep for the 38th time and he told me that he would phone me back. He didn't. So I phoned a little later and told his *messagerie* that I was desperate. At the end of the day, there was a message waiting for me on the caravan phone. He had 'de-blocked the order' and the builders' merchant could now pick up the accessories. No explanation, of course, why the order was blocked in the first place. Over here, it seems, the customer is treated as a nuisance – rather than someone who pays their wages.

Anyway… Sure enough, when I climb down from my elevated perch to check for messages, there's one from the builders' merchant to say that the order has arrived. So I'm feeling quite elated – and not a little proud of myself for having stared vertigo in the face – when I pick up our daughter from the bus stop. A fellow parent tells me there that it's due to be –12 degrees tonight. Tilley tells me that they were shown a film about sexual abuse at school, so victims of abuse would know whom to turn to. She announces that, if anything like that were to happen to her, she could tell her mum and me, my sister and our friend Isabelle, her first teacher. She is getting so grown up these days. Come September and she will be going to *collège*. Only yesterday, it sometimes seems, our little girl was a mere toddler.

*****

Wednesday is always a good day, because Debs takes the day off from work and Tilley doesn't have school, so we can be a normal family again. I fancy a lie-in, but the plumber's due at 8.30, so I take Alf out for a walk on this crisp, cold morning. The distant mountains are as clear as I can ever remember seeing them. Completely covered in snow, they are meringues pressed onto the horizon by some great Mrs. Beeton in the sky.

Francis the plumber turns up on time. It bodes well. Wandering around the site, admiring the wooden framework, he talks and he talks. Debs comes over to join us and the subject somehow turns to essential oils. Francis uses them himself and instantly becomes an expert on the subject. Typically French, he starts to teach Debs about lavender and I can feel her bottling up her frustration. We seem to know so many people who can babble without being able to listen. Still, he has turned up when he said he would and he seems to know what he's doing, so what's a little crass insensitivity between plumber and client?

Later, on the hunt for the particular model of boiler that Francis has recommended, I have a long chat with a helpful man in a plumbers' merchant in some post-apocalyptic industrial estate out in the back end of Brive. He plies me with leaflets to take home and digest. More food for thought, more decisions. Should we abandon the heat-pump route and opt instead for an efficient condensing boiler?

During the afternoon, the rest of the tiles and most – but typically not all – of the accessories are delivered. I am not about to complain, but my delicious relief is rather tempered later by my wife's feedback on the introduction to and first chapter of my book that I have given her to read. She tells me that it reads like I'm trying to be someone else and am not succeeding. I feel like Jo in *Little Women* when Friedrich tells her that she must be true to herself. Her questions compel me to re-examine my whole motivation. What's the book about? Why do I want to write it? I must find the courage to be myself, to be simpler, more direct, more focused and more natural. Apparently, I don't even begin to sound like me until half way into the first chapter. I slope off into a corner to lick my wounds. The girl's right and I value her honesty. It's much more valuable than some glib kind of *very good, darling* verdict. But, heavens, it's hard this whole business of artistic endeavour. Just when you feel happy enough with something to present it to someone else, you discover that you've been kidding yourself. *Rip it up and start again...*

The day, indeed the month, ends pleasantly with dinner chez Muriel. As promised, it's simple and it's vegetarian. Being pasta, it certainly pleases our daughter, who must have been an Eye-talian in another life. The house is warm, welcoming and tasteful – as befits, I suppose, an interior designer.

She's younger than Debs it would seem, certainly younger than either of us would have figured. The wrinkles are maybe due to the fact that she's a smoker. She's from Alsace and has been here for 13 years. Taking possession of our neighbours' house sounds remarkably like the evening when we claimed our old farmhouse: pitch black, pouring rain and a key that wouldn't fit the lock. She and her German husband had wanted to buy a beautiful old house with vaulted ceilings and 200 hectares of land up on the plateau near Milau, but the locals ganged together to stop the proprietor selling up to two apparent Germans. Although they had signed the contract, they decided that they couldn't possibly live in a place where everyone was against them. So they shifted their focus further north to the Lot.

It's surprising to hear this from the lips of a native French woman. There was nothing particularly unusual in our own experience. Small-minded people are small-minded the world over.

On the way home, the alarming thought occurs to me that September to January inclusive equals five months. So does February to the end of June. We are effectively half-way. Roughly speaking, we have another five months in which to finish everything and meet the TV deadline.

February 2004

Perhaps it's because February is a shorter month than usual that I don't feel too unkind towards it. There's also the little matter of my wife's birthday to look forward to. She'll be 47; she's creeping up on me.

The heavens seem to be looking favourably upon her anniversary. The morning is beautiful and the temperature is back in positive territory after the recent cold. I'm keen to get on with the roof, but typically there is no sign of Christian all morning long. The Carpenters, however, turn up to do some more boarding and it's just like old times again with two big overgrown boys cursing each other out. For the want of something useful to do, I spend the time moving tiles onto the roof. Two at a time, tucked under my left arm, as I climb the ladder and add them to the nearby stacks I create in preparation for shifting each stack into place higher up the roof. It's tedious and difficult work and I can't help but think that there must be an easier way of doing this.

While the men banter below, I think back to the film that The Kid and I had seen together at the local cinema the day before: *La Prophésie des Grenouilles, The Prophesy of the Frogs*, an animated cautionary tale of ecological neglect. It was beautifully done – and suitably prophetic. I had looked upon it as an opportunity for bonding, as we have been a little more distant than usual, probably due to the exigencies of this build, but Tilley's friend Lucille turned up with her sisters and an adult chaperone, so I didn't get much of a look-in. Nevertheless, she thanked me so sweetly and so spontaneously when I tucked her up in bed that all was worthwhile.

Christian finally turns up around 3pm. Mike quips, 'We apologise for the late running of the 7.30 from Waterloo'. When Christian does work, he works methodically, but I can't stand this unreliability. Life would be so much easier if I could just do this whole roof myself. Besides, I'm racked by guilt about Bob Ze Builder. When I mention to Christian that his ex-*business partner* might be turning up on Wednesday if his car is back on the road, he plays the prima donna. Clearly he's not happy about the prospect. There seems to be genuine bad blood between them now and I'm caught up in the middle of it. Christian proceeds to point out all the defects in Bob's workmanship, again, and I'm regaled with the saga of a duvet, which he lent to Bob only to get it back two days later, dirty and dishevelled. Bob doesn't wash, he doesn't respect people, he doesn't do this and he doesn't do that. Perhaps he's right, but I still feel like a bounder, because I've promised him this work for so long and it doesn't seem quite fair. C.f. the Hutton Report, in fact, which has now cleared our oily Prime Minister of all blame for David Kelly's death and pinned it instead on the BBC. Scapegoat City and the weapons of mass seduction.

Christian does occasionally have his uses. 'Why not get a farmer with a tractor to help move all these tiles onto the roof?' he suggests. Why not indeed? I leave him to his devices and go off to the local farm in search of Jean-Louis and/or his brother, Alain. The pair of them are at home, having a break for a coffee and cigarettes before they go and do what has to be done in the bovine concentration camp.

Whenever I speak to either brother, I try to shut off from my conscious mind those poor cows, giving suck to their young in total darkness. I join them for a *petit café*, which tastes suspiciously instant, and organise the hire of their hands and tractor for Wednesday.

*****

My poor deserving wife's birthday is miserable. She spends her morning off washing and pegging out clothes in the brilliant sunshine, while I wait in vain once again for Christian's arrival. Leaves on the track no doubt. Tilley is at home for the February break and we are looking after Lucille for a few days, which is great for our daughter but not quite so great for her parents. She's a sweet girl, but she talks non-stop and their combined youthful energy is not necessarily what the doctor ordered.

In the afternoon, a client tells her an appalling tale of the gang rape of her granddaughter, perpetrated by a monstrous ex-husband and his evil cronies. Despite her training as a therapist, she can't clear her mind of the revelations and is therefore in no real mood to enjoy either the candle-lit dinner I have prepared for her or the girls' high jinks. So she goes to bed early, tired out. The end of an imperfect day.

At least Bob has phoned during the afternoon to say that his car isn't going to be ready until Saturday. My own private Armageddon has been postponed for a few days. Ideally, Christian and I will have finished the roof before he gets here, so I can present him with a fait accompli. But progress is slow. While we are trying to fix the edge tiles in place – from which we will work our way to the mezzanine roof in the middle of the construction – Monsieur Fromage points out that they aren't overlapping as they should do. Fortunately, we have screwed them in place and not used nails. So, with Christian on the edge of the roof and me up a rather precarious ladder, gripping the rung as if my life depends on it, we manage to *get it right next time*. The Carpenters are not impressed with Christian. I feel embarrassed.

Good news on the sponsorship front helps to mitigate Deborah's birthday blues. We have been offered free tickets to the next Ideal Homes Exhibition and Red Displays have agreed to supply some shelves for my tapes, CDs and records. At last! The chance to house it all as nature intended. The nearest I've come to proper storage were the shelves my brother built for me from MDF. They stood on the landing of our former home, backless and vulnerable to acts of clumsiness. My nephew's girlfriend once sent a cascade of cassettes tumbling down the stairs. I glared at her before picking up the pieces.

*****

It's the end of a momentous day and I'm sitting alone in the *petite maison* while our daughter and her friend sleep upstairs on the mezzanine level and Debs drives back from giving her talk on her work at the *université populaire*, a kind of Women's Institute affair. All is quiet now after a day of three kids. Jean Louis' daughter, Aurore, joined the girls under my wife's suzerainty while her father and her uncle helped out on the roof. She wasn't easy, apparently. She sits around the house watching junk on the telly and doesn't know how to mix or play with her peers. We're busy rearing a whole generation of the technologically adept, but socially inept.

I'm listening quietly to some *treasures of jazz* from the 1940s and my mind keeps wandering off onto the subject of Bob Ze Builder. My call late this afternoon ruined an otherwise perfect day. The sun shone brightly on us up on the roof all day long. The temperature reached an unnatural 19 degrees and bulbs are busy flowering everywhere, just in time for the next frost. At one point, there were six of us all working in concord. The two brothers took turns in the tractor while the other helped Bret and me on the roof, moving stacks of tiles into place. So the latticework of the roof's wooden frame is now studded with little piles of terracotta tiles.

172

After lunch, Christian joined us with his mate, Michel, a quiet, thoughtful, older man who has worked on churches and ancient monuments. He came to take a look and his calmly authoritative manner filled me with reassurance. He will do the zinc flashing and oversee the work and I am happy enough about his daily tariff, but the cost of this roof is mounting up to a point where it might have been cheaper to have employed a firm to do it (assuming that I could have found one with the necessary window of opportunity).

The Farmer Bros. didn't really want any money, so I offered them both what I am paying Christian – which is probably far too bloody much. They seemed happy to split it between them. But the main thing is that progress has been made. To celebrate at the end of the day, I produced some cake that someone had given us and opened a bottle of wine in the time-honoured fashion. We stood around nattering at the back of the house, looking out on a landscape bathed in the last rays of sunshine. It was beautiful to behold and Alain pointed out the Madonna on top of the Roche de Vic, glinting faintly atop her monument on the hills across the plain.

But when everyone was gone, I phoned Bob to tell him not to come, because the roof is mainly done. Understandably, he wasn't happy. He accused me of dishonesty. I was *pas cool*. I couldn't defend myself, but just had to take it all and squirm. Now that I reflect, of course, I can point out that I had offered to pick him up at the station so he could come by train while he was waiting for his car. And I can point to the alcohol.

Nevertheless, I'm thinking of paying him for a couple of days. Probably not necessary, but isn't that what you do when you sack someone? Compensate them? And I shall write him a letter, explaining my side of the story. Maybe I'll even find him a couple of days of work on some task that doesn't demand rigorous attention to detail. We can't afford to be a charitable organisation; I shouldn't feel so personally responsible for someone else's shortcomings. I like the guy, but his work appears to be as sloppy as his lifestyle and ultimately he brings these problems upon himself.

The sound of a car bursts my reverie. My gal is home safely. The talk has gone very well it seems and she's got several new bookings out of it. Tomorrow she is running a course for eight people at her clinic. And then she and The Kid travel by train to England to visit friends and my mother-in-law. Way *oop north* where the sun don't shine.

*****

The TV team is back again. Tom and Sasha are here to film me living and working as a single man. This is a test. If I can't supervise the house and get back to some serious writing during the ten days they will be away, I should be driven from this land and cast out in the desert. Already, though, the invitations for dinner are coming in. All in the best possible intentions, but people just don't get it that there are times when *I vant to pee alone.*

After depositing the girls at Brive station early this morning and waving them off on the train to Paris, I drive to Bretenoux to deposit my letter and an envelope with a day's wages for Bob. The Carpenters reassured me that I would have been a mug to wait for him with my tight deadline and the propitious weather. And I sure as hell **am** a mug to be paying him a day's wages. After all, if he couldn't get here when he was needed, that was his tough luck. No room for sentimentality in the tough world of construction.

I'm rather hoping that Bob isn't at home, so I can drop the money and run. But he's there, so I have to take my medicine. We talk to each other on either side of a symbolic metal gate. Bob reiterates what he has already told me on the phone. It's the principle of the thing: letting him down at the last minute after he has busted a gut to get his car ready. He reiterates that he has been learning his trade for ten years *blah blah blah.* It's uncomfortable, but I'm relieved that I have faced him like a man. I hope he reads and reflects on my letter, but at least I know that he doesn't think of me as a *gros con,* it's just that he was angry when we spoke and the timing was terrible.

174

In the afternoon, they film me painting a mixture of warmed linseed oil and turpentine to the wooden undersides of the eaves as some sort of protection against the elements, while Michel gets on with his work quietly and methodically. He is making the flashing for the valleys on either side of the mezzanine projection. It is a strange and intriguing system. Instead of one complete strip of zinc, he sheaths the edge of each individual tile that abuts the valley. The thinking behind this is that, if there is a problem anywhere with the flashing, you can remove the offending tile, replace the zinc sheath and slot it back into place. It's a work of art. Like all artists, though, there is a tendency to fuss over the creation to the point where you wonder whether they will ever finish. As the paymaster, I'm secretly wishing that Michel were more of a Cézanne than a Seurat.

My own work, with paintbrush and a flask full of warm linseed oil, is rather more prosaic. I'm happy enough, though, to jabber away for the camera while I paint the stuff onto the wood. The smell reminds me of happy days as a boy, oiling my first cricket bat with my dad. I get onto the subject of my fantasy cricket world, about which viewers surely won't want to hear. Clearly there will have to be some savage editing before our programme is broadcast.

When we break in the afternoon and while the camera is at rest, I quiz Michel about the intriguing sticker on his car. SOS Papa. It's an organisation formed by fathers who have been denied access to their children by law. This quiet man in a beret, who looks like some kindly rural character from *The Railway Children*, has it seems been fighting the court's ruling for years. Lugging his bulging dossier here, there and everywhere. Last summer to the European Court in Brussels. It has cost him thousands, but – even more to the point – the untold hardship of not being allowed to see his young son and daughter. Of course, I don't know both sides of the story, but I do know that the law is generally an ass and I do know that Michel appears a gentle and dignified man. It seems entirely credible when he tells me, with tears welling up in his eyes, that his children would prefer to live with him.

When evening comes, my back is aching from all this physical work and I find myself mentally and physically exhausted. I go to bed early, but – for once in my life – I am not sleeping well. It's customarily two visits to the loo at the moment, which is a pain I could do without. Alfred Lord Sampson usually opens an eye as I creep by, while snoring away in his basket, smelling reassuringly of McVitie's wholemeal digestive biscuits.

*****

Our friends, the Jacksons, are off to England en masse today and they have asked me to house-sit for them. Some creature comforts will be very nice, thank you. Our little house has been a godsend, but there's no substitute for a proper family home. Even if it's another family's.

Before they depart for the motherland, we drive over to St. Bazille de Meyssac to borrow Steve's concrete mixer for the ridge tiles. I ride in style with Tom and Sasha, who want to record the momentous event, but I keep a wary eye on the rear-view mirror, because Christian's van could pack up at any moment. We roll up outside a little house built on some kind of bluff, so the rear elevation seems twice as high as the front – rather like those amazing Georgian townhouses around the Royal Crescent in Bath. This one, Steve explains, was the house of two dirty brothers, who lived like tramps. One of them slept with an open-plan WC in his bedroom, while the stairs to the first floor were simply the drawers of an old chest. But Steve has done a good renovation job and it looks clean, habitable – and saleable.

We load the *ce-ment mixer* (*putty, putty*) into Christian's van and stop on the way home to stage a little action shot, which will almost certainly never get used. Back on site, I join Michel and Christian on the roof before the pair of them go off to the Bonne Famille in nearby Sarassac for the customary goddamn two-hour lunch. I get to stage some calls in the caravan for the sake of footage. Ever since surprising a mouse in the oven, a big mouse that stared at me in a similar state of shock, I now sing loudly every time I step into the caravan. Harvey isn't interested in patrolling the caravan and the awning for me. We owe him a living it would seem.

The phone rings for real. It's Bob – and my heart sinks. *Shiver me timbers*, he's read my letter and is genuinely touched. He doesn't want to take the money without doing some work to earn it. So I tell him that we'll sort something out when it's time to work on the inside of the house.

And when will that be, Sasha enquires? When indeed? I tell her that we might finish the roof by the end of the week, in which case I can start focusing on the next stage. Moving the bales, once Dutch Eric is back from the sub-continent, will be the next of the Munros to climb. I've already been fretting quietly about cutting and re-tying the bales. Will I remember anything from my course?

It's a beautiful crisp day and Alf barks at traces of passing airplanes high up in the sky. The trouble with these two-hour French lunches is that they work later to make up the time lost. So, by the time we call it a day, Sasha and I are freezing. If Tom is, he never shows it. He's imperturbable, like a handsome young Buddha. No wonder Tilley the Kid worships him.

When I get to the Jacksons' house in Montignac, I luxuriate magnificently in a hot bath with my current book. Despite my best intentions, there's no way José that I shall be working on my own book this evening. After a hasty pasta and salad, I spread myself out on the capacious sofa to watch Kubrick's *Eyes Wide Shut* on their new DVD. It's far from the minor masterpiece I have hoped. It's beautifully shot, but the plot is preposterous and Tom Cruise is irritating. Even Nicole Kidman is fatally flawed. When I think of *Lolita, Dr. Strangelove, 2001, Paths of Glory* and other *meisterwerks*, this seems nothing more than an old man's pretence for filming lots of lithe, naked female flesh. (Can't have been too arduous, though.)

*****

It's Friday 13th. At least no one will be working on the roof. I've paid off Christian for the time being and Michel is off to the Aveyron to pick up his children. It will be the first time in years that he's had them to stay with him. He's a happy man at last. Over lunch outside in yesterday's glorious sunshine, he told me how the hatred towards his ex-wife used to wake him up at night. He opened his mouth to show me the gaps where his teeth have fallen out and described in typically French detail the digestive disorders due to marital discord. Appalling what can happen when love breaks down. As terrible as the crime was, you can almost understand what drove that Welsh farmer to get his oldest boy to phone his mother and tell her what he was going to do: gas all his children with exhaust fumes. It still brings chills just to think about it.

So, no work today, the roofer's gone away. It's very frustrating, because the end is in sight. But I'm stuck with a perfectionist and an impostor working in tandem. We all worked on the ridge yesterday. Needless to say, the *accéssoires* supplied by the manufacturers weren't suitable and after several fruitless calls to local depots, Michel decreed that we would just have to do it *á l'ancien* with some bog-standard Roman tiles. He started off the process and then Christian followed on. If, as he says, he **has** laid kilometres of ridge tiles in his time, he can't have done it very well. Michel took over and he will finish the job himself when he comes back from his paternal sojourn in the middle of next week.

Now that I've effectively laid him off, it has become clear to me why Christian can't get it together to turn up of a morning. He sleeps badly from a guilty conscience. He knows that he has been bull-shitting me and he is scared that one day soon the truth will out. He will be confronted with a situation for which he is not equipped. He succeeded in undermining my confidence in Bob, but at least supplied Michel before any serious damage was done. Maybe

Citronelle was right to fire him from the radio station after all. I feel like I have been suckered into this whole mess.

Happily, things are going well in England. Debs told me on the phone how Tilley gets up early, gets into her wellies and her cheap coat from Oxfam and goes to help Ros next door with the sheep and the lambing. My mother-in-law's poisonous partner isn't there for now and the girls are having a ball.

I am not a dog-minder; I'm a free man! Alf is with Baladou Sue and his shaggy mate, Peluché, while I'm based at the Jacksons', so I bunk off in the afternoon to go into Brive for a trip to the music library, just to make sure that I wasn't dreaming about their jazz section. When I take my (difficult) choices to the desk, I tell the woman there that I haven't seen a better range in the biggest jazz shops in London and she seems chuffed.

In the evening, when I should at last be writing, I head over to Jan's to honour my dinner invitation. With Eric still in India, she has found it tough to cope with everything on her own: maintaining their organic smallholding, feeding the chickens, walking the dogs, stoking the fire and so on. So she's as tired as I am. After dinner, we flake out in front of their telly to watch Polanski's *The Pianist* on DVD. Some have said that it's not as good as it bills itself to be, but we both find it marvellous. Adrien Brody in the title role is a genuine star and I love the way that much of the action is seen from behind curtains or through holes in the wall, a little like *Rear Window*. It's as powerful and as shocking as *Schindler's List*, beautifully shot and acted and a worthy winner of the Palme d'Or.

It's long, though. So I don't get back to the *petite maison* till gone 11pm. My original plan was to stop off here, shut Harvey in for the night and then go on to the Jacksons' house for another night of comparative luxury. The lure of bed, however, is too strong. Dedicated writers would put an hour in at this point, but I'm too tired to think straight. I manage a page or two of *The Beatles' Anthology*, but it's far too cumbersome to be read in bed.

*****

Too much socialising for a man with a deadline to meet! On a beautiful Saturday morning, after making a couple of curries for later meals, I meet up with Nick Thompson at Collonges La Rouge for a two-wheel sortie to inaugurate the Corrézian tourist office's new cycle route.

A whole crowd of us congregates around the ancient covered market in the heart of this remarkable blood-red village. It's the original *l'un des plus beaux villages de France*, of which we have six or seven in the Lot, and a gathering like this would be impossible in the summer when the tourists are milling around in their hundreds. Today it's the turn of some motley cyclists. The French take their cycling and their milling about seriously. We manage a good hour's worth of milling: initially up on the main road, where pockets of cyclists chat oblivious to the cars that try to get through, observed by indolent gendarmes who seem determined to do sweet Fanny Adams to earn their inflated salaries; then down by the market place, where we take a breakfast of miniaturised patisseries and coffee in plastic cups while nasty little black nylon publicity anoraks are handed out and dignitaries make the inevitable protracted speeches. Nick and I mutter darkly about this national or regional inability to start events on time.

When, at last, we set off – in waves – it's cold but beautiful and the circuit is indeed worth the event. Astride my old Raleigh, which Debs and I bought off a young student in Sheffield, I cannot compete with the technological improvements in evidence. It's not a race, but I don't even manage to keep up with Nick, who is not even as fit as I am. By the time we get back to Collonges, I'm sweating in my fleece and my snide anorak. The final climb up through the picturesque streets of this impossibly picturesque village is a killer. We mill about for a little longer and then disperse with a purpose probably provoked by the anticipation of lunch.

Dinner with Mike, of The Carpenters, and his wife

Hazel on Saturday evening – British nouvelle cuisine: curry, followed by Camembert cheese, followed by sponge pudding with golden syrup and custard *à ma grandmère* – is followed by Sunday lunch at the watermill with Fi and Giles and other friends. This is crazy. What was I thinking of, accepting so many invitations?

Before lunch, we walk to the next mill along this idyllic hidden valley. Looking down on it from the edge of a bluff, Fi explains how it has been preserved as a museum. Theirs, of course, is a family home – and one of the most beautiful I have yet found in a land of beautiful family homes – but it's a good job that it's February. God knows how they keep warm in the deep mid winter, when everything – inside and out – freezes over.

We have a lovely lunch of fish pie and salad with a memorable lemon tart that Giles has made for dessert. Unfortunately, I sit beside a woman who spends an inordinate amount of time talking about herself. We met last winter at Giles' birthday party, but she wouldn't remember me from Adam. Inner Me wants to cry out, *For God's sake, woman, can't you just listen to yourself?* Outer Me, fashioned by a middle-class Protestant English upbringing, nods politely, while making a mental note never again to cross her path.

After lunch, we watch a new-look England rugby team demolish the game-but-hapless Italians. They win by about 50 points and the slaughter makes me uncomfortable.

I drive home via Baladou to pick up Alf, with the telephone number of Clive the plasterer tucked safely in my pocket.

*****

A frantic full-on day follows the frivolity. Working alone yesterday, I cut up some planks of scrap wood to cover up the west wall in preparation for the arrival of the bales. *The bales, the bales!* I have enlisted Bret's help to move them, and the Flying Dutchman is now back from India.

Michel dropped by while I was busy with saw to tell

me that he had got his dates mixed up and wouldn't be back till Thursday. He came with his two kids, who call him *Papa*, and I have never thus far seen him look so happy.

While rootling around for something in a box in the awning, I found a creature staring at me like Jack might have regarded the giant at the top of the beanstalk. I let out a cry and threw the box outside. I tried to shoo the mouse off, but it turned and ran back into the awning – swiftly followed by another rodent. It's war! Later, I bought myself a couple of crude mousetraps from the agricultural co-operative in Martel. I'm a grown man and there should be no need for such weaponry, but the little critters make me *noyvuss*.

This morning, we all meet up at Christophe's farm. Dishy Tom is back (alone) to film this key part of the narrative. Eric is bubbling with tales of India: the children playing cricket in the street with improvised bats; the delicious food and the disgusting pollution; the discarded plastic everywhere – that blows across the land and finds itself way to the oceans, where it suffocates turtles and the like. The smog of Mumbai is particularly shocking. 'But the people, Mark! The people,' he enthuses. 'They're so beautiful, so friendly. Ya, all that poverty and they're so full of life.'

The bales look well. Still nice and yellow – and still as dry as biscuits. But they're loose and friable and I'm concerned about their potential for cutting and shaping. Bret, my reassuring, optimistic friend, reckons they'll be fine. Eric backs the trailer up to the mountainous pile stacked high under the hangar. We make a rumpus in the hope that any rats will scurry off and Bret scales the heights to toss one bale after another to me, so I can stack them on the bed of the trailer. We manage only about 80 before having to tie them down with tarps and some enormous ropes that Christophe lends us.

And then their journey begins. Slowly and gingerly. Tom, Bret and I follow the tractor at a snail's pace in my car, anxiously watching the tractor's leaning load. We separate at a crossroads, so I can drive to Quatre Routes and buy some red diesel for the tractor.

Back at the site, from the rear balcony, we spot Eric's tractor making its indomitable progress across the meadowlands that tend to flood in winter. It is a relief when the tractor comes chugging down our track. We get unloaded quickly and stack the bales on the pallets I have put down for the purpose. I realise, however, that there's not much available dry space left for the 300 or so more that are due to arrive.

Eric trundles off back home at his stately pace, while Tom takes Bret and me to the PMU in Martel for a spot of lunch. Covered in bits of straw and looking like Wurzel Gummage, Bret chats away nineteen to the dozen about the state of the world and his concept of freedom. There's not much on the menu even for a faux vegetarian like me, so I plump for salad and chips, while Bret orders some awful concoction involving pigs' innards. He tells us cheerfully that it's pretty disgusting and spends the rest of the day *repeating*.

We get back to Christophe's after lunch for another load. For all the stopping and starting for photo opportunities, the load seems more stable and this time it seems to go more quickly. The only trouble is that, by the time we have stacked the bales on my pallets, most of the afternoon has gone. There isn't the light or the time for another load. We drink some beer and toast what we have achieved so far and I finish the day off by sweeping up the loose straw to obviate the fire hazard.

The girls are due in London, but I am unable to reach them at our friends in Crystal Palace, so I go back by torchlight after dinner to try the caravan telephone again – still without success. There is a dead mouse in one of the Lucifer traps I have set inside the caravan. Poor little creature, spread-eagled by the sink. Fortunately, there is no blood. With my new gardening gloves, I dispose of it outside. The battle has been won, but not necessarily the war.

*****

Quite apart from the premature buds, the worst thing about such unseasonable warmth as we have been experiencing this last week or so is that lulls you into a false sense of security. I wake up this morning, pull the curtains and see snow everywhere. It's as if I have woken up from a dream about Polynesia to find myself in the Antarctic.

Despite the conditions, Michel turns up as promised to work on the roof. Dishy Tom turns up to film him at work in a winter wonderland. He poses the pertinent question, 'Is it safe to work on the roof when it's snowing?' In truth, though, it's light powdery snow and, once the morning sun gets to work, it all begins to dissolve.

After flunking a few more of Tom's questions, I follow Michel up onto the roof – such is my desire to get it finished. It looks great, but there remain some details to complete – and, as with all things, it's the details that take the time. Up there holding the flex of the angle grinder for him while he cuts the ridge tiles down to size, I envisage him slicing his leg with the spinning blade and being rushed to hospital. Mercifully, we get through the operation without incident and can pass onto the safer business of mixing the mortar in which to bed the tiles.

At lunch I feed him on leftover curry, which seems to suit him quite well. We talk about the family situation, as we often do. He shows me an old newspaper article about a hunger strike he undertook. Even though it's not ancient history, it shows a much younger man (with teeth presumably intact). His son, he tells me, has been able to make up his own mind about the situation, but his mother has programmed his little sister from an early age. So the poor lad is carrying all the weight on his shoulders from his inability to tell his sister the truth of the matter. As Michel says, however, one day – when she is old enough – the truth will sink in.

I leave him to his slow, methodical work in the afternoon and take Alfie with me to Brive. First, I need to withdraw some more money to pay people. I do it, as always, with studied insouciance despite feeling self-conscious and under scrutiny. *What's this bloody foreigner doing, withdrawing all these large sums of money? He must be living a life of luxury with his ill-gotten gains.* Then I go to the clinic to sort out some paperwork and to sell an ISA to raise some money to hand over to my workers. Finally, I take Alf out on the lead to order a couple of pizzas as a snack for the girls when they get back.

Waiting at the station for the train to arrive with all the other expectant friends and relatives, I'm all a-quiver and can feel Alf's excitement at being in a crowd. The train is bang on time. It's just like a scene from a film, as I take their cases and help them down the steps onto the platform. The Kid chatters away about all the costumes she has seen in the Victoria & Albert Museum, but Debs has hurt her back, lugging a heavy suitcase around while having to worry about connections. Re-united in this still foreign land, we drive home in a car that smells of pizza toppings.

*****

Up on the roof. Still. Michel works on. When I see him lovingly sponging his mortar, I'm tempted to take him by the shoulders and shake him. *Just get a flaming move-on, man!* But he's ever reliable – and he's thorough. I feel confident that our roof won't leak. It's almost there, just the little triangular *houteau* to cover now: Gilles' architectural embellishment, his little *fantasie*, conceived to give me a view of the valley when I'm up working on the mezzanine level. I can't believe it'll be more than the equivalent of a sea-peep and if it ends up taking Michel another three days to negotiate its intricate structure, I'll drive down to Figeac and tug his beaded beard till his eyes water. *You and your flaming architectural fantasies!*

When Michel arrives this morning, it's freezing cold and the water in the hosepipe has frozen solid. The temperature goes up and down like a yo-yo, indicative of planetary melt-down. Once the sun comes out, it turns the frosty terrain to mud. It sticks to everything and we trail it across our pristine roof.

When Michel doesn't need me, I spend my time nailing my off-cut planks to the uprights of the framework for the west wall to provide more protection for the rest of the bales when they arrive. An old farmer with a deranged dog stops by en route for his field, where he wants to inspect his mole traps. He thinks that this is the finished wall. God help us if it were; the draughts would be glacial. So I'm thinking of daubing *TEMPORAIRE* in bold red letters big enough to be seen from afar.

Then the man from Wiessmann turns up to talk about the heating system. He suggests a condensation boiler for the time being and a heat pump at a later date when we can afford one, linked perhaps to a solar hot water system with panels sited on the south-east facing roof. Solar panels would be a splendid symbolic gesture, but I wonder whether the trees and the orientation of the house would render them redundant in winter and therefore economically unsound. To be discussed with Deborah.

Michel, give the man his due, works on till dusk. It's almost seven before he calls it a day. But still no sign of the Digger Man, who has promised to drop by to discuss the *fosse septique*. His no-shows are predictable now.

In the evening, we go out *en famille* to honour our second local invitation, this one from Michelle and Jean-Claude, who live further along this *crête*, not far from the bus stop. Their house is hidden by high hedges from neighbours and by the woods from the main road that winds down to the station below. Their American letterbox suggests that they will be a little more out of the ordinary. And so it proves. Their house is cosy and tasteful and peopled with guests: a couple of Parisians who are restoring the amazing medieval chateau in Curemonte, and an artist who lives in Martel. The Parisians know many of our friends, including Jan and Dutch Eric, whose praises they sing to everyone. *Such hard, hard workers! You wouldn't believe…*

186

Jean-Claude whisks me away for a game of French billiards. We've all just been talking about the brilliance of Charles Laughton's *The Night Of The Hunter* (which was shown recently on Arte, it appears), so clearly the charm of the bourgeoisie is discreet tonight. Playing billiards with Jean-Claude makes me think of Paul Newman's money-making scam in *The Hustler*. Not that I'm a Fast Eddie by any stretch of the imagination. In fact, I don't get the point of this game without pockets. It strips all the fun out of playing on baize. It seems perverse in that respect, and curiously French. They don't do fun.

Yet fun is precisely what we have. Michelle is scatty and loveably eccentric. Once married to an American and an ex-pat resident of Maine and Connecticut, she has never made a vegetarian meal before, she tells us, but her couscous is fabulous. Jean-Claude can be a little overpowering – particularly in contrast to Henri, with his boozer's nose, his ruddy complexion and snow-white hair, and his gentle manner that masks a sly sense of humour – but he clearly has a good heart. Indeed, everyone is warm and welcoming and full of positive words about our nascent house. We go home to our beds feeling flushed by conviviality.

*****

By contrast, the next couple of days are far from fun. The plumber is hounding me for a decision about the boiler and I can't get hold of anyone from Wiessmann or Chaffoteaux and Maury, which may mean that I have to go with his recommendation. The Digger Man, despite the hours I've spent either on the phone or hanging around, is still a figment of my imagination.

And today I have a blizzard to contend with. Just as the *météo's* red alert has warned us. Trying to hang a tarp across the expanse of the north-eastern façade in the face of a stiff northerly wind proves a Sisyphean task and almost reduces me to tears of frustration. It also makes me worry that a straw wall might not be strong enough to resist such a wind, let alone a tempest. I'm beginning to think that some kind of metal grill – to provide a key for the render and strength for the bales – will be necessary, despite our hope that we could do it all without mesh.

Meanwhile, up on the roof, the tarp protecting Michel's work around the triangular *houteau* has come adrift and it's flapping around in the wind like a distress signal. Michel himself has phoned to tell me that he can't get here because of a problem with his tyres. While most are happy enough to let me stew, he has gone to the trouble of chasing up my number. It's appreciated as much as his absence is not. Only a couple more hours of work and then the roof will be finished. *Curse his tyres. Curse this snow.*

The wind starts to swirl, blowing the snow in from all directions. Dishy Tom and his camera should be here to record me rushing about like a headless chicken, trying to hang tarps over all the apertures to protect my beloved bales, fighting them off as the wind wraps them around me, cursing like a foul-mouthed Lear, so cold that I can't feel my fingers, so miserable that I want to hang myself from a mezzanine beam. With a rapidly developing cold to boot, I'm ready to sink to my knees and weep in self-pity.

Finally, I gather up all my bits and pieces and leave nature to do its worst. I trudge back past our neighbours' tennis court to the *petite maison* in the teeth of this bitter blizzard. I would have made a lousy polar explorer. As soon as conditions deteriorated, I'd start whimpering. My fingers are so numb, I can barely get them into my back pocket for the key to the door.

Having just about thawed out by the Calor Gas fire, I remember that I am supposed to be picking up The Kid from school and driving to Brive to meet up with Fi and Giles at the bowling alley to celebrate Giles's birthday. Needless to say, the car won't make it up their drive. But I think of Fi and Giles having to negotiate their perilous track. Would they give up if there's a birthday to toast and beer to be drunk? Would they, heck as like. So I steel myself for another go. This time I go slippin' and a-slidin', roarin' and a- spinnin', growlin' and a-cursin', serpentining all the way to the top of the drive. Now I feel more like the Slim Pickens character in *Dr. Strangelove*, waving his hat and whooping as he rides the A-bomb to Armageddon.

France is geared up for snow. The main roads are always promptly gritted and the journey down the motorway to Brive is remarkably uneventful. We pick up Debs and Juliette, Tilley's best friend, whose mother has deposited her at the clinic for our safe-keeping for a couple of days.

Bowling alleys always smell of well-worn second-hand shoes. The thought of all those sweaty feet makes me feel slightly uncomfortable wearing the flat-soled shoes provided. A little squeamishness doesn't hold me back – although I don't drink nearly as many beers as Giles and his more enthusiastic cronies, who order *giraffes* (as they're called): long-necked plastic tubes full of the amber liquid with a tap at the bottom.

While I am practising my Dude moves from *The Big Lebowski*, Debs whispers in my ear. Fi has told her that she is pregnant – after many years of trying. I suspect that my clever witch of a wife has had something to do with this. That prescription for the tongues of bats and the warts of a toad. I'm so excited for our friend and so proud of my wife's efficacy that I want to broadcast it – but it's still a secret.

*****

2004 is a leap year. February runs on for one more day – and an eventful one at that. It's hardly the relaxing Sunday that we both need. It's freezing cold and we're both suffering from head colds and blocked passages, which won't clear up as they might if we had the luxury of a day in bed.

Didier and Nadine turn up to pick up their daughter. Didier is a kind, softly spoken man who lives, we feel, in the lee of his moody wife. A demanding mother, we also sense a certain frisson between her and her daughter. However, she's on good form today at least, interested to see the house and to talk about its concept. When I describe all that remains to be done – floor, ceilings, stud walls, gas, electricity, water, heating and so on – I realise that I've been concentrating so hard on the outside that I've somewhat overlooked the inside. It sounds like there's a mountain still to climb. Didier has offered to come over during the Easter holidays to help out for a couple of days.

I leave them all to it and go over as arranged to meet Dutch Eric at Christophe's farm to bring some more bales over to the site. Debs was due to come with us to give their little girl another treatment, but she is completely cured after the initial session, so it's nice to feel that the debt of a winter's storage has been repaid. We load up the trailer and head for home.

When I get back, Debs and the others have gone off for a walk with the dog. Standing on the back balcony, I scan the landscape in search of a little orange tractor and its load of big yellow Weetabix. Time passes and I fail to spot him anywhere. There's nothing of that description crossing the flood plain, nothing trundling along beside the single-track railway, nothing climbing the narrow shortcut that would take him up to this crest.

I find him stuck at a particularly steep part of the track where the ice hasn't melted. So it could be worse, but he can't go forward or back. There is no one around in the local farm to ask for help. There's nothing for it but to abandon the tractor and drive off to Jean-Louis' farm and look for help there. Fortunately, he's at home. He's waiting for a lorry to arrive to take the veal calves off to their final destination: a brutal, bloody end to a mercifully brief existence as prisoners in the dark.

Jean-Louis and his tractor have little problem in extricating Eric's load. By the time we get to our house, however, it's gone three and we're both hungry. We join the others for the last of the lunch at a very crowded round table in the *petite maison*. After lunch, everyone walks over to the big house to help unload the bales. I think Didier and Nadine were imagining that they could actually construct a wall while they were here. People seem to think that it's just a matter of plonking a few bales down on some bamboo poles.

Eric decides to leave the tractor and trailer here. I drive him home and get back just in time to wave goodbye to our visitors. *Alone again, naturally.* Now that the bales are all here, sheltering under our new protective roof, the Big Day is fast approaching. The acid test. Will I be able to assemble them into recognisable, functioning walls? Walls that won't blow over in a gale. That evening, I re-read all my literature on the subject. Inevitably, I dream of building straw walls.

March 2004

March may be a bit of a nothing month, but it doesn't stop it being just over four weeks before we have to quit our temporary lodgings. Still, the countdown to the certain ecstasy of moving into our own house has begun. We can see it taking shape from the little bathroom window here. Whether it will be in any state to accommodate a homeless family is another matter. I'm all for camping under our new roof, but Debs has pointed out that it will be totally impractical. Let the search for a short-term let begin.

After all the preparation, the day has finally arrived when Bret and I lay the first bales. Dishy Tom is here with Vicky, a new cove from the production team, to film the momentous event. I have spoken to her before on the phone and pictured a little girl who still plays with dolls, but she's in fact what one might describe as *grungy*.

Bret clocks in, all bright-eyed and bushy-tailed, full of life as usual and full of good ideas. I start by leading him through some basic principles, but cannot remember how to tie the slipknot that I was taught on the course and it soon becomes obvious that I am teaching my grandmother to suck eggs. He already knows far more about this than I do and shows me the *Bret-knot*. It will serve. Our future, thankfully, is in the hands of someone capable.

We start by notching the first bale and laying it in place beside an upright. Then we genuflect and carry out a mock Japanese ritual. Alas, I have forgotten my camera, so must rely upon Tom's video. Whoever said that bale walls go up quickly wasn't reckoning on a first morning, spent largely on experimentations with different cutting implements. Perhaps because the bales are so dry, the chainsaw only seems to tear the straw out. My disc cutter is too small and it's only when we try out a bigger burlier borrowed version that we dare acknowledge that this whole venture could just work.

After lunch at the PMU, where Bret warns Vicky about the *andouilette*, or pig's penis as he calls this awful offal sausage, we carry on in the afternoon sunshine. Jean-Claude, the man with the pocket-less billiard table, turns up to see what's going on and we have an enlightened conversation about the folly of deforestation. He used to have a house in southern Spain, but sold up when he realised what was happening to the water table there.

Despite the distraction, by the time I go off to pick up my daughter from the bus stop, we have laid about a course and a half. It's exciting and encouraging and not a piece of cake – you have to think carefully and then think again about what you're doing and the sequence you're doing it in – but, with the disc cutter and all Bret's good ideas, it's feasible that we can build these walls in under a fortnight. Of course, that's when all the fun and games start: shaping window seats, reinforcing hanging points, sighting power sockets and preparing the straw for rendering. *Let's just cross that bridge when we come to it, shall we?*

In the evening, the three of us play a card game that Juliette has taught Tilley. It's called *tas de merde* or pile of shit, and it makes us all laugh. Debs and I watch Michael Moore's film about America's love affair with firearms, *Bowling For Columbine*. I look forward to Charlton Heston's obituary.

*****

Sasha arrives with almost a full film crew. Kevin cometh later. This time, their presence is quite disruptive. Everything takes double the time, because they want to film this and they want to film that and would we mind just...? And with this kind of audience, Bret never shuts up. When we stage a bit of corner-rounding, the chainsaw starts to smoke and, more worryingly, I spot a little column of grey-blue smoke curling out of the top bale. But the 2000-watt disc cutter and the lethal knife that Bret has fashioned from an old shutter brace work well in tandem and we're already up to the sixth row on the west wall. At this height, I can't get the bamboo stakes in to pin the row to the two bales beneath it, so stability may be compromised.

There's an extra body this time in the shape of a journalist, who's here to write a chapter for the book of the programme. He interviews me over lunch at the PMU, where the waitress is in particularly odious form. It grieves me to think that we are providing them with all this unmerited custom.

The journalist is a rather scabby individual of 26, with bleached straw-like hair hacked off just below the ears, a straggly goatee beard and a general look of scurf and dandruff. Some mother must love him. I'm not terribly impressed by his questions, which seem merely to scratch the surface. Back at the house, Sasha asks me a far more penetrating set of questions about, for example, my motivation. We seem to settle on the notion that this house derives more from a lifestyle than an aesthetic impetus. In short: *better house, better way of life*. Perhaps she wants to prepare viewers who are expecting a rather more lavish and more consciously architectural construction. Kevin tells me that ours is the only house in the series that has any kind of environmental credentials. How depressing.

When the best of the light vanishes, the crew packs up and goes off to film Debs at work in her clinic. She is consistently treating over 20 people and their problems each week now, so she's well and truly knackered and could probably do without the intrusion.

At the end of the day, Bret and I have a bitch about the journalist. We would both love to be full-time writers, so the presence of a mere kid, who is already making his living thus, is irksome. Someone half my age has been commissioned to write the kind of book that I have been plugging for years. I stamp my little feet and we agree that life is not fair. This guy, however, is probably not writing what he wants to write in his heart of hearts.

*****

Checking the budget this morning, I discover to my consternation that there's about €27,000 left to pay for everything still to come: electrics, plumbing, internal walls, rendering, heating system and so on. This at a time when I get an unforeseen bill from the architect for a further €900 to cover the drawings he did for the mezzanine. Foolishly, I believed that they were all part of the service. Our budget is evidently awry. The maxim seems to be correct: *think of a budget and then add at least another 10%*. At least.

No wonder my ears are blocked, again. I'm snuffly, full of catarrh, cold and generally dilapidated. We went to bed early last night to watch a video of *Twelfth Night*, but fell asleep after 20 minutes. Just long enough to wonder – what with all the elisions in the script – what Olivia's motivation is for getting dressed up as a man and ingratiating herself in the court of Orsino. We both thought we knew the play backwards, yet find that we don't know it at all.

Bret comes over early and working hard with him takes my mind off the financial worries. After making real strides in just a few hours, we have a late lunch together before he has to leave on one of his frequent missions of mercy. He spends his life helping friends and his adopted family. Either he's incredibly selfless or very insecure or both. He's certainly helping me much more than I could have ever imagined. So much so that I'm beginning to wish that I had employed him to oversee this venture from the kick-off.

While waiting for the star of the show to arrive from Toulouse or wherever it is that they're picking him up from, my financial concerns spur me to chase up potential sponsors from my Formica-top caravan desk. A frustrating business, though, when you don't succeed in contacting anyone. Has their initial enthusiasm turned lukewarm? Are they now out to avoid me? *If that's Mr. Sampson again, tell him my maiden aunt's just died. Anything, just get rid of him!*

Everything stops for Kev. When he gets here, there's a buzz in the air. People start behaving with such a sense of purpose that you wonder whether he holds the power of life in his hands. This is not to denigrate the man; I am getting quite fond of him. It's just that stars have this quality, this magnetism, which turns them into human heaters. People gather around to warm their hands on his aura.

Mr. Media is impressed with what we have done. He genuinely seems to like the house after the doubts he harboured before Christmas. The mezzanine has turned it from two matching rectangular boxes into something a little different. On seeing the walls, he comes over all unnecessary. A literal bale-hugger, he presses himself against the wall and caresses the scratchy surface of the straw; he turns round and backs himself into a corner and then shuffles down to sit on the ground. He loves the stuff. He's like a kid with a new teddy bear. It's both comical and reassuring. Our wall has met his criteria: they're nice and strong and regular. It's like getting a clean bill of health from your doctor – and it pleases me no end.

He himself has built his office or outhouse from straw bales and is thinking of building a new family home with the stuff, because it's so robust and, lest we forget, a waste product. We've got to be doing the right thing here. After debating the comparative merits of the load-bearing (without a wooden frame) and the non-load-bearing approaches, our conversation somehow segues into the health of our respective digestive systems. Cue subsequent interview on

196

our side terrace-to-be about my current stress level and my budgetary fears. Even with hovering cameraman, it feels like a cosy chat with a man on my wavelength, a man who understands the vagaries of internal organs.

Soon after the crew goes off to the comfort of their hotel rooms in nearby Martel, a Parisian couple from a nearby house turn up for a nose. She, a small mousey woman with a short-sighted air, wanders off after a brief chat. Her husband, however, a white-haired man in a nautical cap, lingers... and lingers... and still he lingers. We stand on the plank over the drainage trench between the porch and our muddy land, while he regales me with some spiel about ordering parts for a veteran car club. I'm not sure whether or not he is asking for my help, but he rattles on with barely an intake of breath, so I can't even jump in with an *excuse me*. Time ticks by. I have to tidy up before going off to pick Tilley up from her class excursion to the *château fort* at Castelnaud. Finally, I put my hands up in abject surrender and tell him that I have to go. I run for the car and leave him to find his own way off site. Mental note: *beware the man in the nautical cap, for he understandeth not that people have better things to do than listen to twaddle.*

A great big coach arrives at the school and 16 small children climb off. Our daughter descends with Lucille, the pair of them animated as usual and quite unconscious of my presence. It's good to see her so happy and buoyant. In the car, she laughs and laughs. Not only is Alfie there on the back seat, but – unbeknownst to me – Harvey the cat has sneaked in, too.

*****

Time marches on apace – and with it our straw walls. I leave Bret to it one afternoon, while I go over to Christophe's farm to help Dutch Eric bring over another load of bales. We're getting near the bottom now of the once great pile under the hangar. It's clear that the rodents have had a time of it this winter and I have to discard several precious bales. Eric totters off with his precarious load in his old Renault tractor, while I follow anxiously behind.

When we meet up again at the site, Bret is tying bales with blue plastic twine and the *Bret-knot*, accompanied by The Specials on my tinny ghetto blaster and chilled to his marrow by a northerly wind so biting that I'm almost happy, once we've finished unloading the bales, to step back inside the caravan to renew my efforts to contact critical parties. But still no one seems to want to talk to me: Francis about the floor, Clive about the rendering, someone else about the gas boiler, another about the guttering. Only Paul, my trusty electrician, phones me back. He has offered to do a day next week, but unless Francis does his bit first, there's really little point.

Nothing for it but to sweep up the loose straw at the end of the day. It's great material, but it makes so much freakin' mess. Still, I can forget about it this evening, as I forgot about it last night for a couple of hours at the cinema in Biars, where I immersed myself in Sophie Coppola's charming *Lost In Translation*. Confirmation, if ever I needed it, that Tokyo is one of the last places on earth I want to visit.

Tonight Tilley and I pick up our friend Sophie at the car park in Turenne and drive to the theatre in Brive, where we meet Debs for an evening of dance. A *jazz ballet* choreographed by Geraldine Armstrong, formerly of the Alvin Ailey school. There's some lovely dancing and some great gospel music, but we all get a bit hot and bothered up in the gods, seated too near a party of voluble school children. My mind keeps wandering off to get ensnared in the complications of the final stages of this build. Our daughter enjoys herself immensely, though.

*****

The walls near completion. Bret and I have reached the sixth and penultimate course. We will stop when this course is finished to compact the straw with spare roof-tiles, just enough to allow us to slide in the final bales between the sixth course and the ring beam.

I go to Meyssac in the morning to withdraw some

money for my right-hand man and the guy in the bank mistakes me for a computer technician come to repair their system. It must have been my woolly hat.

On my return, I find my good friend Smiffy has turned up. Alf is rushing around the site with Polly, Smiffy's scruffy and adorable terrier. He has put on weight and tells me that he is taking tranquillisers after all his recent domestic problems. Back in England, he reveals, he has taken out a loan to buy a longboat, which he plans to moor on a canal in the Warwickshire countryside, just south of Brum where his mum lives. He blesses this house: following ones heart's desire is not easy, as he well knows. Before leaving, he offers his help while he is over here. I know that it is sincere and that I can count on him. It's the mark of a genuine friend.

Come the afternoon, I go to see the osteopath for another treatment, primarily this time for the persistent blockage in my ears. I fall asleep on his couch. At the end of the session, while summarising the prognosis and outlining his prescription, he picks up all the little scraps of straw I have shed on his Hessian carpet when taking off my work clothes.

On my return, Gilles, the architect, is busy photographing the construction with his new digital camera. It seems a miracle of technology – to create an image by using mathematical binary code, a series of 0s and 1s in other words – and it makes me wish that I'd thought to buy one from the outset. Gilles points out all that is wrong with the house, as if to rub my nose in the fact that we haven't employed him to oversee the operation. Because Michel has done the ridge in the old style, the mortar is likely to crack and lift tiles in the future; and The Carpenters should not have put the waterproof plastic up against the facia on the mezzanine walls, he should have used a framework of battens in order to create a passage of air. And so on. It's all rather depressing and I don't really want to hear it.

In the hope that Clive, the plasterer, might still turn up, Bret and I work on till after six (which means leaving my daughter in front of the TV with a video to watch and leaving our dog to look at me accusingly, because it is way past his *walkies*). With driving rain predicted, we finish up by securing our Dutch friend's massive tarp over the north-eastern wall.

The phone rings in the caravan. It's Francis, the plumber. Somewhat out of the blue, he tells me that he'd like to start work on laying the heating tubes for the *plancher chauffant*, or under-floor heating, the following Monday. It's clear that we haven't properly discussed his estimate. I want to use cork for the insulation and he advocates tailor-made polystyrene sheets. So I make a series of frantic calls to significant others to see whether they can juggle their plans to fit in with this eleventh-hour arrangement. Tomorrow, I must arise and go to the suppliers to look at these sheets and then, if necessary, cancel my order for the cork at the health food shop in St. Céré.

Fortunately, Debs has had a cancellation and is back early enough to cook dinner, while I take Alf out for a walk in the crepuscular gloom and try to make everything slot neatly together in my head. My sainted wife is devastated. She has lost the beautiful Hopi Indian necklace I bought for her from a native American street vendor in Santa Fé two years or so ago. It must have slipped off as she was walking through the streets of Tulle early this afternoon, on the way to her supervision group near the old cathedral.

Whether it was something that Gilles joked about this afternoon when stubbing out his cigarette on our concrete floor, I don't know, but I awake – mercifully – from a nightmare of conflagration in the early hours. The call of nature rouses me just before our bare walls come crashing to the ground. I glance through the loo's tiny window to make sure that it was but a bad dream.

*****

It's clearly Open Day at the dog's meadow today. First, it's the young couple who want to build in straw somewhere nearby. They've come back to check on progress. I hear

200

about some interesting technique that they use in Morocco and similar places: a waterproof lime-based wall plaster, which could be suitable for the bathroom and shower room.

Then friends arrive from our old village. They arrive in Jacques' BMW and emerge, immaculate. Nicole, with her bobbed peroxide-blonde hair, is wearing her customary tight leather trousers and pointy black boots. Jacques, as usual, looks like a photograph from a catalogue aimed at the older man. He's had the good sense to bring the sturdy Wellingtons he always wore whenever he walked past our old house to and from the field in which his horse, Chloë, lived her solitary, ruminative life. I see Jacques as a representative of the last fortunate generation that will be able to retire early on a good pension and live out the rest of their days in comfort. I don't count the rich, of course; they will always have the wherewithal to live a life of leisure. Jacques is not rich, but quintessentially *comfortable*. Post-retirement, he has already been on a couple of exotic equestrian holidays: to Rajasthan and to Patagonia.

Before our move, we were invited for aperitifs one Sunday morning to view the photos of Rajasthan. They live together, unmarried, in the house that Jacques built. The surrounding garden is manicured and soulless. The interior, we discovered that day, is preternaturally spic and span – like the clean clobber with which they cover limbs honed in their home gymnasium (where surely the slightest lingering odour of sweat is banished by aerosol). Everything has its place; nothing is left to create the slightest semblance of what might become a mess. You could eat your meals off their polished floors. It was eerie. Conversations with Jacques, who takes the trouble to enunciate his words clearly, like a politician might do, often reveal him as a cultivated man. Yet there was nothing to suggest it in that sterile house.

Here today, though, they are both refreshingly down-to-earth. They, too, are positive about the house (and the view). It's good to hear their benediction: we have done absolutely the right thing in leaving behind our village. In fact, Jacques would like to quit it and build another new house somewhere a little less conspicuous.

They stay long enough to share a bottle of cider and a bag of pistachio nuts outside the *petite maison* in the midday sun. Jacques produces the album of photos he took in Patagonia and I flick slowly through some stunning views of the southernmost Andes. He looks as if he were born to ride a horse. He could be Steely Dan's original *audacious cowboy*.

After lunch, I have two more – local – sets of visitors. Firstly, the young farmer with his wife and daughter from the nearby village. She, it appears, teaches at the *collège* where Tilley will go after primary school. He is a genial quietly spoken man with teeth encrusted with tartar, and incredibly wiry hair that cries out for a topiarist. They tell me kindly that our only daughter would be most welcome to come and play dolls with their only daughter.

Soon after they go, the farmer who sold us the land turns up with a crony. I am pleasant enough to this strange mumbling, shambling man, despite the fact that he seems to think that he has some kind of residual proprietary right to walk across our land whenever he sees fit. I also want to raise the matter of the condition of the pen in which he keeps his hunting dog. He slopes off with his mate, however, before I can summon the courage to do so.

Unfortunately, the one person who doesn't materialise is Clive. When I reach him on his mobile, he promises that he will turn up this weekend. What else can one do but hope? You can't give him a bollocking, much as you might like to, because he's clearly very busy and you're too dependent on him to upset the man.

*****

Having seen the interlocking polystyrene sheets and discussed the matter long and hard with Debs, we decide to opt for the pragmatic approach again. These sheets are clearly tailor-made for under-floor heating, but neither of us much like the thought of insulating our floor with something chemical and toxic. It's like the rubble-trench footings and the concrete compromise we had to make: if I had the confidence to do it by myself, then I would certainly have chosen to use cork.

At the same time, I checked out the Fermacell boards that we want to use instead of standard plasterboard. They're made of re-cycled paper and gypsum, and although you stick them together with glue, they seem to be a healthier option. If price is any guideline, they're reassuringly expensive.

Incredible how much everything costs. Soon after the return of The Carpenters, who are back to finish the wooden panelling on the external mezzanine walls and to start fitting the doors and windows, a delivery-lorry arrives. It bears a modest load – 12 lengths of drainage pipes, some joints and angles, sufficient concrete blocks to build an inspection chamber at each corner of the house and some gravel – and it comes to over €400. Enough to reduce a grown man to tears. Everything seems to be spinning out of control.

There's nothing for it but mechanical work. In the startling warmth of a premature spring, Bret and I work in t-shirts on the drainage trenches around the house. It involves a judicious use of stones, gravel, plastic pipes and spirit levels to create a light but sufficient gradient to carry the rainwater safely away. It's back-breaking toil. Bret asks why on earth I haven't hired a mini-digger for the task? Answer: because I haven't thought it through.

That evening, I catch up on paper work. In order to open a professional account at the builders' merchant that will supply the Fermacell boards – and qualify no doubt for about one or at most two per cent discount (because it's a big chain and, if you threaten to take your custom elsewhere, they merely shrug) – I have to fill in several pages, make several copies, provide tax statements and other supporting documents. I'm surprised that they don't want to know about my blood group.

Which serves as an unwelcome reminder of our tardy application for our girl's first passport. We have already reserved our crossing for the impending trip back to the UK, but have heard nothing from the Passport Office.

*****

The fitting of the French windows that will, hopefully, fill this house with the light we were deprived of in our previous house, has brought the cavalry back. Just the two of them again this time: Vicky comes bearing bars of Cadbury's Milk Chocolate for Tilley with a grungy friend to direct things in Sasha's temporary absence. Clearly, they think that the event is significant.

They're right. As The Carpenters work in the glorious sunshine, answering questions direct to camera like seasoned veterans now, I can see how the work qualifies as another *symbolic moment*. Suddenly a space has been transformed into a house. Now you can enjoy the sensation of standing inside looking out – not through gaps in the walls, but through glass.

Today, I can do little more. My back is bad again and I need a good massage. Yesterday, I had to tuck a cushion behind the small of my back in order to drive down to Cahors to look at floor tiles. Then I drove up onto the arid *causse* for a meeting with the guy who will supply the extruded aluminium guttering in the copper colour that our architect has specified. He said no more than he had to, so the meeting was brief but positive and I was back by early afternoon – just in time for the Digger Man, who delivered a lorry load of river gravel.

Suddenly, he seems to be putting himself out for us. Maybe it's because his daughter has been to see my wife. He told me how *hyper content* he was with her progress. She is less stressed at school and altogether better *in her skin*. I glowed with pride. Although snowed under with work – mainly the installation and maintenance of swimming pools – he was able to confirm that he could install our septic tank next month.

Unable to do anything taxing, I move the remaining bales onto the back balcony as the first stage of cleaning up in preparation for the under-floor heating. After school, I bring The Kid back on site with me rather than leaving her alone in the *petite maison*, so she can do her homework outside before the temperature dips for the evening.

'Why are you doing that, daddy?' she asks.

It does seem sometimes that I am spending an inordinate amount of time shifting things from one place to another. Moving stuff in… and moving stuff out. *Ask not of Sisyphus, child, why he labours thus. Just think of the colour in which you want to decorate thy bedroom.*

My daughter's presence reminds me that it is now too late to make my umpteenth call of the day to the Passport Office. We don't know yet whether or not we will receive her document in time. With all the terrorist activity in Europe at present, it makes you wonder whether there's some cosmic reason for the delay. Are we meant to go? In any case, it's neither our child's fault nor concern. Conscious of the tough time that she, too, is having currently, I suggest that we drive down to the water mill on the outskirts of Martel so we can walk Alfie and maybe even give him his first swim of the year.

*****

For someone who used to plan his revision down to the last half hour to be thoroughly prepared for exams, I'm leaving things precariously to the last minute. There's less than a week to go before we set off for England and I haven't even organised a dog-sitter or a cat-feeder. Debs doesn't know; I've been fobbing her off with bluster.

While the weather has taken a predictable turn for the worse, everything slots magically into place in less than 24 hours. First the postman arrives with our daughter's passport and my relief is liberating. Our postman is a genial man, who drives his little yellow van (with or without a black-and-white cat) around the countryside. I give him a guided tour of the house. He professes to be *un peu étonné*. I am equally a little astonished when he tells me about someone on his route who has installed geothermal heating. Sometimes, it seems like a very lonely business being allegedly a kind of eco-pioneer and it's surprising when you hear of others doing the same thing.

Indeed, later that same day, I have a visit from a rather earnest be-spectacled woman, who wants to build a straw bale house with her husband a little further south. Bret and I have been recently discussing whether we could run straw bale workshops for €250 a day. While wishing to help others, we also want to be paid for the expertise we have developed. However, her project sounds a little too modest. She tells me about an organisation of volunteers who call themselves Les Castors du Lot. She also tells me about a low-cost under-floor heating system that uses wood-chippings for insulation under a lime screed. All these opportunities I'm learning about too late.

Debs drops by with Tilley to say that she has bumped into Muriel, our near neighbour, who has agreed to feed Harvey while we are away. They are off to see the schoolteacher, the wiry-haired farmer with the egregious tartar and their daughter. By the time they get back, I have popped the question to Thompson & Thompson about our Alf. Last minute dot com delivers. My wife and others of her kidney will say that if you put your trust in the universe, the unseen forces will deliver. I should look beyond logic and have more faith.

The visit to the family tries the patience of both visitors. They're nice well-meaning people, but Madame the teacher, apparently, lacks confidence in anything but her academic subject. Desperate to please, she insisted that Debs should drink something other than water. Under pressure, she suggested tea, but Madame confessed that she didn't know how to make tea. So Debs then suggested a little coffee, which threw Madame into a state of consternation. She served up some instant coffee that was fairly undrinkable. All this didn't help to lighten the atmosphere in which the two girls were supposed to play. So it was all awkwardness personified and both 'my girls' were relieved to get away.

206

*****

We take Sunday afternoon tea with the Squirrells at our old house, which has been magically transformed into their own domain. With a burgeoning circle of friends and acquaintances, they have passed the severe test of their first winter here with flying colours.

Before the guests arrive, Ingrid takes us down to her studio in our former basement apartment to show us her work in progress on the piece of sculpture that she intends to give us as a house-warming present. How come so many talented artists are beset by self-doubt? Reticently, she pulls back the dust cloth to reveal... (*cue drum roll*) one of the most beautiful pieces I have ever seen. Our momentary stupefaction no doubt triggers a jolt of fear within Ingrid's matronly bosom. I am quite overcome. We had expected a little pot or something, but she has made us a female figure about five feet tall with arms outstretched in welcome. The detail and the glaze are exquisite and the overall effect is that of one of Sir John Tenniel's magical illustrations for the Alice books rendered three-dimensional. Our Lady will sit, I can see it now, on our side terrace to greet callers at our side/front door.

*****

Back in the UK for the first time in ages. There's always a frisson of expectation in the car as we travel north. We leave early, allow plenty of time and take it leisurely. Alone in the back, our daughter's patience is remarkable. It was ever thus. During our first epic journey to the Alps – across the lonely wilds of the Massif Central – she spent hours and hours patiently learning to tie her shoelaces.

Our route is so familiar now we could almost do it in our sleep. And because it's so familiar, it becomes apparently ever shorter. This time, we go the extra two or so hours to Calais, so we stop off at Le Touquet to eat our picnic and wander along the beach. Tilley's excitement at seeing the sea is infectious and keeps my mind from wandering off onto forbidden topics such as under-floor heating. Le Touquet is basically a bourgeois gambling joint. British punters used to hop over the Channel for a spin on the roulette wheels. Judging by the ghastly nouveau riche houses that line the road leading to the beach, there's *loadsamoney* here. If some of it comes from the casino tables, most of it comes probably from servicing the people who come to place their bets.

We stay at my sister's industrious house. My brother-in-law's business has expanded again. Now he's employing five or six people, who work in the room at the back that they have converted into an office. Wind farms must be one of the few growth industries in the UK. Soon they will have to move into a bigger house to accommodate this burgeoning concern.

Tilley the Kid is in her element. She loves it back in England – and she loves the attention that my sister heaps on her. My parents are rather more guarded. They represent something of a challenge to her: she feels that she has to earn their love. One evening we eat there, always a challenge in itself, and the conversation turns to my mother-in-law's odious *boyfriend*.

'What do you think of him then, Tilley?'

Our nine-year old girl, sitting there like a child who should be seen and not heard, reflects momentarily before replying, 'He's a bloody arsehole'.

There is a brief shocked hiatus before an explosion of laughter around the table. She's dead right. Out of the mouths of babes and so on.

We leave her with her extended family one day to take the train up to London for a day at the Ideal Home Exhibition, courtesy of the tickets we have been given by a potential sponsor. The crowded, uncomfortable train, is a reminder of daily life on our overpopulated island. We have come with an album of photos, some plans of the house and some of Debs's new business cards. We have even set ourselves a goal of three new sponsors, so we're keen but a little apprehensive.

It's the first time I've ever been to this annual show. I

once went as a child to the Northern Irish equivalent in the King's Hall in the Belfast suburb of Balmoral and spent some of my pocket money on a brooch for my mother, a rather kitsch red rose seemingly pressed under Perspex. Olympia must be at least twice the size and there are people milling around everywhere. We spot a stand selling built-in wardrobes with beautiful sliding doors. *Why not?*

We speak to a friendly woman with a brace on her protruding teeth. Her reaction is so unquestioningly positive that we both feel that she must have misunderstood us. *Shurely shome mishtake.* But no. She understands perfectly. It's a small business she runs with her husband and she's very keen to use our house as a showcase for some of their products. We all get very excited and a little carried away.

It's a huge boost. For maybe the first time in my life, I realise that I have something valuable here. For once, it's not a case of others selling to us, but of us selling to others. This recognition swells my confidence and imbues me with a sense of... well, power. We both become quite euphoric, approaching anyone and everyone with *sang froid*. This is what it must be like to be rich: see something you want and go for it. By the end of our foray we have firm offers of two fitted wardrobes, some oak dining chairs and some lovely quirky lamps made by a delightful South African. There's interest, too, from a firm that makes water softeners. It's not something we've considered before, but our water is so hard and if someone wants to give us a machine to soften it, who are we to look such a gift-horse in the mouth?

After five hectic days of what never really amounts to relaxation, we head for home. Our journey south on the other side of the Channel begins at 2.30 in the morning, just after the clocks go forward. When we arrive back at the *petite maison* in the middle of the afternoon, our daughter bursts into tears. She is missing everyone already, missing England, missing her cousins, missing being part of an extended family – and probably missing all the attention. Did we really do the best thing for her in moving to a foreign land, where she would grow up admittedly in beautiful countryside, but so away far from her family? Perhaps a terrace house in suburban Sheffield would have suited her rather better. Whatever you do as a parent, it could always be better. Hopefully she won't hold it against us later on.

*****

The final two days of March provoke another crisis of confidence. When I open one of the new doors and step into our eerily silent new house, I see before me a great expanse of white polystyrene floor over which a network of red plastic heating tubes have been laid in intricate serpentines. But when I describe to Gilles what the plumber has done, he tells me that he should have done it another way: you start by marking out the rooms as we have done, but then you put up the internal walls, lay your insulation and finally pour your *chappe* zone by zone. By doing it all in one as Francis has done, either you build the internal walls now and hope that the polystyrene will support their weight, or you build your walls on top of the *chappe* and sounds will resound throughout the house.

Panic sets in. There is only one thing to do in such circumstances: phone Monsieur Fromage. He suggests that the plumber's way is a pragmatic alternative approach. Bret, too, is reassuring. For every problem, his code states, there is a solution. But then I make the mistake of talking to Lucille's father, who is building his house concurrently. Being French, he does things according to the book. He comes over to take a look and shakes his head and wags his finger. *C'est pas bon ça. Naa, you don't wanna do it like that, you wanna do it like this...* So whom do I believe?

Predictably, that night I have a nightmare about under-floor heating systems. I wake up in a cold sweat at 4.30 and fail to get back to sleep again.

The following morning, I receive a pair of e-mails. One from Vicky informs me that they might need to shift the programme deadline forward a week or two to the end of June. The other, from our absent neighbours, tells us that they won't be moving back till mid May. We have a reprieve! Let joy be unbridled: we can stay in our Wendy house for a few weeks longer.

April 2004

As my wife and I open the door to the house, there's a crash and a thud. My first fear is that something structural has collapsed. In fact, we find that a little bird has fallen from the roof and it's lying prostrate on the polystyrene sheets. Debs tip-toes over the tubing and picks it up. She cradles it in her hands and strokes its head. As she feels her hands get hotter and hotter, she holds out little hope for the bird's recovery. But suddenly it flies off and up into the roof. It seems like some living, breathing metaphor for all my recent concerns. *All will be well*, says the sweet bird of youth.

I've brought Debs over to show her the under-floor heating tubes and to explain what Lucille's father has told me. The plumber hasn't done things the correct, French way. I have that awful sinking feeling again: not only that things are spiralling out of control, but also that I must confront someone. In this case, of course, Francis. Rather than dilly-dally (for once), I pick up the phone and do it straight away. Probably a mistake, because I haven't prepared my spiel. Francis gets the hump and counters by accusing me of not having confidence in him *blah blah*. It's about as bad as informing Bob by telephone that he wouldn't be needed on the roof.

However, I insist that Francis comes over to talk about it face to face. I need to impress upon him that, in trying to direct operations with minimal technical knowledge, I have to be guided by the architect. He's never taken the time to talk through his commitments to allow me to marry my busy schedule to his, so it's understandable that I should be worried and confused.

By contrast, Clive the plasterer keeps our latest attempted rendezvous and immediately reassures me that it has been worth the wait and the aggravation. He may look like a big, tough skinhead, but he's calm, mild-mannered and… he *listens*. We stand on the balcony together, leaning against the handrail, and I spot a bird hopping around on a mound of mud. Our rescued bird? The conversation meanders onto the subject of divorce. Strangely, his girlfriend is also an aromatherapist. She is hoping to set up here, so I suggest that she rings Debs for some worldly advice.

By the time Clive leaves, I am confident that he can do the job at a time when my schedule demands it. He's not cheap, but he comes with a list of testimonials as long as my arm. The chance of keeping to budget now is so unlikely that I'm beginning to become blasé, almost ready to throw money at the operation just to get the bloody thing finished. It's funny. Debs bumped into a former client of hers, who moved away from our area to build a family home near Beaulieu. He told her how much he enjoyed the endeavour. One of the hardest things about it was to keep all his helpers occupied and happy. *Helpers, schmelpers!* All our friends seem to need the money as much as I need their benevolence. My experience has been purgatorial. At least Capability Clive has lifted one big weight from my shoulders.

Later that day, I drive over to Biars to see Bob Ze Builder. He's working as part of a team in an old hotel that's being refurbished. He wants to show me a product they have been using, which he feels might be useful for our house. It's a kind of eco-mortar, which contains a mixture of wooden and synthetic fibres. I'm touched by Bob's concern and it's an evident peace pipe, which I grasp with enthusiasm despite my doubts about its suitability in this case.

The next stop is to pick up Tilley from school and take her over to Baladou Sue's for some piano practice just before her exam. Why are the French so obsessed with exams? You're supposed to learn an instrument for fun. But our daughter is already such a perfectionist and therefore so paranoid about this flaming exam, that Sue and I keep hearing angry thumps whenever she plays a bum note. This system contrives to remove any element of enjoyment. Later in Martel, we wait outside the medieval tower where she has her lessons. Pacing around the courtyard, with piano music wafting out of a leaden window on the second floor, I try to reassure her, but The Kid is not for comforting. When it's her time, I take her up the stone spiral stairs and we bump into Jessica and her oldest daughter, Rosie. Tilley derives reassurance from Rosie. From the waiting room, I glow proudly to hear my daughter run through her piece almost note-perfect. *Crisis, what crisis?*

*****

Bret and I finish moving the mountain of gravel and pouring it into the trenches around the house. With the Easter holidays here now, child-sitting duties mean that I won't have so much time for intense tasks like this one.

As we sit together over a picnic lunch I have prepared, Francis the plumber turns up for the face-off at 20 paces. It's a frustrating business and I wish that there had been a British plumber to employ for the job, because – like so many French people – he simply doesn't listen to you. Trying to employ a foreign language to get a word in edgewise throws me off my carefully rehearsed speech. For every considered thrust on my part, I am met by blah and more blah. Still, we come to some kind of understanding. My head has been a little like the chamber of a volcano, with channels of magma pushing against a fragile plate, but this clash of the Titans seems to have settled things slightly. An eruption is less likely for now. I decide to go for Francis's pragmatic option of pouring the floor on top of the under-floor heating installation and then building the internal walls on solid ground. If it risks greater internal resonance, so be it.

When Tim comes by in the afternoon to pick up a couple of planks of wood in his customary seigniorial fashion, I tell him that I would never again work with Francis. Deep down, I suppose, I blame him for recommending the plumber quite so strongly. In truth, though, I have no one to blame but myself for a lack of due diligence. The deadline is too impending to change track at this point. It's Francis and be damned.

Later, I talk to a Monsieur Barthe on the telephone. He runs a small family concern south of Toulouse that produces beautiful clay floor tiles. In a funny little piping voice, he thanks me very politely for my proposal of sponsorship and offers to sell us first-quality tiles at a second-quality price. Not quite as generous as I had hoped, but not to be sniffed at. I'm learning that it's better to talk. Occasionally, people will bite on the strength of an e-mail. More likely, though, they will waver, park the message and then forget about it. Just like journalism really. Were I more ready to phone up editors, more ready to risk rejection, then I might have more commissions for articles.

*****

Chez Jackson to pick up The Kid at the end of the afternoon, Steve and I share a beer on their terrace and enjoy the beautiful early-evening sunshine. In his musical North Carolinian drawl, he tells me how he and Jessica met and fell in love and, after a sojourn in Pennsylvania, ended up in this part of France as a pair of glass blowers bringing up a pair of daughters. In an oblique sort of way, he asks me about whether we'd be prepared to sell our middle plot of land. Evidently, he's got an idea of building a new family home. In an oblique sort of way, I say no. We'd be happy to have the

Jacksons as neighbours, but the middle plot is our de-militarised zone between our house and the Mannakee house-to-be on plot 3. Why would he want to put himself through all this when they already have a beautiful family home? I guess Steve is one of life's inveterate risk-takers.

*****

We drive to Carennac on the Dordogne with Tilley and Alf in the car and Vicky and Sarah following in the hire-car behind. They are here for the next inept instalment. It's Wednesday, my wife's day off. Her exhaustion is compounded by a night disturbed by our daughter's own perturbations.

In the lee of some of the beautiful medieval buildings that make this one of the *plus beaux villages de France*, we walk along the footpath by the edge of the river under the gaze of the camera. Up and down and then up and down again. Happy family enjoying a walk by the river. In fact, pre-adolescent daughter mutters darkly whenever we reach for her hand.

After another couple of *mises en scène*, I race off to Brive and manage to get to the bank just before the doors close for the customary long lunch. During the fallow period between midday and 2 pm, I put up a curtain rail in my wife's clinic and eat my snack lunch, before heading off to the depot of a company that pours liquid *anhydrate chappes*. Alas, there is no one in the office and I have to wait 40 minutes in the car for the secretary to dawdle back after an even-longer-than-customary lunch break. This benighted lunchtime culture here. The time one wastes waiting.

Their estimate is less than I had bargained for, so I write out a cheque for the deposit. In a few more days, we will have a solid floor to walk on. More importantly, we'll have a solid base on which to build our internal walls.

Back on the land, Francis is at work on our pipes. Maybe my confrontation has had an impact after all. All that bluster might simply be a defence to mask insecurities of his own. I go down into the *vide sanitaire*, the crawl space underneath the platform on which the house sits, to help him. For all the bent posture, I realise that this is not very difficult. Something I should have done myself. If I'd thought to buy the materials, I could easily have put it in place and paid him simply to come and make connections and check for leaks.

When it's time for him to pack up, I emerge from my dark confines to stretch – and find Debs entertaining our American friends from Wisconsin, here on one of their periodic visits to their second home. They have just taken delivery of a new Volvo estate, which they will ship back to the States. We give them a quick guided-tour during which John gives me the lowdown on the Green Bay Packers' frustrating loss to the Philadelphia Eagles in the NFL play-offs earlier in the year. He is gratifyingly surprised by the level of my knowledge about our team in particular and the sport in general.

Our daughter joins us. After they leave, we all pick up loose straw from the polystyrene sheets in preparation for the pouring of the *chappe*. It's probably pointless, since the straw will no doubt be buried harmlessly in the liquid floor, but it involves Tilley and gives the impression that this is a family venture. We comment on how it feels warmer inside this still draughty house than it does inside the *petite maison*. The straw is already working.

When the girls are both asleep and the house is quiet, I treat myself to a concert that my father has recorded for me on video. It's James Brown live in London. The Godfather is over 70 now and obviously doesn't dance like he used to, but the funk still fuels him. The show makes me regret not going to see him in Brighton when I had the chance – on the grounds that he was too old at 60. Another ten years and, if I survive all this, I shall be such an age.

*****

Crawling around on two spare polystyrene sheets with a tape measure. The final desperate last-minute preparations before the company comes to pour the *chappe*. I've taken copious photographs, but figure that I need to measure where all the heating tubes will be buried in relation to the intended internal walls. If we have to fix the bottom rails with screws, it will be as well to know that there isn't a heating tube directly underneath. Tilley awaits at the *petite maison* with her friend, Rosie Jackson, who is beginning to sound more and more like her American father every day. She is a strange mixture now of English rose, French gamine and American beauty.

After lunch, a van-load of desperados arrive. Young men with attitude knuckle down to the job of finding a level with a spinning laser. They then place weird little tripods on the polystyrene floor and wind them up or down to the level of the laser beam. The finished level will be a little higher than anticipated, which means that the 2cm-thick terracotta tiles from Monsieur Barthe's company will be a little *juste*, as they say. Which might also mean that we have to build up the levels of the door thresholds throughout.

I realise that my hopefully amicable chatter will probably serve as lunchtime banter. *Tonnerre du Brest! Quel tosser, cet Anglais...* So I slope off to continue my task of painting the back balcony with my customary mixture of warmed linseed oil and turpentine. It's not the best day for such labour. There's a cold wind blowing and a shower threatening. I watch it move across the plain and wonder whether it's worth the risk to continue.

When the mixer arrives, everything happens very quickly after all the protracted preparation. They simply pour in this milky liquid via a giant hose attached to a king-size compressor. The men, however, stomp all over the floor in their Wellington boots and little pieces of polystyrene rise to the surface like stones washed up by the sea. All very weird. It dries like porridge with a kind of brown-sugar crust, which they'll polish off in a fortnight.

I chat to the driver about the landscape and the weather. I know now that Ussel, the effective capital of the Haute Corrèze, has three times more rain than Brive. And if you live somewhere beyond an invisible line between Vayrac and St. Céré, you have half the rainfall of Brive. Which suggests that we probably have around two-thirds the rainfall of Brive. The man speaks with the authority of a full-time meteorologist, so I do not doubt him. I don't know whether to be worried or reassured.

After they leave, I check inside the *cave* and find water dripping from the concrete ceiling. Now I'm worried. This can only mean one thing: there are cracks in the *hordis* through which the screed is running out. When I come back tomorrow morning, the heating tubes will be visible once more and the floor of the *cave* will be six inches or so higher. Perhaps, if I just lie face down on the floor of the cellar, I will be petrified by quick-drying gypsum. I think better of it. There's a dog to walk and feisty young girls to feed.

First thing next morning, with considerable trepidation I open one of the French windows. God is sometimes merciful. We have a solid floor. It's not yet dry enough to walk across, but the liquid gypsum hasn't drained away through cracks in the concrete. Oddly, I can see impressions of the heating tubes buried underneath. They look like fossilised snakes.

I close the door on it all and give myself up to Easter.

*****

Easter is a strange moveable feast. You feel that you should celebrate it, but are not quite sure how. Fortunately, this year, the decision has been made for us. We gather at the Jacksons' homestead in Montignac, where Steve has lit the little stone bread-oven for baking purposes.

It's a quite stunning day and we are due to be joined by the Mannakees and their two children, and by Laurence and Susan and their daughter, Ella. Laurence and Susan live in Bexleyheath and are staying in their house just across the road from the Jackson domain for the holidays. A permanent move here is mooted. In the meantime, the Jacksons can use their house in the summer, when they turn their own place over to paying holidaymakers. After all the disturbance we have been through since moving from our old house, even top dollar wouldn't tempt me to consider the idea.

Tim and Gilly are on top form, as they often are when it comes to a party. We talk quite happily as friends again, and I make sure that the conversation doesn't stray onto building sites. Emboldened by a glass or two of champagne, I sidle up to Laurence – a balding man with a paunch and owl-like glasses – and question him on his reputed love of music. A former literary student at York in the heady days of the 1960s, he is an arts consultant now. He used to promote music concerts and specialises in raising funds for concerts, tours and other musical ventures. Back in his youth, he tells me, he saw the likes of Miles Davis, John Coltrane and Lee Morgan when they passed through the nation's capital. As a promoter, he once put on Laura Nyro, a mutual heroin. Vividly, he describes the experience of being alone in the hall while she rehearsed her entire repertoire as if for him and him alone.

With all the food that everyone has brought with them to cook in the bread oven, we indulge in a huge feast. Afterwards, we men take the girls and the dogs out for a longish walk while the women folk hide the Easter eggs and the chocolate euros for the subsequent hunt. During my chat to Tim about the joys and heartaches of being a parent, it becomes apparent that he has been sincerely angered by the TV programme's suggestion that the build might affect our friendship. I suggest that Kevin has just done what he always likes to do: sow a little seed to create some drama that really doesn't exist.

After the egg hunt, when we are all indoors on the Jacksons' capacious sofas, gathered around a roaring fire, Tim relates a funny tale about an old guy who keeps cycling past them as he and Geordie Mark work on restoring the stones of his current project. *Vous faites les pierres?* he calls out each time. *You're doing the stones?* Steve speculates whether – at this precise moment – the old chap is telling some friends how every time he cycles past them, the two English guys answer his question in exactly the same manner. *Oui, on fait les pierres!*

Having failed to convince Jessica that we should help her wash up, we drift off home around eight. It has been a wonderful day: just the kind of thing, Debs suggests, that she had wanted for our daughter at Christmas. She hasn't seen me so relaxed and animated for yonks. Even Alfred Lord Sampson has had a fine old time of it, gambolling with the Mannakee dogs, Gemma and Blondie. As a coda, the three of us sit at our round table to look at charts supplied by Ecos Paints and decide what colour our new walls should be.

*****

The Easter interlude has reinvigorated me. Onwards and upwards! So much still to be done. Monsieur Fromage reminds me on the telephone to remind the Digger Man about the septic tank if we really are hoping to camp in our new house when the neighbours return. He also offers to lend me his scaffolding for the rendering stage and won't countenance any hire charge.

Bret arrives, similarly refreshed by the break and raring to go. We get to work on the 7th and final row of bales. However, we only manage to get about six bales cut to size. The cuts are complicated; it could take us as long to get this final row in place as it did to erect the previous six rows. In fact, we spend an inordinate amount of time talking and planning. How to hang the ceiling boards? What materials I'm going to need for the next stage? Who needs to do what and by when? It's of enormous benefit to have someone so dependable with whom to talk things through, but frustrating when we're not actually physically doing something to advance the construction.

The following day is Bret's last before he goes off on a camping trip with his adopted family to the south of France. Dutch Eric will take his place, but I will have to lead *him* and not the other way round. His imminent departure means that we work with renewed gusto. We finish the 7th row, but need an 8th row for the mezzanine section. It involves going back to the chainsaw and cutting without the guard to stop the machine getting constantly choked up with stray bits of straw.

Meanwhile, the sponsors are growing restless. There's no news about the lime, so I haven't been able to order the materials – even though Capability Clive is imminent. The company that makes re-cycled glass worktops need a detailed plan before they will consider any kind of deal and we haven't begun to think about kitchen design. The water softener company is blowing more cold than hot now. If we don't get the living area finished in time, the various companies I have approached about displaying their goods in an apparently finished home will have no option but to back out. This TV programme is a double-edged sword sometimes.

On the home front, Tilley's recent sleepless nights are wearing her parents out. Debs has developed an abscess in her mouth. She has been keeping it at bay with tea tree essential oil, but yesterday she was forced to go to a dentist in Brive. The sadist drained it without giving her any local aesthetic. My poor wife is in pain and so tired that the shadows under her eyes are beginning to look as dark as Duke Ellington's.

Bret and I work on till the light fades inside the straw house. With visibility giving out on us, we get the last bale in place and shake hands like a pair of tunnel-diggers breaking on through to the other side. Recent demoralisation has given way to sudden, unexpected elation. I can let him go off on his camping holiday now with my blessing – even if tempered by the knowledge that I will have to make decisions again entirely on my own.

*****

We're looking after the Jackson house once more, while they spend a few days with family in the UK. After another grim night courtesy of our daughter's sleeplessness, Debs has decided to cancel her first client, get The Kid her breakfast and take her to school in the hope that a bit of quality time with her mum will settle our child. She came into our bed last night. We don't normally sanction this, but we were both so tired we didn't have the strength for a battle of wills. I spent an uncomfortable night, sleeping on the edge of the bed, dreaming at one point of fish that kept leaping out of a big tank and writhing on the ground around me while I agonised impotently.

I slip out of bed, so I can leave them to grab an extra half hour's precious sleep. I stand by a window, sipping my matutinal hot lemon and watching the drizzle spatter the glass, with a heart heavy at the thought of another day on site followed by another evening of wrestling with imponderables.

After breakfast, in the letterbox at the top of our drive, I find a letter from the lime producers. It's full of meaningless technical data, which seems to suggest that, because we're not going about things in the prescribed French way, they're not going to help us. It's a blow, but at least it means that I can order the materials for the rendering of our walls. On the whole, I'm deriving much more success in terms of sponsorship with small enterprises. These big industrial behemoths seem set on letting me down at the eleventh hour.

Eric arrives in time for the promised delivery of the Fermacell boards for our ceilings and internal walls. The big ones are heavier than their plasterboard equivalents – and awkward to carry. We have to work fast to get them under cover before the drizzle turns to something heavier. We chat about the demonstration of plastering with a lime-and-hemp mix that we'd both been to during the weekend and lament the negative connotations of hemp, which is in fact something of a miracle crop.

The weather stays kind for as long as we need it to. With the boards stacked on pallets under our sheltering roof and covered with plastic tarps just in case, the heavens open. Not long after, I notice to my horror that water is pouring down onto the bale walls from above. Up on the mezzanine-level balcony, I realise that it's coming in via the round window and via Michel's intricate flashing. Fortunately, Eric has a calming influence on me. There will always be teething troubles, he suggests. We just need to identify what and where and put it right while we can.

Before driving off to the builder's merchant to order the lime, I telephone my friendly contact at the manufacturer – just to check that I have understood the letter correctly. I'm geared up for an argument, but he proves as nice as pie. The letter was apparently just to cover their backs. They will provide me with a pallet of their *Batichaux* for the external walls.

Nevertheless, I learn that delivery will take longer than I have bargained for. So, at the end of the day, I phone Capability Clive to see whether we can put back the rendering and plastering for a week or so. While this is bad news in terms of our ultimate deadline, Clive is as cool as a cucumber. *Shouldn't be a problem, Mark.* Music to my ears.

*****

My dear friend, Jacqui, and her family are here for a few days, taking time off from the Alpine snow to stay in our near-neighbour Muriel's little *gîte*. It was a source of comfort and joy when we first ended up in France to know that my best friend from college days lived just across the Massif Central. But France is a big country and the drive from here to the Alps takes anything up to ten hours.

Their son, Loïs, has turned into a very good-looking adolescent and our trainee adolescent is turning summersaults to try to attract his attention. Judging by her general showing off and her range of silly voices, she is smitten. It hasn't helped her sleeping, though. Last night, Debs got up and read to her in the sitting room to the accompaniment of our child's histrionics. The other day, *oor kid* fell asleep on the massage couch for a couple of hours. She's clearly overtired and perturbed by this period of transition.

Still, with old friends here, we can turn to other matters. The sun has come back out for them. Today they went out *en famille* for a cycle trip around the *causse de Gramat* and came back sunburnt. We all gather later for aperitifs with Muriel and her *companion*, V, who serves us rum from her native West Indies. They are as potent as my grandfather's dry martinis used to be. As V knocks them back, she becomes ever more loud and opinionated, sounding off about the abuse of the French welfare system by legions of immigrant wastrels. The Africans and Arabs are draining it dry, and meanwhile the indigenous entrepreneurial talent finds itself stultified by too much legislation and forced to move elsewhere. Of course, there are elements of truth, but it's rich coming from the mouth of this husky dusky Caribbean islander, the product of a multi-cultural society.

Overnight, the weather turns foul. It rains all day for our long-planned trip to Toulouse. Tilley, though, is happy to be picked up from school by Jacqui, Claude and the *beau* Loïs, while Alf can spend the day with his scruffy mate, Peluché, at Baladou Sue's.

The plan is to check out Ikea and then drive on to the Barthe factory to look at the floor tiles we plan to buy. Our nerves are frayed, however, and we manage to get lost – as usual – on the *autoroutes* around Toulouse. We lose an hour at least and, by the time we find the shop, we are barely talking to each other. It's my first time in a French Ikea, but nothing has changed: it could be Wembley or it could be Walsall. No wonder the founder of Mundo Flat-pack is one of the richest men in the world. Still, the experience of drawing up a wish list improves our moods considerably. We re-locate our entente cordiale in planning the final stages of our home-to-be.

The Barthe factory lies south-west of Toulouse. The stunning backdrop of the distant snow-capped Pyrenees guides us there through the flat, drab countryside. For a family enterprise, it's bigger and busier than we have imagined. Conversely, Monsieur Barthe himself is taller and younger than the squat balding man conjured up by his funny telephone voice. It's a little embarrassing to be treated like visiting dignitaries. We both feel like impostors, as he talks us through the history of the company and such like. In turn, he listens politely and with much apparent interest to our own tale. Then he hands us over to his secretary, who guides us to a huge greenhouse, where their range is displayed in its entirety. Here we find our projected lot of four pallets full of tiles of all kinds of shades of terracotta. Truly a mixed bag, which appeals to us much more than dull uniformity.

Before we take our leave and head for home, an assistant gives us a guided tour of the factory itself, where we can follow the process of making one of these *tomettes* from start to finish. It's rather like wandering within a painting by Breughel: the largely Algerian workers in gloomy labyrinthine passages; the strange little chimneys that respire every ten seconds or so and blow out puffs of sulphurous coal smoke. The main oven itself is as big as a 5-a-side football pitch. Our guide tells us proudly that it hasn't once been extinguished in the last 52 years.

Back home, we show Jacqui and Claude the secretary's *devis* with all the products she has added on for the complicated business of sealing the tiles. They protected their own terracotta floor tiles with a mixture of all-purpose linseed oil and turps. Claude even phones his cousin to get a recipe for us. Spray them twice with two-thirds turpentine to one-third linseed before doing the joints, followed by a final coat of equal parts linseed and turps. This is good news, because it cuts the final cost down by about a half.

*****

Ah, the vagaries of what a Dutch colleague of my father's used to refer to as *springtimeweather*. I'm keeping a constant eye on the forecasts with a view to the rendering. Clive will have to come when he's blocked out the time, so it's more about co-ordinating the removal of the temporary protection. When I check, the bales seem remarkably dry and healthy.

My current principal endeavour is preparing the straw to receive the render. I've bought myself some cheap hedge-clippers with telescopic handles from Lidl and I find myself constantly staring at the walls like an Englishman might regard his manicured hedge, then snipping here and snipping there. Whenever there are a few free minutes to hand, I make up little faggots of spare straw with which to pack out hollows, gaps and indentations. I'm getting quite obsessive about my quest for the perfect straw wall.

I'm also spending frustrating amounts of time searching for glass-fibre netting with which to help fashion the internal window reveals, and diamond lathe for the two most vulnerable walls. At the same time, I'm trying to organise The Carpenters and the roofer to attend to the leaks at the side of the mezzanine.

With all the dramatic meteorological shifts, I find that the caulking of the round windows has fissured badly. It will let more rain in when it arrives, as it soon will. In fact, these windows have not been done at all well and I feel let down by The Carpenters, whose attention to detail – as Bret has kept suggesting – has not been as thorough as it should.

Fussing around on site on Saturday morning while Debs and our friends are out on a long walk somewhere not too far from Rocamadour, more visitors arrive. A Dutch acquaintance has brought two English guys over to have a look at the building. Steve and Dave are two ex-army buddies who have moved over here to set up some kind of building business together. I imagine army vets to be killers in civvies, but strike up a rapid rapport with both of them. They're impressed by what I'm doing and we're all keen to do whatever we can to help each others, so quickly reach a deal. They offer free labour for a few days when we're ready to do the rendering and I offer any practical help I can give to Dave, who is instantly converted to the idea that he should use straw bales as internal walls in his barn conversion.

During the afternoon, Bob Ze Builder turns up with a ginger-haired friend, who has driven him here. Having just recently got his car back on the road, Bob lost control of it on a bend when over the limit and not only crashed it, but also – and rather typically – lost his license in the process. When he finishes his current job, he'll be able to work here, but will be dependent on friends for transport. He's here to work for the day's pay I gave him a few weeks ago, so I set him to work making some zinc flashing for the bottom of the wall that will abut the back balcony. In less than three hours, it's all done – and done apparently rather well. So I thank him for his proficient work and suggest that he has repaid his debt to society.

That evening, we are invited for aperitifs once more by Muriel and V. We cut it as short as possible and retreat into the *gîte* for dinner and the bottle of champagne that Debs and I have been saving for a special occasion. Perhaps it's the *V effect*, but Jacqui comes down with a migraine and has to retire to her bed. We follow suit soon after for an early night, which – for once – is not ruined by our daughter's nocturnal demons.

*****

Our friends head back home at the end of the weekend. The following morning, Juliette's dad, Didier, comes to help out for a couple of days. He arrives in brilliant sunshine, so I set him to work on the north-west wall, preparing it for the metal mesh, while Eric and I drive to the builder's merchant in Souillac to buy the sheets of diamond lathe.

Bret turns up after lunch and shows us the extra roll of belly *grease* that he has accumulated on his camping holiday. He also shows me proudly a folder full of printed sheets of paper. He has finished the first draft of the novel he has been working on. It feels bad to bring him back to earth with a bang, but what we need to do now is to stitch the sheets of lathe to the outside wall with a couple of bale needles that Bret has made from lengths of rebar. The idea is to wrap the plastic twine around the notch at the tip and then push the needle through from the inside to someone on the outside, who in turn loops the twine through the interstices of the lathe and does the same thing with another needle from the outside to the inside.

First, however, we need to determine which way round

to put the lathe. The guy at the builder's merchant has told me his opinion, but Bret thinks the other way round is logical. I try to raise Monsieur Fromage to cast his vote, but there is no answer. Finally, Didier phones the builder's merchant and speaks to someone who confirms that Bret is right. As usual. So either the guy's colleague is incompetent, or (and this is always likely) I have misunderstood what he told me.

I leave the three men to their work, while I catch up on correspondence in the caravan. The sponsors are clambering. Since we haven't even designed our kitchen yet, it looks like I will have to decline the offer of a work surface of recycled glass. Then I discover that the company that is to supply the ventilation system isn't actually offering to give it to us. The price they quote is more than what Paul the electrician has estimated. I also learn that the heat pump I have been considering is currently being trialled. So there's no guarantee that it will perform as suggested.

Rain clouds are gathering when I emerge from the caravan. The guys have made good progress with the mesh, but work is suspended to hang up the huge tarps that Eric has lent me for the duration. The rain is preceded by gusting wind, which doesn't make the task any easier, but we succeed just before the first large drops start to hammer against the taut plastic.

Didier stays with us overnight. His company serves as a great excuse not to spend the evening working out the location and the dimensions of the pine shelving, which could possibly be on offer from a firm in London.

*****

I've put back the rendering now till the week after next. With all the constant chaos of the construction, I've rather hidden away the fact that we are supposed to be leaving our temporary residence at the end of the same week. We have several options: go cap in hand to our neighbours and beg for an extension; or go cap in hand to friends and ask for shelter; or clean up the caravan and move back in there; or camp in our embryonic home.

The TV crew is here again, including an Australian photographer called Tyson, who's here to take photos for the book of the programme. When I tell Kevin about my vague notion of moving in to the new house in a fortnight, he guffaws. Maybe my wife will come up with one of her last-minute miracles.

Dishy Tom arrived a day before the rest of them and he has been helping my team of charming male assistants with the job of defining the window reveals and stitching in the sheets of metal lathe. Didier has gone back home after falling off a ladder and giving everyone a scare.

In the relentless rain yesterday, we also had to unload rolls and rolls of Bâtiplume: insulation made of feathers and sheep's wool, which I managed to buy at a factory price direct from the company somewhere over in the Rhone Valley. It came in a huge lorry driven by a miserable SOB, who moaned constantly about his assignment and did nothing to help us empty the trailer. We proceeded to roll them down our *chemin* and store them up among the roof trusses. There are white feathers and bits of straw everywhere now and the whole place smells of a farmyard.

The Carpenters and Michel the roofer put in guest appearances to attend to the waterproofing of the mezzanine. When we all sat down for a break, Tom told us a hair-raising tale of his drive here from Rodez airport the night before. After a civilised dinner in the former mining town of Decazeville, he got back in his car only to be chased by some mad French driver for 50 kilometres or more. We could see that poor Tom was clearly still shaken in recounting an incident that reminded me of *Duel*, that early Spielberg film featuring a faceless truck hell-bent on running Dennis Weaver off the road.

Tom is now back in the role of runner – dashing hither and thither for the crew. I ask him if he would buy another roll of the glass fibre netting from the builders' merchant for me. Just a little gesture in lieu of all this now rather

230

unwelcome disruption. But he hums and hahs about having to spend an extra €90 that they haven't bargained for. This cheap television makes me cross. There's plenty of money for food and drinks for the crew. I'd far rather that they spend some on our material needs rather than staging, for example, a specious dinner this evening at the pizzeria in Martel's market place.

Unsure of what it's all in aid of, Debs and I gather dutifully to meet up with Kevin, Tim, Paul the electrician and The Carpenters. We chat about our reasons for living in France and the different attitudes of French and British artisans to life, travel, work and the universe. It won't make riveting viewing.

I sleep badly that night, worrying lest, after all, we have fixed the sheets of metal lathe on the wrong way round. I want to sneak out of bed and phone Capability Clive, but he won't thank me for the interruption. I'll just have to grin and bear it until his next visit.

May 2004

There are times when I feel almost sad to see the TV crew go. I've never been in a theatrical troupe before, but my wife's tales of her thespian past suggest the bitter-sweet quality of a *wrap* or a final night. The sense that you've been in it together, that you've triumphed against the odds and now it's all over. Perhaps I shall feel like that in July when this particular show winds up and its various players head off in search of projects new. For now, however, I am only too happy to see them pack up.

The early morning – a particularly fine one after all the recent rain – features Kevin's simulated arrival by train from Brive. So we go down to the local railway station to stage the scene. Debs and I are on one platform, while Sasha is across the tracks on the opposite platform, fussing about with her microphone. Tyson meanwhile is shooting stills and ordering me to give him more *body shape*. When Kevin arrives, we pack him into the Berlingo and drive up the hairpin bends to the top of the hill. We do this two or three times before the director professes to be happy with it.

Later we stage a bit of simulated rendering for the

programme, because itineraries don't coincide with Clive's limited availability. Our capable plasterer is happy enough to oblige if they are prepared to pay him for his time, but it all strikes me as a luxury we can ill afford at this juncture.

Clive confirms that he can work with the lathe. We haven't screwed up. But he delivers the unwanted news that we should put it on all the exposed wood, inside and out, or the render just won't stick to it. As it is, his showpiece with hawk and trowel confirms our belief that the render must be blown on in order to stick to the straw behind the lathe. So I suppose the simulation has been worth it if only for the *quod erat demonstrandum*.

While all this goes on, Debs wanders about with pencil, graph paper and a tape measure, trying to plot where the kitchen and the shelving will be sited. Tyson and his assistant buzz around her, taking photographs, talking about her business and generally distracting her from the task at hand.

Right on schedule, the guttering team arrives. The process of extruding a 25-metre length of copper-coloured aluminium gutter from the back of the truck is intriguing. Fortunately Clive is still with us to direct the operation of moving it – like a mighty boa constrictor – to the back balcony, where we lift it into place while it's fixed to the edge of the wooden eaves with an electric screwdriver. All this in the rain, which has masked the morning sun. It's a fairly rapid operation, which will surely make for good television.

It appears that Bret and I have built our inspection chambers a little too far out from each corner of the house. We'll need to modify the down-pipes to make good our mistake. Nevertheless, the gutters do look rather good. I can tick off another stage completed.

Once everyone has gone and peace has been restored to our rural idyll, there is just time to go to the bank in Brive to move the money around that will pay for all this. After this… well, that's just about it now in terms of our ever-mounting budget.

The following evening, Gilly celebrates her 40th birthday. It's a welcome opportunity to let off steam and forget about the events of another stressful week. I had a dream the night before that Bret, Eric and I were all fighting a fire in a big office block. At one point, a whole gang of builders in the adjacent block were hurrying down enormously long ladders in an attempt to get away early for the weekend. Then Eric and I found ourselves running down a railway track, trying to get to Sheffield station. I had to get to Boots for a record sale. We picked up two abandoned mobile phones. They didn't work. All very strange and no doubt laden with significance.

Gilly's party is rather more transparent. The gang's all here. The Jacksons look like celebrities in a *Vanity Fair* magazine: Jessica in a dress that transforms her into a cousin of the British royal family; Steve in his wedding suit with a rockabilly string tie and pointed Italian shoes, smoking a huge aromatic Havana cigar. Bret was planning to go as Einstein, but couldn't quite get it together in time. He wears instead an absurd Charlie Brown tie and a blazer small enough to look like a straightjacket.

Tim's mother suggests to me that *you young people shouldn't mind roughing it from time to time; we've all done it in our time.* This I seriously doubt. I resist the temptation to head-butt the old crow and leave her for a throng of energetic dancers. The music is reasonable, but far too loud, so everyone has to shout to make themselves heard. You can't converse in such conditions and it reminds me of all those student discos where you point to your ears and shake your head in response to some unheard comment.

Debs and I slope off with our over-tired daughter around two o'clock when the party is beginning to wind down.

*****

On our 14th anniversary, I'd like nothing better than to stay in bed. Instead, I drive to Souillac to buy yet more sheets of expanded metal lathe, with which to wrap all the woodwork. How terribly romantic.

My good friend Smiffy turns up to help with the seemingly endless task of preparing the straw walls. He arrives with a new beard, Polly his dog – who rampages with Alf like a pair of long-lost playmates – and a tiny kitten with a damaged tail. The sight of this big bearded bloke feeding the helpless creature with a miniature bottle of milk he's bought from the local vet is very touching. The kitten was one of four: abused and thrown away like the remains of a picnic in a plastic bag. Smiffy found them in a bramble bush while out walking Polly, who has become the kitten's surrogate mother.

I give everyone their respective tasks and leave them to get on with it, while I busy myself with urgent correspondence in the caravan. There's an e-mail, for example, from Derek, our neighbour. We have still done next to nothing about our imminent departure and I use the reply as an opportunity to beg for a stay of execution – until the weekend following their return. By then, the first part of the rendering should be over and I will be in a better position to concentrate on our evacuation. To assuage my guilt, I offer to arrange for someone to come and do some much-needed gardening. The vegetation is rioting once more. *Spring garden on fire...*

I also send off dimensions to the Shelfing Store and the MD's reply really does suggest that they are offering to supply all our needs. *Great nooze.* Proper purpose-built shelves for all our books and assorted clobber for the first time in all the years we have spent together as squirrels in love.

Bret spends his day measuring and cutting lathe, keeping just ahead of everyone and stopping only for a cigarette. Smiffy jokes, however, that Bret – now known by Eric as The Dude following his viewing of *The Big Lebowski* – also never stops talking. I find this a little rich coming from my voluble pal.

Tilley the Kid joins us at the end of her school day on the promise of being able to feed the kitten. Inevitably she wants her, but I have to remind her that we have nowhere yet to live and there is the little matter of her own cat, Harvey. A jealous guy.

Debs and I toast our continuing marriage with a glass of very fine wine that a client has given her. The client in question has told her that my wife's healing hands and empathetic nature have changed her life for the better. How many must she have helped in a similar way over the years since I made the idle suggestion that maybe she should train to be a masseuse? It must offer at least some compensation for all the exhaustion it entails.

*****

From our vantage point above the flood plain, you can watch the weather come in from over the north-eastern horizon. Storms gather like the great wave in *The Poseidon Adventure*. All through this volatile spring, we have been bathed one minute in glorious sunshine, then lashed the next by brief torrential downpours. Our tarps flap around like sails in a typhoon and then settle down once more as the storm moves on.

We are engaged in a race against time, Bret, Eric and I. All of us are now busy sticking masking tape all over the windows and doors to protect them from lime-splatter once Clive and colleague get to work. When the rain sweeps in from across the valley, we simply move inside and work on the internal facades. During this process, The Dude points out that The Carpenters have hung the doors in such a way that there's no space for any render behind the hinges. If, one day, we have to replace a door or a window, the lack of clearance will make it almost impossible to lift off the old and slot on the new. I have looked upon those chippies as almost divine-like beings. They are mere humans and I shouldn't have taken everything they told me as gospel.

Later, while I'm on the phone to my wife by the front door, my attention suddenly wanders to a wet patch on one of

236

the bales. There's a puddle on the floor. I have to cut my wife off and call the boys over. We go up once more to the troublesome mezzanine balcony and realise that the concerted efforts of the tradesmen have not resolved the problem. The water is running down the post to the ground and wetting the bales that are notched around it. *Quel horreur!* It's a straw-bale nightmare.

This really knocks the stuffing out of me. I have been trying to focus on a trip to the little cinema in Souillac to see Wim Wenders' *The Soul Of A Man*, the first part of Martin Scorsese's series on the blues, but now my enthusiasm has gone. Capability Clive is due to start rendering next Monday and we haven't yet finished our preparations, but I'm almost ready to stop caring. *Please sir, can I just have my life back?*

Eric and Bret try to make a joke of it and I do my best to put on a brave face, but I really feel like crawling into the caravan for a good cry. Bret recognises only too well the strain that I'm under, even though others tell me that they've never worked with someone so seemingly calm. This morning, for example, he hands me a CD full of comedy clips he's made for me. Although it's one of the most touching gestures that I can remember, I'm not sure whether I'm in the best humour to listen to comedy.

The distraction sets us back and we work until early evening to catch up. Another touching gesture, but I am mindful of the ever-increasing burden of having to pay for all this labour. I must have spent about €100 alone on all the tape for the doors and windows. It's nerve-racking to look at your bank statements and see them emptying as fast as they are. By the time I've swept up the loose straw and trudged back over the field past the tennis court it's 7.30pm. Alf hasn't had an afternoon walk – again – and our poor daughter is becoming a latchkey kid: just left to her own devices once I've picked her up from school. She's sufficiently conscientious to sit down and get on with her homework, but I'm well aware of the strain she, too, must be under.

Debs gets back late from the clinic. After dinner, we sit

down to discuss our lodging options. My erstwhile idea of camping in the new house is clearly deranged. Sue has made some vague promises about her house in Baladou, but is still unsure when she plans to go back to the UK. The caravan is still haunted by the ghosts of heat waves past. But our friend Jessica has mentioned a woman in her village who wants to let her family's 1950s house somewhere in the same commune. Debs points out that she's earning well and that our daughter will benefit from the security and having the Jacksons' daughters so close by. Harvey can stay indoors for a few weeks, and Alf will be fine wherever his basket goes.

The weekend is frantic. While Debs packs some of our less essential stuff in boxes and cleans up our neighbours' *cave*, I am on site eight till late fixing electrical sockets to little scraps of wood equipped with long wire staples so I can secure them to the straw in readiness for the first coat of render.

Capability Clive turns up for a look with his mate, a rough diamond with intricate tattoos and a broad Somerset accent. They mention the need to protect the eaves with black plastic and to screen somehow the roof spaces from splattered render. God, it's never-ending. I want them to go!

Then Gilles, the architect, turns up on his scooter. Among other things, he tells me that Paul's VMC is probably a waste of time. We'd be better off with a fan in each bathroom and a hood over the cooker. He also suggests turning a hose on the mezzanine wall to simulate rain and see where the water might be coming in.

I want him to go, too.

*****

The first lesson of plastering or rendering straw bale walls is this: If you're going to start on the inside walls, start with a thin coat.

The Bad Day at Black Rock starts badly for The Dude. He phones to say that he has filled his car with diesel by mistake and he has broken down en route. Soldier Dave has come over for a deco today, so I send him off in his Land

Rover to rescue my right-hand man.

Clive's mate arrives early with a hired compressor. Mike's nickname is Effin' or F-In, in honour of the frequency with which he punctuates his broad Somerset speech with colourful nouns, verbs and adjectives that share the same Anglo-Saxon root. 30 metres of tubing attach the compressor to the hopper in which the mix of lime and sand is placed and then blown onto the walls. When we start the process, I can see that it takes a big strong man to hold up the hopper and hold it still while the lime is forced against the straw. Not something I could ever have done myself.

We start on the inside of the north-west wall, the one that will take all the weather. The contraption makes a right mess everywhere. The force of the projected *crepi* soon shreds our protective wraps on the doors and windows. Never mind; I'm relieved to see how well the lime sticks to the straw.

Then, my heart stops. I realise that the top bales are coming away. *Whoaaaaaa!* Running outside, I can see clearly that there is a gaping chasm between the straw and the metal grill we put up. This is awful. It's as if my world is collapsing like a house of cards. We can re-build the wall of course, but if we can't plaster it without pulling it over again, we're snookered. Even Bret for once looks shell-shocked. F-In/Clive, however, don't panic. They find the biggest plank available, nail a smaller cross-piece to the end and use it to push up the bowing wall. Then they secure their makeshift device to the roof trusses with some battens and get back to work. This time, they approach it a little more gingerly. We will start with a thin coat and alternate between interior and exterior walls, so that the weight is more evenly distributed.

Clearly, too, I should have pinned the top row of bales to the rows underneath it with bamboo stakes, even if access was difficult. So, while Bret fixes yet more plastic to the undersides of the eaves in order to protect them from flying lime, Eric drills holes through the off-cuts of Fermacell boards that sit on the uppermost row of straw in order to bash bamboo stakes into place. Fussing around like a mother hen, I do anything useful that I can until it's time to drive into Martel to buy yet more plastic and tape from the agricultural co-operative and pick up our daughter from school.

When we get back, F-In/Clive are tidying up after a productive day's work; Eric and The Dude are up ladders outside underneath the giant orange tarp; our near neighbour, Muriel, is conducting visitors from Toulouse around the house; Soldier Dave is packing Rosie, his Rotweiller, into his Land Rover; and The Carpenters are busy caulking suspicious areas in a no doubt vain attempt to stem the leaks in the mezzanine. I look upon these works and marvel at such concerted industry.

*****

Momentum gathers apace now. As if we've gone from 45 to 78rpm in the space of a couple of weeks. We're hurtling towards a deadline and a conclusion. The second day of plastering goes better than the first and we now have a scratch coat on the internal balcony wall. With the sun shining, F-In/Clive then flamboyantly pull off the tarps that have been masking the front of the house for weeks in order to start outside. Then the gas company turns up to bury our gas tank not far from where they're working. Muriel's German friend, Werner, who deals in solar panels, drops by for a look. Heat pumps, he tells me, are merely a way of getting you to use electricity as your heating source. Solar panels are the way to go.

'Not one of France's nuclear power stations has got any kind of indemnity insurance,' he tells me, 'because it would be so expensive. Yet every professional has to have some such insurance in order to practise.'

When Werner has gone, Clive calls me into the house to look at a problem with the doors and windows. As Bret has already noted, they are too close to the reveals, which makes rendering very difficult. It's all too late now, so I just tell him to do the best he can. The more I see of the chippies' workmanship, the more reservations I have. The trusses are not spaced evenly enough to allow you to fix the ceiling boards directly to the undersides; the decking of the balconies slopes towards rather than away from the house; the mezzanine leaks; the big posts of the front porch haven't been propped above the level of the concrete to prevent the bottoms rotting. I should have seen these things, but they are pros, God damn it. It's demoralising, because I've paid them well and I suspect that they would have taken more care with their own homes. When I share these feelings with my wife, reasonable creature that she is, she reminds me that Monsieur Fromage never wanted to take this on in the first place. It was my own insistence that he was the only carpenter that I wanted to work with that swayed him. In other words, as is often the case, *you only have yourself to blame*.

Our English neighbours have arrived back, so our departure is imminent. We're frantically cleaning and packing whenever there's a spare moment. Debs was figuratively treading on eggshells, worrying about being in the way and overstaying our welcome. It's a throwback to her childhood ruled by a cantankerous father. But she speaks to Ro when they cross paths outside the *cave* and feels better as a result. A tennis player of some style and competence, Ro even suggests that Tilley should make use of their court if she's interested in playing the game. True, we're thinking of taking her to tennis lessons in Martel, but I suspect that her interest is less to do with the sport (as she looks a sure bet to inherit her mother's sport-neutral gene) than the fact that her friend, Ione Jackson, wants to flex her forehand.

*****

A new micro-phase of our family life is ready to begin. Our bags are packed and the boxes are ready to go. The *petite maison* looks like an advert for Flash. The house to which we are taking all our portable clobber is a house of the most execrable taste. It belonged to an old lady, now deceased, and reminds us all of Mad Sad's house in our old village: kitsch, concrete, dark, heavy and oppressive. When I looked at it yesterday, empty and abandoned – with a store room in the *cave* as big as an underground car park chock full of bottled preserves – I noticed that there aren't enough sockets. And those that I could see are often in the wrong place. I guess life was less electrically convenient in the 1950s when the house was built.

Meanwhile in our own house-to-be, almost overnight our walls have undergone a transformation. They have become the fat curved embraceable forms that you see in the textbooks. Capability Clive has been scratching them with a lethal-looking tool of his own devising to give them the look of Mexican adobe. The pair of them have been working like Trojans. Who can begrudge them their substantial fee? Not much fun breathing in lime all day long and getting it all over your clothes and your hands. Just humping bags over to the mixer that turns all day long, my own delicate writer's hands are as cracked as the Limpopo in the dry season.

The Army Boys, have been here to help out. Steve has been suffering from terrible hay fever and Debs has offered him a couple of treatments in return for this help. And Dave has persuaded me not to put Fermacell walls up in the kitchen area simply for suspending eye-level cupboards, but to leave the rendered straw walls apparent. He's fallen in love with them and is quite set on using bales in his barn. Who needs regular right angles when you can have these glorious voluptuous curves?

Talking of which… Vicky is back with a pot-bellied beauty in low-slung jeans to operate the camera for another exciting instalment in the life of this build. They get me to have a go under Clive's tuition and I don't make too bad a fist of it. Slow but steady: a luxury we can ill afford. I'm better employed tidying as we go.

Towards the end of the afternoon, I drive off to Martel to pick up my child and thence to Souillac for a speedy shop at E. Leclerc. Because of the road works, I can't seem to get out of the supermarket car park. So I leave Tilley in the car with strict instructions not to talk to strange men and hoof it over to the hire plant. I have arranged with F-In to meet him on his way back home just before they shut up shop at six. If he doesn't make it in time, I'll have to pay for the compressor for the weekend. So I stand anxiously by the gates, dressed in lime-splattered work clothes, clutching my beaten-up leather-effect briefcase, peering up the road in the hope of spying the car of the foul-mouthed man from Somerset. Gone six and there's still no sign of the 7th Cavalry. The man marches out from his office to lock up the gates and... *hark! Here come da compressor* with seconds to spare! All is delivered and paid for and I can breathe a big sigh of relief. I even manage to find my way out of the supermarket car park at the second attempt.

Vicky has picked up her customary pile of newspapers from the airplane for us, so that evening Debs and I treat ourselves to gory articles about torture and executions in Iraq. Oil has hit $40 a barrel now. We're in for a long and difficult epoch.

After an hour of looking through the papers, I'm about ready to drink bleach. How do these commuters, who buy their daily paper to read on another crowded train, manage to preserve their sanity? Maybe they don't.

*****

A frantic weekend begins by packing up the Berlingo and dropping off a load of boxes at the new house, before taking Tilley over to stay with her friend, Phoebe, for the weekend. We find the place devoid of humans, but eventually I track Gilly down to her vegetable garden, where she's hot and busy in the sunshine, extricating strawberry plants from a tangled mass of undergrowth. It's the last beautiful day of a beautiful week. Perfect weather for drying lime render.

Back at the house, I find a freshly shorn Clive at work with brush and trowel. Surely it wasn't possible to cut more hair from his scalp, but his barber has managed. I help the outsize softy pack up for the morning. By the time I wander across our neighbours' land to the *petite maison*, Debs is back from her morning's work. Her final client has cancelled, so we have the luxury of an extra hour to spend on the final touches of our spring clean.

By the end of the afternoon, we are sufficiently established in our new temporary residence to prepare a culinary contribution for the evening's soirée at Bret and Corinne's. Oriental eggs: a family staple.

They go down well. Somehow, we contrive to be the first to arrive. I also come bearing my CD-writer, which has just packed up. The Dude has a look at it for me, but pronounces it buggered. One of the few activities that has dulled the mental trials of all this project-management has been the making of CD compilations. Now, it seems, the pleasure is denied me.

Dutch Eric and Jan arrive. Then Christophe, seller of straw, turns up with Chantal, his lovely wife, and three children. Lee and Claire, who run an organic farm on the opposite side of the plain, arrive with Logan, their little boy, and a friend called Loz, who looks rather like a goblin from the *Lord of the Rings* trilogy. We share a bottle of champagne before making inroads into some cheap local plonk. It's the kind of stuff that turns your lips purple, so it's a great excuse not to drink more than a polite glass with our communal meal. Good as my eggs are, it's Chantal's strawberry flan that takes the prize. Helio, their oldest boy, collects the plates in order to polish off the scraps.

Dead on our feet, we are the first to leave – just the other side of midnight. A Sunday spent unpacking and arranging our new accommodation awaits us. But first, that warm comforting cocoon, that place where all conscious mental activity shuts down. *Bed, glorious bed.*

*****

The bills, the bills! It seems that they arrive every day now. I'm writing out cheques, willy-nilly. I owe Bret and Eric small fortunes. I haven't had the courage of late to sit down and tot up by how much we have exceeded our forecasts, but we must now have run over our total budget. Everyone says it'll be worth it in the end.

The Dude and I are now preparing to put up the

ceilings. This involves chalk lines and complicated mathematical calculations. Without him, as The Sweet were given to yell in the dire 'Blockbuster', I wouldn't *have a clue what to do*!

After the death of their last dog, Mars, who wasted away from cancer, he has brought with him the family's new pet. They found him, abandoned and running free: a black dog, with a muzzle like a shark's and weird offset eyes that lend him the air of a hellhound. Unfortunately, Alf is uneasy with Reglisse (or Liquorice) and there are frequent territorial disputes and much marking of uprights with squirts of concentrated canine urine.

It's a beautiful day. The house seems remarkably cool inside. Bret complains that it feels damp, but I suspect that it's the sensation of drying lime. In between helping my hired hand put up the frameworks for the two main ceilings, I spend most of my time picking off the paper and masking tape that we spent so much time applying before the plastering. I manage only about five doors before it's time to go and pick up Tilley the Kid. She and the school have been out for a long walk to a local landmark and back. *52 kilometres!* a gaggle of parched girls inform me. *You wouldn't believe it!* I don't. On closer questioning, I estimate less than ten. But they all got a free pencil case for their efforts, with a small bottle of Evian water inside.

Eric has been hard at work all day with his strimmer on our neighbours' considerable garden. A parting gift from winter's grateful squatters. At the end of the day, he tows the concrete mixer back to the Jackson house in Montignac for me. Tilley rides shotgun and joins Rosie and Ione in their pool when she gets there. I follow on a little later, once I've directed the delivery of our six pallets of floor tiles from Barthe & Co.

And while this is going on, Monsieur Boussard arrives from Figeac to discuss the solar installation. A friend of our architect's, he's a man in his late 50s (I would think), with a long grey bush of hair and beard to match, who looks a little like Gandalf or Dumbledore. He's a quietly spoken, lugubrious type with a healthy line in cynicism. The government, it seems, is reducing its grants and tax incentives for domestic renewable energy at a time when the cost of raw materials (particularly copper) has risen by about 30%.

The cooker in our new accommodation is electric, which seems the most wasteful form of appliance. Cooking the evening meal on unresponsive rings transports me straight back to the world of my childhood. It must be the faint hum of the current and the sharp smell of burning whenever anything spills onto the glowing element. Both my parents and my paternal grandparents cooked with electricity and I remember the fascination I had for my maternal grandparents' old gas cooker. I've been a gas-man ever since. It's a tricky process of readjustment, but I manage to serve up something palatable to eat on a dining room table, which appears almost indecently large after living in a caravan and then a Wendy house. *Space, the final frontier!*

*****

Sitting at the large table in the early morning, reading with my first pair of glasses, which I bought yesterday in Brive at a pharmacy. The girls tell me that I look distinguished in them, but as far as I'm concerned it's another nail in the impending coffin. From 20/20 vision to specs almost overnight.

In spite of the morning mist trapped in the valley below, the sun is streaming through the double windows that open out onto a balcony designed for exercising old ladies with crutches. I get up and open the window to admit Harvey. Debs must have put him out during her troubled night. The tossing and turning might have been due to yesterday's abortive trip to Ikea in Toulouse. This time she came back with an estimate for a kitchen, but no bed and no desk. We are the *weeping, weeping multitudes*, content in the name of our flat-packed dreams to put up with all manner of indignities in those blue overcrowded, under-staffed stores.

Back on site after the overnight rain, I find the front wall stained by water either side of the big front doors. Bret and I hang another tarp to offer some protection, but there's no doubt that the mezzanine has been badly done and in need of some serious repairs.

Bret has been getting it in the neck from a wife who misses having him around because he's spending so much time on the dog's meadow. It makes me nervous to hear this in view of all that's still to be done. Moreover, Eric phones to tell me that he can't come back till next week. In spite of the rain, the sudden hot weather has turned the topsoil to concrete and they're having problems planting. What a precarious existence these agricultural types lead.

We make a start on the ceiling boards. It goes well until the interruptions. First, Geordie Mark and French girlfriend to check on progress. His French is a little better than it was, but still quirky to say the least. *Ca va, pet?* he enquires solicitously. She in turn has little or no English and one has to wonder how they communicate meaningfully.

And then Debs delivers our daughter along with Juliette, who will be staying until the weekend, before hurrying off to Brive for another stint at the massage couch. Tilley is suffering from allergies at the moment and she retreats into the caravan for a cry. And then Juliette starts crying because her friend is crying. This doesn't help the construction of our ceiling. Nor do the dogs. I lash out at Reglisse, which makes Tilley cry all the more.

At the end of a difficult day, I telephone EDF to explain that payment on a bill is overdue, because I received it late. The woman at the other end of the phone signs off by wishing me *Bonne journée, Monsieur Mark Théodore.* You got to laugh. Then I open a letter from the supplier of a cheapish telephone service to the UK, which addresses me as *Sampson.* This one cracks me up. Helpless with laughter, I stagger about like an old wino. The girls don't know whether to laugh or hide.

We parents notice that evening how much more helpful

our daughter becomes when her friend is staying. According to Juliette's parents, Tilley is very helpful whenever she stays with them, while their own daughter also barely lifts a finger unless there's a friend to impress. *When I were a lad...* We try to be fair but firm and demand a modicum of filial respect, but maybe, like so many modern-day parents, our love renders us over-indulgent.

*****

On Saturday morning I drive Juliette up onto the plateau on the other side of the plain to hand her over into the safekeeping of her father. The sunshine and rain have combined to produce stunning springtime fecundity in the Corrèze, *the green country*. Having helped out on the house over Easter, Didier is keen to hear my progress report. Juliette meanwhile gets into the back of the car to join her older sister, who is all budding breasts and teenage attitude now. There seems to be little love lost between them right now.

After my delivery and my wife's return from her work, we have a weekend's respite. Off *en famille* to the mill for a weekend with Fi and Giles. Now that our diminutive elfin hostess is pregnant, she carries her little bump like a kid hiding a football under her shirt. Our host revels in his new role as father-to-be, though this doesn't prevent him from fulfilling his self-appointed duty of supplying (and drinking) endless alcoholic drinks. Since we are staying overnight, I let my hair down for once and feel myself getting more garrulous and light-headed with every offer accepted. Dickie is here again, working on their bathrooms once more. Clive turns up early in the evening, already a little drunk – and very funny. He is in a fine mood because Manchester United have just beaten Millwall 3-0 in the FA Cup and somehow he has contrived to watch the first half twice in different bars. 'Because of the time differential,' he tells me, though I can't quite figure out the chrono-logic. We talk about our dogs. His Batty, apparently, has been a bit *facetious* of late. I think he must mean *fractious*. I laugh it off as I knock back another *pastis*.

The subliminal roar of the river lulls us to sleep in our bedroom overlooking the mill-race. Alf wakes me around 7.30 the next morning, wanting to go outside for a wee. There is no one abroad and little chance of getting back to sleep, so I take him out for a walk. Little wonder that Debs and I find May the most beautiful month in this part of France. Little wonder, too, that Brigitte Bardot (reputedly) wanted to buy this place. The peace and the serenity here are quite magical. If I believed in hobbits and elves, it would be easy to mistake this place for Rivendel.

Later, we have breakfast together outside under their arbour. Dickie has brought Shreddies and two kilos of bacon with him from the motherland. The hour together is precious and not long enough, but Giles must go and paint someone's swimming pool to help keep this place together. He reminds me very much of my brother, while Fi is almost like a sister to my wife.

On the way back to our temporary home, Debs drops me off at the land. The walls have dried out now. I spend the rest of the day cleaning up our windows and doors with humble household vinegar.

There are a couple of e-mails from sponsors for my attention. Kinetico is close to offering us a water softener, but there are questions to ask of Francis the plumber before I can supply the missing information they need. Choice still wants to supply our fitted wardrobes, but they want my assurance that they will be filmed by the TV cameras – and I just can't give it. So I write a long e-mail in which I promise to do my utmost to publicise their wares. Those cupboards are a luxury that neither of us wants to relinquish.

*****

Little more than a month to go. Sasha is back now – with yet another camera-person: a mild-mannered guy with frizzy hair and a bulky body. Fortunately, she can record steady progress with the build. The ceilings are virtually finished and we're now discussing how to construct the interior walls.

I don't really want to use aluminium rails and am not sure how to fit the floor rails if we can't use screws because of the water pipes, but Bret seems confident that glue will do the trick and I guess that will have to sway me.

The mezzanine is still leaking. Gilles has asked me to fax him some sketches, but it's the last thing I can face doing of an evening, when all I want to do is to unwind. Besides, I've got a raging toothache at present. I'm afraid it's an abscess underneath my crown, and I've made an appointment with Bret's dentist in nearby Meyssac. Last night, I even resorted to a painkiller. None of this helps with my decisions. Which wood-burning stove to go with: a Clearview or a France Turbo? What about the boiler? Should we entertain the heat pump? The deal they're offering doesn't seem that good.

If Sasha is unable to film my cerebral cat's cradle, there are a few comings and goings throughout the day to record. The Army Boys drop by and offer us their services for the week including 14th June, when Eric will be away, walking in the Alps with Tim and a few others. Dave talks to Sasha about a great bit of theatre he has come up with. How about filming him in full climbing tackle, shinning up the outside of the mezzanine to paint the uppermost woodwork with the linseed oil paint we have ordered?

Later, a man from the DDE – the local equivalent of the Department of the Environment – rolls down in his car to take a look at the lie of the land. He's considering an application for planning permission from the man who owns the tiny strip of triangular land in among the woods: the same strip that he offered to me for a *knock-down* price of €15,000. Obviously, I'm anxious that this man withholds his planning permission. But while I'm chatting to him and trying to convey a good impression, bloody Reglisse jumps into the back of his car and won't come out. Bret and I plead with him, but he sits tight on the back seat. Clearly, there's little grey-matter in that hammerhead shark's head of his. In the end, I hold the door open while The Dude yells at him and pushes the beast with all his fairly considerable might. The ridiculous scene could make good television, but it won't endear the man from the department to us.

*****

Another new day – and it starts badly. While walking Alf in the early morning around our new surroundings, a ferocious Alsatian attacks us both. I fend it off with a stick and Alf bares his teeth bravely, but we are both shaken by the experience. My mother was once attacked by a German Shepherd (the canine variety) and set about it with her shoe. Her oft-told experience has always made me wary of these dogs. Maybe this one preyed on my unease and Alf's natural submissiveness. We won't be walking that route again.

Our house is taking firmer shape by the day. The Carpenters are back again to lay the poplar boards across the mezzanine beams. It's suddenly bigger than I'd credited it before. And it's all got to be sealed!

When that is done, they attempt to rectify the leaks by raising up the two corners of the decking. It may be better, but I'm very sceptical that it will do the job satisfactorily. The Dude, for one, has serious doubts. He has been taunting Monsieur Fromage about shoddy workmanship and Mr. F. has been defensive and quick to counter. While we are marking out the internal walls with a network of blue chalk lines, which cross and intersect like a Mondrian painting, the two of them almost go eyeball to eyeball. Mike and I manage to make peace. It's the first unpleasant incident since my early argument with Tim, which isn't bad I suppose for nine months of work. I sympathise with Bret and am touched by his concern. He has become so involved with this project that he probably feels that any poor workmanship reflects badly on him. But I still feel loyal to Monsieur Fromage. If he now looks mortal and fallible, I mustn't forget how I counted on him in the early months and how I may never have entertained this whole venture without him.

It's a relief in more ways than one to visit the dentist. My gum is throbbing underneath its metal crown as I lie back in the chair to be poked and prodded by a young man so clean and so pristine that he looks like a Persil ad. He gives me a prescription for a mouthwash to see whether it's a localised infection of the gums. But if this doesn't work, it will mean removing the crown to probe deeper.

My sister and brother-in-law arrive at the end of the day from Toulouse. They have flown over to look at the old ruined house at the bottom of the land. They want to put in an offer. The Kid is as keen as mustard; she adores them both. Debs and I are both chary of any association with negative talk about *les Anglais* bumping up local prices with their silly money.

My sister is covered in a rash from head to foot, probably as a result of having been injected with a dye for a barium meal. The cortisone she's been on for years because of her asthma has probably caused her osteoporosis and no doubt has something to do with this current eruption. She is quite a case study in the side effects of 'traditional' medicine.

While they look over the house next morning, I try to manhandle the massive ladder that Monsieur Fromage has lent me, so I can climb up and apply my patent warm linseed mixture to the posts and beams of the mezzanine. They report back that the house is in reasonable order, but very small (and overpriced, I add). The girls come over later to take them to look at a plot of land. This gives me a chance to finish my labour in peace. I love the smell of linseed and turps in the morning and there's something quite restful about applying it to planed wood. The hardest part is the ladder manoeuvres and, by the time I call it a day, my legs are covered in bruises.

The land proves no good. It's situated right by a concentration camp for geese destined to wind up as pâté. So the ruined house is back on the agenda. Alan shows me all these elaborate calculations on his laptop, which are supposed to illustrate projected returns on investment. I'm still not convinced. The house market over here is as inflated as it is back home and no doubt due soon for a *correction*.

After a *grasse matinée*, as the locals call a Sunday-morning lie-in, I go over to the house to treat the new mezzanine flooring with *caseine*, while everyone else visits the bric-a-brac market at Quatre Routes. It's a natural product, which coats the wood with a milky sealant. However, despite reading the instructions attentively, I get myself confused by using 2-litre bottles for measuring the water. Rather than spreading like milk, it goes on more like liquid Evo-stick. Still, the finished product doesn't look bad: it gives the wood a nice honey-yellow coating that will, hopefully, protect it for many years.

Alan and Jo take us all out for lunch in the market square at Martel. There are English voices to be heard everywhere. May, that most beautiful of months, is on its way out. June next, then July.

Soon you won't be able to move for tourists in this ancient and picturesque square. Soon the deadline will be upon us. Soon there will be no more time.

June 2004

Monday. Pentecost. My sister has gone back to the UK, while Alan, her husband, has gone to Lyon for some interviews in connection with wind-farms. They still seem to be serious about the ruined house at the bottom of our land, which suggests more-money-than-sense.

Bob Ze Builder is back. Because he's lost his license, a mate drives him here and deposits him for the day. Bob gets stuck in without delay, mixing up some filler with which to cover the ceiling joints. He works at the double, which makes me nervous. I wish he'd take it easy, stand back and reflect a little more about what he's doing.

When Bret arrives, we embark on the aluminium rails, paying particular attention to the grid of Mondrianesque chalk lines that guides our work. Dutch Eric arrives after lunch and I have a full complement for once. We make enough progress to take a little time off to look at the plans for the kitchen that Debs brought back from Ikea. The four of us agree that the cooker has been badly situated and that we should return to the drawing board.

After Bob and Eric have gone home, I phone the secretary at Red Displays to discuss the shelves for the CDs, tapes and records. From the corner of my eye, I spot Bret wandering around outside as if drunk. Instinctively, I fear the worst for some reason and can't concentrate on the phone call.

I find him inside the house, in a terrible state. Feeling dizzy and queasy, he's worrying about his heart. He's been diagnosed as having a slightly arrhythmic heartbeat and has suffered similar panic attacks in the past. We sit on the stack of Fermacell boards and chat about paranoia: how focusing on one particular, sometimes tiny, thing can ripple outwards till you feel that your whole life is out of kilter and you lose that precious sense of being in control. Meanwhile, I'm thinking: *Oh my God. He won't be able to work any more. I'll be snookered – and just at the point when the end is in sight.*

The next day, Bret phones me while Eric and I are putting up boards together: slowly and tentatively, like two unable seamen without their commander-in-chief. A case of Eric the purblind leading Mark the blind. Bret tells me that the attack was possibly a reaction to a session he had the week before with the osteopath, bringing up stuff from the past. As to when he can come back, he just doesn't know. Eric has noticed recently that The Dude's eyes have been twitching in the way that they used to do when we first knew him, a Canadian *immigré*, unsure of himself and anxious to ingratiate.

Without him, progress slows to a crawl. Eric and I make elementary errors in cutting the boards to size. To compound matters, I have to go into Brive to pick up the internal door that will separate the bedroom area from the living space and the kit that will become the stairs up to the mezzanine level.

Meanwhile, Debs is facing a lull. Numbers of clients are down at a time when we need every penny we can get. This does mean, however, that she will have a little more time to sort out the kitchen lay-out – while I wrestle with decisions about the heat pump and sighting the solar panels.

On the way back from Brive, I follow the blue van of the local gendarmes all the way along our ridge. I'm convinced that they're looking for an Englishman, who's employing friends rather than bona fide artisans to build his house. Then I remember what Alain, the farmer, told me when walking the dog first thing this morning. Someone has burgled the little house at the edge of the woods – for the second time. So crime happens here, after all.

*****

The first week of June is a long and frustrating affair. Bob's mate has been unable to bring him over, Bret is on the mend but unable to tell me when he'll be back, and Eric can only work in the afternoons. He'll be off on his Alpine adventure next week, and the prospect of Bob and I alone is scary.

However, when taking Tilley back to our digs in Cavagnac, we spot what must be a hoopoe at the side of the road: a beautiful coloured bird with an exotic crest. They winter in Africa and come over here for the summer. Seeing the hoopoe fills me with hope, as if it's some kind of sweet bird of aestival promise. It doesn't help Tim Henman, though. Tilley and I watch him lose the semi-final at Roland Garros to a young Argentinean, who wears his baseball cap the wrong way round.

That evening, we parents have to have serious words with our daughter about the lack of assistance around the house. We ban TV for the weekend, which goes down like a ton of bricks. However, before driving to the site the following morning to spend a day treating the internal wood with linseed and turpentine, I drop The Kid off at Laurence and Suzan's, who are back in France for a week, so she can play with their daughter, Ella. I suspect that the two girls will be watching a DVD together at some point. Laurence hands me two CDs by Laura Nyro. I am, as they say, *made up*.

On Sunday morning we take breakfast on the concrete balcony in full glorious sunshine. Our words to our daughter have had an impact and she has prepared a special breakfast for Mother's Day. It's such a beautiful day and I light up one of my periodic Gauloise cigarettes to go with my coffee, but this is a mistake. Tilley looks mortified. She has been lecturing me of late about smoking too much. She wants me to cut down from eight to five a month. I point out that it's a genuine pleasure and that I take in little of the smoke, anyway. But seeing her expression underlines how much I have underestimated her concern. She's genuinely worried that I might be damaging my health irreparably. Besides, I was reading an article in *The Week* about the damage done to marine animals that ingest old cigarette butts washed away off beaches. I promise to cut down to one per week maximum, with a view to giving up altogether before long. Then, of course, she feels guilty that she has pressurised me into this decision!

Too hot on the balcony, we step inside into the sitting room, whence you can see through the open windows a grey-blue shadow across the hills on the horizon. The birds are singing in the trees outside and Laura Nyro is playing big plaintive chords on her grand piano. If only time would stand still at such moments, instead of continuing to race ahead to the longest day.

Still, it will all be over soon. It's the anniversary of D-Day and Arte has been broadcasting fascinating documentaries about the landings. Somehow, history seduces us into taking it all for granted. Yet, the scale of the operation was astounding. The project management entailed! *Phew, what a head-scorcher!*

*****

The Dude is back on site, but all is not necessarily well. I pick him up at his house on the way back from having a tooth filled at the dentist's in Meyssac. Corinne is outside, working in the garden. She seems frosty with me and on the verge of tears. Everyone, in fact, seems close to breaking point. She is suffering because Bret is working flat-out on our house, and Bret is suffering because he's under pressure from me and from Corinne, and I'm suffering because I'm under pressure, period. I feel guilty about taking Bret away from his wife and need to talk to Debs about paying him a little more. I'm sure that Corinne thinks that we are exploiting her man. True, we're probably not paying him in a way that's commensurate with his value, but it's all we can afford and I certainly don't take for granted someone who's now a real friend.

Bob arrives soon after we get to the house. Despite a bad start, when I snap a board while trying to saw off a portion from the top, we all get on pretty well together and make visible progress.

Both Paul the spark and Dumbledore drop by in the afternoon. Although he's here to discuss the sighting of the solar panels, Dumbledore explains that we should cut a little trench in the slab right across the living area, because there's a danger that, when heated, the slab will dilate and the floor tiles will lift. The plumber, of course, curse his cotton socks, has never mentioned this.

Paul, bless his socks, is always accommodating, always prepared to discuss things. He has come to fit the electrical conduits into the internal walls with a view to locating the sockets. But he asks me awkward questions about heating the water, which highlight what a daft thing it was to sink the gas tank in the garden if we're still even contemplating a heat pump to provide the under-floor heating. It's quite unpardonable that we haven't finalised our heating system this far into the project.

At the end of the day, Bret presents me with another long list of materials to buy. It's never ending. Money goes west every single day. Debs tries to gee me up by reminding me how exciting it is to be building our family home. *And don't you enjoy working with friends?* Well, yes. At times. But the relentlessness of it all is like a Chinese water torture. Drip... drip... drip...

*****

My toothache has returned, so it's almost certainly an abscess under the crown, which means big bucks and precious time.

It could be worse. This morning, Debs has one of her *premonitions*. The last time she had one was while driving to Brittany to join some friends in their *gîte* on the north coast. She dropped me off at Caen, so I could catch the boat to Portsmouth for a week's work across the water. All the way there, she had kept her feelings of unease to herself for fear of transmitting them to her susceptible husband and even more susceptible daughter. Half an hour after deposing me at the port, the car started to make some worrying noises. She pulled over just before the steering packed up on our Peugeot 205.

Today, something tells her to take the same silver-coloured car in for its new front tyres. They could have waited a few more days, but something troubles her. In changing the tyres, the mechanic discovers that one of the brake pads is cracked and on its last legs. Potential disaster is averted.

After much soul-searching, we have decided to raise Bret's hourly rate. We can't afford it, but he's indispensable and worth it. Today, The Dude, Bob and I manage to finish the internal walls that demarcate the three bedrooms. They're small and imperfectly formed, but they're quite big enough for our needs. Cutting them down to a minimal comfortable space has allowed us to augment the living space, which is as it should be: a bedroom, after all, is for sleeping in. The wool-and-feather insulation between the double skin of Fermacell boards and the two eventual offset fitted wardrobes should muffle the sounds and safeguard everyone's privacy.

At the end of our daily labours, Bob takes a look at the problematic mezzanine. He cannot understand, for one thing, why Michel has done the flashing in the way he did. I hear Bob's wounded professional pride again as he explains how sheathing each edge tile in zinc is fine for flat tiles, but not for our Romans. Surely he should have opted for a pair of plain zinc valleys. I did wonder at the time, but never wholeheartedly challenged him, because I know nothing about roofs. Was Michel exercising his artistry – at our expense? Using our roof as his canvas? Bob proposes to re-do it. He reckons it would take a day, but a day is precious and really, if anyone should re-do it, then it should be Michel. I thank him for his evident concern and suggest that I think about it.

After picking up our daughter from the bus stop, I take her direct to Laurence and Suzan's house for daughter Ella's party of expatriate girls. I don't intend to stay, as there's a dog to walk and a meal to prepare, but there are friends and there are nibbles and there are drinks... Inevitably, I end up drinking more than I should have done, but enjoy the companionship and the conversation in the beautiful evening sunshine. Debs turns up just as the others are leaving, but we stay on for more of the same. Laurence has led a fascinating life. As a student of literature at York, he was taught by the renowned F.R. Leavis, who dubbed my new friend an eccentric because he didn't share his treatise that D.H. Lawrence was a great writer.

We have plenty to talk about and end up eating with them. We get back quite late to our nearby digs, tired but stimulated. Alf seems as philosophical as Harvey, our faux Siamese, is indignant about the delayed meal. I discover that some beast has bitten my left ankle and my lower leg has swollen so much that I look as if I'm afflicted with elephantiasis.

The heat doesn't help. Tilley can't sleep because of it and wanders about all night. Getting cross doesn't alleviate matters. It takes a cuddle in the parental bed and Papa's soft words whispered into his child's ear before, at last, she drifts off into the Land of Lethe.

*****

Saturday night is music night. Baladou Sue comes over with Alf's dish-mop pal, Peluché. Recently shorn of his winter coat, he looks more comical, more mischievous, than ever. Because it's so hot in the house, we decide to leave them in the garden, which is fenced all the way round. We all drive to Brive for the Cesaria Evora concert at the big arena behind the multiplex cinema.

The place is packed with fans of the barefoot diva from the Cape Verdean Isles. Packed and impossibly hot. Everyone sits fanning themselves with their programmes. We sit up towards the back on benches, which become unbearably uncomfortable by the end of the first act, particularly once our over-tired daughter decides to use my lap as a pillow. No one bothers to announce the support act, which I find frustrating and disrespectful, because their repertoire of beautiful music from the same Afro-Portuguese islands is glorious.

In truth, I enjoy them more than the star of the show. She's a funny old thing: a dumpy elderly woman dressed in a big black dress resembling a sack. She makes no announcements and, at one point, sits down for a quick drink and a fag. I find her music – the traditional *morna* – a little mournful and monotonous. It lulls me into thoughts about all that still needs to be finished in the house before July: the jointing of the internal walls, the sanding, the re-jointing, the re-sanding, the plastering, the tiles, the painting of wood and walls, the shelving, the electrical fittings, the plumbing, the stairs.

Happily, Cesaria is backed by a great band, which features fiddle, ukulele, soprano sax, guitar, bass, piano and percussion. The up-tempo numbers keep me much more alert than the soporific slow numbers, which all start to merge into one indefinable dirge.

We slip out during the second encore to avoid the mass

exodus, and it's a relief to be upright and out of the inferno. Back home, we find the dogs where they should be, in the garden, happy and excited to see us.

The next day, however, while I'm up at the house attending to a beam that has already been attacked by *capricorns* (or death-watch beetles), the girls take a walk to the Baylis house, so Tilley can see Ella one last time before they go back to England. They decide to leave Alfie in the garden. Five minutes down the road, they turn to find him walking along beside them. *How did you...?* On taking him back to the house, they find a hole underneath the fence in the front garden. It's too small for our dog, but we realise that Peluché must have dug his way through the night before. The cheeky-chappie would have led our perfect dog astray and urged him, no doubt, to leap the fence to follow him on a nocturnal adventure while we were out in Brive. Then they must have heard the car and hurried back to the garden to greet us, as if nothing were amiss. The canine scoundrels!

*****

On Sunday evening I did my back in – the usual lumbar fragility – trying to move a rose bush in a pot. What with my throbbing tooth and the sudden feverish realisation that I've got the glue for the floor tiles wrong and that I'm starting to make reckless spot decisions at this stage of the build, my self-esteem at the start of another week is low.

At least we have a full complement of foot soldiers. The Army Boys turn up to lend a hand with the aluminium insulation for the mezzanine space. This whole area is proving the Achilles heel of this house. Yes, it will make it stand out architecturally, but what good is that if it leaks and it's not properly insulated? I don't trust this aluminium stuff. They make all these claims about the equivalence of 50cms or whatever of glass fibre, but it just doesn't seem plausible. Moreover, that kind of performance depends on it being applied perfectly. It's my fault for not being there to supervise them, but they cut the stuff flush with the beams instead of folding the edges over.

It's Soldier Steve's birthday. While I'm busy fuming about mistakes and poor decision-making, he's chewing over England's defeat in the European Championships to France. Zidane scored two goals in injury time to clinch it. The England football team, as it tends to do, threw it all away. His obsession makes us all laugh: Bret, Bob, Dave and I don't really give a monkey's.

Soon it becomes a day of frantic activity. The new Kinetico water softener arrives by courier in the morning. I speak to the MD of Ecos Paints in Heysham (of all places), a real Lancastrian who sounds older than I had imagined from his e-mails, and he gives me a firm offer for x tins of paints.

Then, right at the very end of the day, when we are having our dinner on the terrace of our temporary home, Richard and Alison from Choice Bedrooms turn up in their big Audi. They prove to be a hoot. A natural double act. Pretty soon, they are telling us all about their four children with a refreshing and engaging frankness. Richard's view on smacking, for example: *a smack is for today, a punch is forever.* He tells a story about a very funny incident, which might normally be shocking in polite, politically correct company. It involves his breaking his son Archie's favourite Thomas The Tank Engine toy in revenge for Archie breaking one of Richard's window frames. It must be quite a household. Raw material, I would think, for some kind of reality TV programme along the lines of *The Osbournes*.

We'd both have liked to keep them there all evening, but need to start the next round of packing – before we move into Baladou Sue's bungalow during her impending absence – and they need to go off for a meal. They are excited by the whole project and reassure us that they're not expecting anything huge from the programme. Besides, what they're giving us doesn't actually cost them very much in relation to its perceived value.

*****

Despite The Dude's latest, temporary absence (to help his wife get ready for her open day at their homestead), things seem to go exceptionally well for a couple of days. Too well. Capability Clive phones to say that his mate has damaged his foot and will be out of action for two weeks. Clive can spare us two days at the beginning of next week, but after that we're on our own. Bob, bless him, tries to reassure me that he and his mate, Benoit, can finish the job. Even if I believed him, I need them both to do the floor tiles. And then Debs phones to say that Ingrid is going back to England for three weeks from the 3rd July, which will mean that we won't be able to go and get our stuff from the old house in time for the final shoot on the 12th. *So it goes...*

With Soldier Dave and Bob working together (with barely a mutual word in common, although Dave is keen to boost his French vocabulary) on the last of the Fermacell boarding in the mezzanine, a huge lorry arrives. Inside are our beautiful table and chairs from The Apple Orchard. They weigh a ton. Needless to say, the lorry can't reverse down our track, so we have to go and retrieve the cargo. It takes four grown men to lift the table off the lorry. Dave suggests that we strap it to the bonnet of his Land Rover and take it down the *chemin rural* – and thence into our *cave*.

After its hazardous bumpy ride down the little rutted path that runs down beside our house, I find a big scratch across the fine polished surface. We manage to hump it into the *cave*, but my heart feels heavy. We haven't been given the table, only the chairs. We are borrowing it, as part of the deal, so it can be shown as an ensemble on television.

I have accepted the responsibility and been found wanting. What do I do now? Write our sponsor an e-mail and confess the truth? Or keep quiet and hope that we can buy the table at a favourable rate? The trouble is, it retails at £1,700. It will be hard to separate table from chairs; they clearly belong to each other. But even if it's a substantial discount, we won't have any money left soon. I decide that candour is the better part of valour.

*****

Another day, another delivery. This time, it's the man from

Brive with the funny little piping voice. He promised me on the telephone that it will be the finest sand I can imagine (for the final coat of render). He takes a similar pride in his lorry. I have to cut back any overhanging branches as he reverses very carefully down the track. Perhaps I can pitch an article on speed-pruning to a gardening magazine.

The sand, heaped up in a little dune, is indeed beautiful to behold. Clive should be happy. The sandman is a funny little man. *Ooo-la*, he keeps intoning, as he surveys first the view and then our straw walls.

Dutch Eric turns up in the afternoon for a spot of sanding, back from his Alpine walking with Tim and others. We discuss the possibility of his fetching my office chair and the CD shelves in his van. By a convoluted arrangement with Nick, our friend the wood merchant, they have been delivered to a depot in England and thence taken to a sawmill just south of Thiers, the other side of Clermont Ferrand. Nick had hoped to get them into his car when visiting them, but they proved too big for his boot. Eric is happy to oblige. It must be preferable to sanding excess filler. But it's more time and more money.

The plumber turns up with a mate. Together they run some pipes through the crawl space underneath the house, ready to plumb in bath, shower and two loos – which we have yet to buy. I find it hard now to be civil to the guy. He turns up when he wants to, not when I do. Never a word of warning; certainly not a word of apology. That would be too much to ask.

The Army Boys are going back to England next week, so I have to hope that Bret and Eric can supplement Bob Ze Builder. By then, we shall be lodged at Baladou. So it's back to Cavagnac at the end of the day, with daughter and dog, for an evening's intensive packing with my fatigued other half.

*****

And now, the end is near... We must familiarise ourselves with the quirks and idiosyncrasies of another temporary home. Our stuff is now more scattered than ever before. I spent yesterday rushing about between Cavagnac and Baladou and dropping off boxes at Steve's glass-blowing workshop. The rest of the time, Debs and I were packing cartons and plastic skips onto a ledge in Sue's garage. After many precarious trips up and down a ladder, our clobber is packed away with economy and discretion.

In the afternoon, while I went to Brive to buy an internal door and an array of brushes and paint rollers, Debs and Tilley went to see our recent landlady to retrieve our *cheque de caution* and thence to Corinne's open day. It went well. Despite her pathological mistrust of the earnest French alternative scene, my wife even participated in a few workshops.

Sunday is father's day. I am not supposed to get out of bed all morning. So when I sneak into our daughter's bedroom to look for Alf's missing collar, our slumbering princess in satin pyjamas growls *No!* at me from beneath her Ikean mosquito net. Sometimes I worry that we might have created a monster.

Such feelings never last long. She is delightful all day long: attentive and loving. I enter into the spirit of this prefabricated, Americanised celebration of fatherhood by lounging around all morning in our strange new surroundings. The place is surprisingly dark, built as it is with a number of rooms that lead off a central corridor extending from the kitchen to the garage. But it's comfortable, and it'll be home for a number of weeks at a time when the good ship Sampson needs safe harbour.

We have a full-blown Sunday lunch around Sue's dining table. I select a Harry Connick CD from her small collection to accompany the food. There's something ever so slightly tasteless about Mr. Connick jr. He does it all so well: the Sinatresque voice, the Neal Hefti-esque big band arrangements. A talent, no doubt, yet ultimately (to use my wife's excellent analogy) it's all a bit *Stars In Their Eyes*. You can applaud him without taking him to your heart. Kurt Elling, on the other hand, also blessed with a fine voice that suggests Sinatra, has created something identifiably his own.

*****

It's the longest day. I'm never happy on the longest day, since it's all downhill from here on in till winter. But I take a break from sanding the filler to lean on the new handrail of the back balcony and survey the countryside, bathed in the golden light of summer. It hasn't rained for a few weeks now and farmers everywhere have been busy bringing in the hay. There are giant cotton reels dotted all over shorn meadows, waiting for collection.

There's no sign of Clive and no sign of Bob and his mate, Benoit, who's joining the team as from this week. I'm hoping that Ben is better than Bob. Steve, our *Amerikanische Freund*, dropped by for a quick progress report over the weekend. He asked me who had filled the joints and the screw heads. 'Let me tell you,' he said in his rich Carolinian drawl, 'he hasn't done you any favours'. He's put it on too thick and it's dried as hard as a rock. Sanding it down is proving a tiring and time-consuming task. I'm red-eyed and covered in white dust when the phone rings. Talk of the devil. Bob tells me that he and Ben have broken down near Montvalent. He reckons the engine's *foutu*. So God knows how they will get here now.

A white van rolls down our track. It's The Carpenters! They have come to look at the side door, which hasn't been closing properly. They fix it easily enough. The frame has warped slightly, probably because I didn't treat it in time. They also re-fix one of the loose boards of the gable ends, but report that the wood is already beginning to split and warp. *But it's larch, God damn it.* It's not supposed to split and warp.

While they are still here, Capability Clive arrives at last and starts work on the spare room. At first, his *muck* keeps falling off. So he scoops it off, puts it all back in the mixer and starts again – with barely a curse. How I could do with a lesson or two from Mr. Phlegmatic. Second time around, it sticks like Marmite to buttered bread. I check on his progress later and the wall looks heartbreakingly lovely. Heartbreaking because he isn't available to finish the whole job. God help us if I have to resort to Bob!

Fortunately, The Carpenters disappear before Bret turns up to tackle the shower room. We have decided to put boards up against the external walls so we can tile the room, which is little bigger than a walk-in wardrobe. But those walls are about as level as a switchback. The Dude scratches his head and makes hieroglyphic notes on a scrap of paper like some real-life Professor Calculus. I don't pretend to understand what goes on in that mysterious head of his.

As the light outside fades at the end of the day, I flick through the Ikea catalogue in front of the football on Sue's telly to prepare for Wednesday's trip to Toulouse. Remembering the significance of the day, I get up to look out of the window at the long front garden, and watch as it gradually disappears with the remains of the longest day for another year.

*****

My wife is happy to drive to Toulouse the big white van we've hired for the day from the Renault garage near the slip road to the motorway. It must remind her of her days touring around Europe as part of a theatrical troupe.

I have left The Dude in charge of everything on site – which is what I should have done in the first place. Bob and Ben resolved their transport problems and yesterday suggested that I was quite wrong to doubt the abilities of Bob's friend. All day long he worked quietly, methodically and – more to the point – expertly. He was able to make affectionate jibes about his mate's workmanship while effectively showing him how it should have been done.

Today, Clive is working with Bob on our eventual bedroom wall. Clive will deliver his verdict on whether Bob is capable of finishing off the job. This may turn out to be a good tactic. Clive clearly takes a pride in his work. The thought of leaving the rest of it to Bob's tender mercies might scare him into finding the time needed to finish the job himself. One can but hope.

Ikea is quite ghastly. The showroom is swarming with shoppers. We queue and counter-queue for our kitchen order. They send us hither and thither and learn eventually, from a spotty oik at the so-called Customer Services, that they have failed to keep the bed that Debs reserved for us. Which means that we have to opt for something rather more expensive. Although we are both rather taken with the substitute, I'm not telling the oik this. I ask for the name of a supervisor to write to and, in the best French tradition, he refuses to supply one. Simmering with anger, I burst on the way out one of the balloons festooning the doorway. *Arrest me if you dare, punk!*

When we get back to Baladou, Debs hurries off to pick up our daughter from chez Jackson and our dog from Thompson & Thompson, while I get to work unloading the van, so I can deliver it to the Renault garage and pick up our car before it closes. I make it just in time. It's almost a relief to spend the evening doing something mechanical and brainless: shifting flat packs to corners of the garage where they will be out of Sue's way.

Undressing for bed that night, I discover that a tick has twisted itself into a dark and intimate nook of my nether regions. With hand-mirror, lavender oil and the little green plastic hook we bought from the *pharmacie* for removing ticks from Alfred Lord Sampson, I spend a frustrating quarter of an hour trying to unscrew the useless little blood-sucker. It's like a game for some sick Japanese equivalent of *It's A Knockout!*

*****

We're *slip-sliding* towards July and there's still a ton of things to do, but the tactic has worked. I talk to Clive on the phone and he tells me that I can't count on Bob to finish his plastering. He promises to find some time over the next two weekends to come and do whatever it takes.

This is welcome news, because the inside of the house is a complete wreck. Everything is coated with fine white dust. It's as if Mr. Pastry has passed by in the night to sprinkle sacks of self-raising flour everywhere. We, the workers, red-eyed and spectral, look like ghosts of Christmas past.

The plumber fails to turn up to fit the water softener. I find out from his rather objectionable wife that he's been sick. I'd gladly tell her that I'm sick of her benighted husband, but I need him to finish the job. When I think of the headaches he has created, I could sink to my knees and weep. Would that my brother had needed the work and been happy to spend a couple of months in France. But plumbers back home are never without work.

Still... Bob and Ben are ready at last to start laying the terracotta *tomettes* in the bedrooms that Clive has finished. If he is true to his word and comes back this weekend, then we can maybe just about synchronise plastering and tiling, which will give us a fighting chance of finishing the jobs in time.

I leave them all to it and go off early, because I have promised our daughter that I will attend the school's *spectacle* in Martel. It means leaving Alf in the car along with Harvey, who has been travelling back and forth in his basket, as we can't risk leaving him at Sue's unattended, even with a litter tray. Fortunately, because it's a warm day, I find a free parking space under a sheltering tree. Like Douglas MacArthur, I promise that I shall return.

The *spectacle* takes place in a little square not far from the beautiful church in the medieval heart of the town. As usual, chaos reigns. I never learn. Upbringing dictates that I arrive on time and then I spend half an age hanging around, feeling alien and outcast, waiting for things to begin. After a mass samba session, which bears little relation to the rhythms of Brazil, we endure song after tuneless song from the *école maternelle*, enlivened only by the callisthenic directions of their leggy young teacher in white top and very short skirt. By the time Tilley's group appears for their traditional Languedoc dance, I am about ready to bark at the audience of parents and siblings, most of whom are talking, smoking, chewing and/or nibbling through it all. *Be quiet, you madding crowd of country bumpkins! Can't you see my daughter's trying to perform for your entertainment?*

It's a sweet little dance, but all proud parents **would** say that. Afterwards, she and her friends come to find me and I let them walk Alf around the alleys and courtyards of Martel. I'm dying to get home, but The Kid has left all her stuff in her classroom, which her teacher has locked while she goes off to watch her own daughter's *spectacle*. So we hang around until we can retrieve her clobber. Mercifully, Debs has got back before us and prepared supper.

I watch the France/Greece game of the European Championships, fall asleep on the sofa and wake up to witness the delirious celebrations of the victorious Greeks. The night before England, as per, lost a gripping game on penalties. It's hard to believe that our team represents a once-proud nation that not that long ago possessed an empire on which the sun never set.

* * * * *

The following morning, Saturday, Debs goes off to Brive to massage bodies. I load dog and daughter into the Berlingo and stop off in Martel, the scene of my girl's triumph the evening before, to buy vegetables for the week ahead at the bustling market. Tilley is to spend the day with Rosie and Ione in Montignac, but I suggest that we drop by the house to see what Bob and Ben have done. I half-dread turning the key in the lock of the front door. I lead my girl through the detritus of activity to her parent's eventual bedroom. Tilley gasps. Behold, it is beautiful! So tiling is Bob's real metier. I take her for a look at her bedroom and get a kick from her excitement and anticipation.

When I get back from the Jackson house, the cement mixer is already churning. Clive has arrived. I could kiss him. We chat as we work and I learn a little about his background. He was raised in Eastbourne of all places, but he's a country boy at heart and the peace and solitude of rural

France suits him perfectly. He likes his beer and stuff, but most of all, I think, he likes his dog and his old stone farmhouse.

Later that morning, Bob and Ben turn up to carry on with the *carrelage*. I undertake to treat it for them the following day with the obligatory linseed oil. All day long in the beautiful sunshine, the house is a hive of amicable activity.

The evening is blissful. Dinner with Thompson & Thompson at their stately but welcoming house that overlooks a meadow full of sheep. Jan is there, without Eric, but with a friend and baby from New Zealand. They are all ensconced at the pool with my aquatic girls. My gracious hosts give me the run of their upstairs bathroom, so I can wash off all the dust from my day's sanding. This in itself is blissful. I'm happy to sit by the side of the pool with my feet dangling in the water, watching the others cavort in the water.

The light is fading by the time we all sit around the tables laid out under a spreading oak tree to enjoy the meal prepared by Sophie, our delightful anglicised French hostess-with-the-mostest. With their illuminated house glowing just off-stage in the crepuscular light, and the distant sound of cheering from people presumably watching the Holland/Sweden match, I feel for some reason that I'm a part of a canvas by René Magritte. I nod off and miss the man with pipe and bowler hat floating over the house.

Conversation with Jan's friend revives me. New Zealand has long fascinated me, but she doesn't share my romantic idea of the place. In Wellington, where she lives, they rarely get the chance to sit outside on a summer's evening. The rain is endless. Even Auckland, it seems, has very wet winters (with westerly winds). And it's a long, long way away. A 26-hour flight, for heaven's sake. Her baby wanted to get off the plane somewhere just north of Auckland. Maybe we'll stick to France, I tell her.

The following morning, on leaving for another stint at

the dog's meadow, I discover that I have punctured a tyre of the Berlingo. It must have been the rocky shortcut back home. Debs tells me that I was driving too fast. Next time, I'll take the long way round.

*****

The proof of the pudding is in the eating. The weather has been beautiful, very hot outside, but the house has stayed deliciously cool. Which is not something that you can say about me. I'm spending too much time raging against the plumber. There is no sign of him and apparently no means of contacting him. When he's here, he seems to spend half his time running between the *cave* and his van. He tells me that social charges are going up again and that he plans to get out of the business. The sooner the better.

I've also got a line from that Elton John song going around my head at present: *I'm still san-ding!* It's taking up so much time and still it looks lousy: great big blemishes clearly visible underneath the paint. Nor is the painting particularly easy. These Fermacell boards drink it up. Today I abandon the roller that Bret advocates for a big emulsion brush.

The multi-media shop, Cultura, is next door to Mr. Bricolage, where one can buy brushes and rollers. The summer sales have just started and I couldn't help myself. Even though our money is draining rapidly away, I thought, *Sod it! If you can't spoil yourself from time to time, it's a piss-poor show.* And how can one pass up Blue Note Conoisseur Series CDs for three bucks apiece and a lavishly illustrated history of Jamaica's Studio One down from €34,99 to €4,99? You know it doesn't make sense, but what the hell?

I'm almost ready to forgive Bob for his inexpert filling, because he and Ben are doing such a great job on the floor. They are filling the joints in our bedroom with a lime-and-sand mix and the results are beautiful. The lime gets into the pores of the tiles and creates a lovely natural distressed look. I can't wait to show the girls what they have done.

In the afternoon, there's a call from Federico at Smeg UK about the cooker and hood that they've offered us at a healthy discount. Debs has done the negotiations on this one and I keep hearing her wonderful impression of his musical Italian English as I talk to him. *Hhhello, eet's Federico from Smegukay.* Well, Federico from Smegukay suggests that they can be delivered, but we'd have to go to Paris to pick them up. Bugger that, for a game of soldiers. I'd rather pay a little more and buy them locally.

Because The Dude isn't here at the moment, progress is slower than usual. I'm not going to see a great deal of him over the next week and a half. He's got friends coming to stay and is busy with preparations for his 40th birthday party. How can he think of enjoying himself at a time like this? Without him, I stay on until after nine, painting and sanding. The Kid's off school now for the summer and Debs is on domestic duty today. Me, *I'm still san-ding!*

The light down below in the valley is extraordinary. I step outside onto the balcony for a break from the stifling dust and watch the month of June slip into history, bathed in a soft, mellow, golden hue. Only 12 days of July to go now. There's so much still to do, but as the final curtain starts to drop I've become more philosophical. We've given it our best shot. We're only human.

July 2004

Crazy Richard turned up yesterday evening with a fitter and a car full of wardrobe fittings while I was frantically painting the wardrobe spaces. They dropped off the clobber before announcing that they were driving off to San Sebastien to see the fitter's uncle. They reckoned it was a three-hour journey from here. I phoned Tim, because he and Gilly have commissioned a wardrobe for their house. Tim drives fast, but reckoned that it would take them more like five hours to get there.

And yet... they turn up this morning as I arrive for work at 7.40, all bright and bushy-tailed. They have just driven to Spain and back for heaven's sake, after driving down from the UK all day yesterday. Richard must like driving and he must like driving very, very fast. Either that or he's on amphetamines.

The TV crew turns up later in the morning to record a capitalised Day of Frantic Activity. Richard and his fitter are busy putting up the two built-in wardrobes with their lovely coloured sliding doors in the spaces reserved for them in the end two bedrooms. Paul the electrician is in the roof space, feeding conduits down into the bedrooms while sweating and cursing in the suffocating heat. Bob and Ben are doing the joints of the tiles in Tilley's room. The technician from Kinetico turns up to check the installation of the water softener in the *cave*. Everyone calls for my attention, needing snap decisions about this and that. Meanwhile, Federico from Smegukay keeps phoning up about the cooker. In the end, I agree that we will pay for delivery from Lyon. Anything for a quiet life.

But it's far from that. The technician finds a leak in the water softener. And then he wants someone to take a photograph of the pair of us shaking hands for the company's website. And then Ingrid turns up with Our Lady. Poor thing needs my guidance and I am in the middle of helping her move the various body parts when someone calls for my urgent attention and I get distracted and completely forget about her pressing needs. Then, when it dawns on me that I have forgotten about her, I find her out on the terrace, in floods of tears. In all the mayhem, she's managed to drop one third of Our Lady's exquisite ceramic skirt and it has broken on the concrete surface. Wracked by guilt, I could seize a handy whip and take myself off into the woods for some auto-flagellation. There's nothing I can do or say except to give her a cuddle.

When she's had a good cry, we discuss the situation. It hasn't broken into tiny pieces, perhaps with some judicious use of glue... I direct her to the co-operative in Martel, where she will be able to find some epoxy.

Meanwhile, Capability Clive phones to say that he's stuck in Cahors, but hopes to be able to finish his work tomorrow. Bob and Ben seem hell-bent on finishing theirs, while Richard and his fitter erect the wardrobes in time to pose in front of them for the TV camera. I hope to God they will use the footage, because their doors are ravishing and frankly I feel as guilty as hell to think that I might have brought them all this way on false pretences.

Paul emerges like a troglodyte dripping with sweat

from the roof space. With his huge drill and bit and some spare silicone donated by the Choice Bedrooms team, I spend the latter part of the day chatting to Sasha and her camerawoman while helping Ingrid by fixing some rebar into the concrete terrace on which we secure first the reconstructed skirt and then the slender torso with its two outstretched welcoming hands and finally the beautiful head of Our Lady. We fill each section with sand for extra security. You can see the joins and the residual epoxy slime at the bottom of the skirt, but provided she can endure a winter's cold, it's not the disaster it was a few hours ago. When you stand back and see her with the view framed behind her by the wall of the house and the edges of the terrace, the effect is stunning. Ingrid and I hug again, in happier circumstances.

*****

We still owe the men about €3,000. I'm wondering more and more often whether I've spent the money wisely. I seem to have made so many mistakes that maybe it would have been cheaper – and certainly less stressful – if the architect had supervised everything. Once you start spending money at this kind of rate, you begin to get slap-happy. I nip into Stop Fouille, a nearby plastic emporium, essentially for some dishcloths for cleaning the tiles – and end up spending another €30 on assorted *stuff*. I'm wielding my credit cards these days like *Billy El Nino*. The fastest plastic in the west. I just have to trust to my ability to earn some money again to pay for it all.

Bob and Ben, the terracotta men, are about half way through the tiling now. It looks fabulous, even though it's in need of a good clean: another of my jobs for the end of the week. But... *I'm still san-ding!* I was hoping to get our bedroom-to-be painted, so we can get the new bed from Ikea assembled, but it looks like we're going to have to go back into the caravan once we've moved out of Sue's bungalow this weekend.

The Army Boys are for hire all next week and I've

arranged to pay them with some residual sterling still in a UK bank account. But there's only two more days of Bret's time before he goes off on party leave to get things ready for his 40th. What would have been wrong with turning 39 this year?

On phoning Monsieur Boussard, Dumbledore, I learn that not all gas boilers will function in conjunction with solar hot water. So now I've got to check with the elusive accursed plumber whether the boiler that we've finally settled on is compatible or not. Probably another example of a hurried decision gone wrong. Why can't people tell you these things and not leave you to discover them once you've shelled out your money? *Hang down your head, Mark Sampson, hang down your head and cry...*

*****

Today's the day the teddy bears move out of Baladou. Fortunately, we've lodged our daughter for the weekend and the week ahead: initially with Juliette and her parents and then with Phoebe and the Mannakees. That's one less headache.

I leave my knackered wife to pack up and clean up, while heading for the house after a hurried Sunday-morning breakfast. My mission: to clean up the living area, then prime the screed in preparation for Bob and Ben's next push. The loneliness of the long distance cleaner is tempered by The Dude's arrival. Like Clive the day before, he is prepared even to sacrifice his leisure time for us.

He is here to paint. This is his pedigree, apparently. He and his brother used to clean and paint skyscrapers in Canada, suspended in those unstable-looking cradles you see way up above the pavement. This must be a piece of cake in comparison. I admire his technique: a roller on the end of a wooden stick for the ceiling. Back and forth and back and forth with vim and alacrity. He makes it look easy. My own attempt to follow suit dispels any such notion.

By the time Debs turns up with Alf and Harvey and a car full of clobber, our hairy friend in the white singlet has covered whole swathes of sanded walls and ceilings. He loves the Ecos paint that arrived from Heysham, Lancs last week. However, in certain lights – nay, most lights – you can clearly see the patches of filler underneath. My sister would probably do her nut, but we will learn to turn a blind eye to it. Life's too short to fret about a flawed finish.

At the end of a long hard day, we rustle up a meal together in the caravan, which makes us wonder how we managed last summer. We are too tired to vacuum throughout and clear up the faecal evidence of residential rodents, so we decide to sleep on our daughter's mattress in our new house.

It's quite something, really, to spend your first night in the house that you have constructed yourself. As excited as scouts on their first camping trip, we huddle together on the single mattress. The house is as quiet as one of the mice that wintered in our caravan, but I'm a little concerned by the resonance when you walk on the new tiles. Probably something to do with the lack of furniture. My hope is that the acoustics will please me when, eventually, I can set up the stereo. I haven't read of any straw-wall sound tests in *What Hi-Fi?*

*****

And so I face the final curtain... Under a week to go and I'm just about shot. I'm not one who ever has any difficulty sleeping – usually my head turns and whirrs so much during the day my system shuts down as soon as I put the light out – but I'm tossing and turning as I dwell on all that's still to do, so I'm not being replenished during the wee small hours. I've got piles for the first time in my life, my gums are receding and my whiskers are growing unchecked. I must look like an under-nourished tramp. When I phone Bret for a bit of technical advice, though, he sounds about as stressed as I am over his forthcoming party. I shall look upon the party as my reward for getting through this week unscathed.

At least we don't have to worry about Tilley the Kid. After staying with Phoebe, she goes off to spend the latter part of the week with Lucille. She has been very sweet and supportive now that school's out for summer. She loves the house and Debs tells me today over breakfast that she feels very proud of me. I'm chuffed to bits and put some extra love and care into the painting of the brilliant pink she has chosen for her bedroom walls.

I've hired the Army Boys for the week and am growing very fond of them. Dave's calm presence and sardonic sense of humour brings sanity to the proceedings. Bob and Ben are self-governing when together. Benoit keeps Bob in check: he's less of a loose cannon with his friend around and I wish I'd hired them as a double act from the start. Capability Clive drops in and out according to his busy schedule. He's here to finish plastering the pantry, so we can soon start assembling all the modular pine shelving donated by Shelfstore.

Jacqui, my dear Alpine friend, has sent me some of her recent paintings, which arrive by courier. They're lovely and, serendipitously, the colours pick up the colours of our new walls. It's a vain hope, but I figure that if we hang them on our bare walls and the camera lingers on one or more, say, then somebody or bodies watching the programme might think, *Hey! I like this artist. I must commission her to paint some more canvases for my seriously big house.* She has been a struggling artist for as long as I've known and it's time she had a break. It would be lovely if she and Ingrid Squirrell could find fame and fortune as a result of our programme. *Dream on, Saatchi...*

The weather's pretty awful, so it's just as well that we're working exclusively indoors. The rain is feeding the grass of the dog's meadow. It looks long enough for one of those atmospheric tracking shots in which a director like Terence Malick specialises – when you hear only the sound of the wind in the grass and the heavy breathing of the character who shares the camera's point of view. I take time off from the flurry of frantic activity all around me to go up to the farm and almost beg Jean-Louis to mow it all with his big green tractor in readiness for filming at the weekend.

A little later in the week, the day before the advance guard of the film crew is due, the activity is so frantic that we seem to have become characters in a TV game show: the type where the contestants are set some daunting challenge to see whether they have the mettle to achieve the impossible, and you feel their stress as you watch them rushing about like headless chickens. During a 10-minute tea break in which I feel like an internal combustion engine, idling impatiently, Soldier Dave asks me how I'm feeling. I tell him the truth: that I feel worse now than at any other point of my life, with the possible exception of my marital break-up. Genuinely surprised, he tells me that I appear to be one of the least stressful individuals he has ever known. *It's a funny old game, Saint*. Strange, these misleading messages in which we humans specialise.

And so the final days pass: a mad routine from 6 am to 12 am. Sleep is a luxury and meal breaks an irritating necessity. Meanwhile, though, my wife's business has picked up again after a recent, worrying lull. Traditionally, the summer months have been fallow, but now she's busy, busy, busy. Her two-week holiday has begun – one week to help on the house and the other for a trip to the UK right after we move in for a nephew's lavish wedding.

*****

The advance guard arrives in the friendly form of Vicky. She's here to lend a hand before the full team arrives at the weekend. When she witnesses at first hand what's still to be done before the deadline, the worry shows on her face. We go into a crisis talk together, as a result of which I negotiate a bit of financial help for my crew. If she wants the shelves and the kitchen assembled – even though there's nothing yet to put on the shelves or stock the cupboards – then the production company can damn well pay for some help. I know full well that, as soon as the broadcast and the subsequent repeats and overseas sales start to kick in, the revenue will come pouring into their coffers like a never-ending jackpot at a beneficent fruit machine.

I appreciate the fact that she's keen to help, but recognise that her motivation is far from selfless. For all her soft words and affinity, we are effectively *products*. Alas, too, she's clearly been skilled at the Bob Ze Builder School for Loose Canons. I have to keep an eye on her, and I don't have an eye to spare. I find myself, probably with some justification, getting irritated and prickly. It's all very well for her to slap paint on our walls in order to get things ready for the TV deadline, but what happens after the deadline has passed and the crew has packed up and moved on to another subject? We have to live in this house. So I *talk* to her and feel good about myself for having done so for once, rather than merely internalising all the angst.

I suggest that her time might be better spent in going to the garden centre nearby to source plants to create a misleading sense that the house is lived in. *Oh, and while you're at it, maybe you could buy some lunch for us all, so we can stay on the job for as long as possible*. Dave, who has taken a shine to Vicky, likes to think of himself as a man who can stay on the job for long periods. They're wags, these soldier boys. I can imagine him having fun with his mates on manoeuvres, but I'd like to ask him one day how he would have felt had he been called up for a war somewhere. I suspect that he would have been very professional about it and treated it as a job – in the same way that this is.

At the end of each day, my cohorts go home to their various abodes and Vicky goes off to her hotel in Martel. Debs and I then work on throughout the evening before collapsing exhausted onto our temporary bed in our bedroom-to-be. We prefer it here to the caravan, because it gives us an illusion of occupation. In the extraordinary hermetic silence within our thick straw walls, we can lie and chat and imagine what it will be like to live again among our *schtooff* (as a Spanish friend would have called it). I can't wait to reclaim all those long-forgotten boxes. In trying to induce sleep one night, I conduct a mental inventory and realise that it's stored in eight different locations.

*****

Saturday. The last day of frenzied – and my, it's frenzied – activity. After this, there's nothing more that can be done. *We've given it 110%; you can't fault the level of effort; it's in the lap of the gods now* – and all those other sporting clichés. The Army Boys finish assembling our wooden shelves, then put up our new double bed and finally create the kitchen we brought back from Ikea. Despite the occasional *I can't seem to find...*, all the bits and pieces appear to have been provided. Debs cleans; Bob and Ben and I paint. Vicky fetches and carries and attempts to prettify the exterior and provides us all with drinks, snacks and nourishment. Clive turns up for an hour or two to finish plastering the window reveal in the bathroom. Because of the lack of clearance above the window, he is forced to use ordinary plaster rather than sand and lime. At this stage, I'm so numb that I wouldn't mind if he used wallpaper paste.

It's chaos. Cartons and bits of flat-packed kitchen everywhere. And yet... And yet... It's strangely invigorating and a little bit enjoyable. We've got to that stage where you're ready to laugh hysterically. There's a pervasive sense of esprit de corps, or – as I like to quip – *esprit de corpses*. At one point, our American friend, Steve, and his wife, Jessica, *swing by* with the glass wall lights we have commissioned. I leave it to my wife to direct their operations. It doesn't take long to secure them to their spots on the wall and we take time off to admire their handiwork. They're beautiful: true, functional art.

A little later, Jan turns up, without Eric but with lovely flowers from their smallholding. She and Vicky arrange them strategically throughout the living area in an attempt to suggest occupation. And while they are thus gainfully employed, and almost at the point of giving up hope, I hear the sound of a tractor out back. Jean-Louis, bless him, has come to mow the meadow. I wave cheerily at the man in his cab from the balcony: a scene from an adult version of *Trumpton. And there's Mr. Sampson the Project Manager waving to the farmer in his big green tractor...*

Towards the end of our last-minute-dot-com, we all assemble on the back balcony for a cold buffet provided by our munificent benefactors. We are joined by some of the crew, who have now arrived for the final shoot. Tomorrow and the day after, all hell will break loose.

Debs and I send our co-workers on their way with a heartfelt hug and any money that they are owed. We could crack on ourselves, but I have put my foot down on behalf of Bret's party. It's fancy dress – of a kind. We go quickly through our mess in the awning to locate a few props. With an old tatty black wig and some of my wife's kohl around my eyes, a pair of black jeans and some dark glasses, I *am* Keith Richards. Debs dresses as an indeterminate vamp. On the drive over, we get a few double-takes from the locals as the Berlingo sweeps through their sleepy hamlets.

My grungy Stone is a little close to the bone. Our outspoken French friend, Evelyne – who makes some very funny asides about the unsuitability of mini skirts on certain female bodies – is particularly alarmed by the state of my body. It makes her sad, she tells me, that every time we see each other, I appear to have lost more weight. I'm so used to weighing 9½ stone, that I haven't really given it a thought. It's true, though: I've tightened the belt I'm wearing by an extra notch. Evelyne, I feel, would like nothing more than to serve me a big juicy steak. Being French, she neither understands nor approves of our vegetarianism.

The Army Boys have come along for the *Fête de Joie*, as The Dude has christened it. Every year, the circle of friends widens a little more. I chat to Steve's wife by the bonfire. She gives me the impression of someone close to tears. They're living with Steve's parents in their house somewhere near Pompadour, in the northern Corrèze. Steve is OK; he's got his friend here and they've got their work. But she is homesick and dispossessed. I feel that they're not long for this brave new world. Either a marital break-up or a return to the motherland seems on the cards.

Smoking, as I do, one *clop* a week, my smoker's drawl is a pale imitation of our Keef's, whose voice has been excoriated by a 60-per-day habit over the course of his disreputable lifetime. So my on-stage presentation hardly does justice to my state of emaciation. However... I raise a few laughs in wishing Bret a happy if rather belated 40th birthday, praising and thanking him for contributions to our new house and presenting him with the pocket computerised organiser, which Debs and I have bought him via the shop where Bret mends laptops and printers when he's not working with me. Our friend is genuinely delighted.

The new house is out of bounds now, so when we leave all the stragglers around the campfire not long after midnight, we sleep the sleep of the exhausted in our caravan for what may be the penultimate time.

*****

Saturday night and Sunday morning. We are effectively excluded from our house by the crew and confined to the caravan, which becomes our *green room* for the next two days. Lucille's dad returns our daughter to our safekeeping, but we can't offer him much more than a glimpse at the supposedly finished product within.

This is the full TV Monty. Everyone's here except Kevin, who arrives tomorrow for the final time. There's equipment galore, including a crane of sorts that allows the camera to swoop in and over the house, and a trolley that enables some dramatic tracking shots. Seeing the arc of the camera on its crane reminds me of the legendary opening sequence of Orson Welles' *Touch Of Evil*, where the camera follows the Charlton Heston and Janet Leigh characters on their evening walk through a Mexican border town and ends with a dramatic explosion. They had to get that right first time for obvious reasons. There's a little more room for errors here.

Everything unsightly outside – and there's a lot of it, given that it's still officially a building site – has to be removed from shot. So the big orange tarp over the sand pile, for example, has to be removed and folded up and hidden in the crawl space under the house. Periodically, our presence is requested in the house, which seems big but incredibly empty, by the Australian photographer, for all kinds of arty shots destined for the book of the series. He promises to e-mail us some of the best images, but I don't hold out much hope. Nice as he is, we suspect hot air. The way that we have been excluded from our own home is symbolic of the way that these media types treat you: nice as pie to your face, but ultimately you're really just in their way. As soon as they've gone, any undertakings made will be forgotten.

Happy enough to leave them to it, we three enjoy some quiet horizontal time on the caravan's banquettes. It's blissful weather for the occasion and while we're not stifled as we were last year in the awful heat of the *canicule*, we're all suitably soporific.

Kevin arrives with a fanfare of trumpets the following morning. While awaiting his arrival, my wife waxes lyrical about the lichen colour with which we have painted all the internal wood and the look and colour of the walls and the beauty of the floor tiles. Bless her! She's like a little kid in her big new family home. Physically, emotionally and financially spent (as I plan to tell Kevin), I'm more concerned by the trolley's tyre marks on our tiles.

We start with the usual ridiculous mock-ups, which surely fool no one. The knock on the door. Kevin peers inside. We walk over together to let him in. *Hello Kevin! (Fancy seeing you here.) Kiss, kiss; hug, hug.* If it's all a bit of a charade, I suppose everyone knows it is, so it becomes a kind of knowing, tongue-in-cheek double bluff. Actually, we are both genuinely happy to see our intermittent *deus ex machina*. This time, it means the end is nigh.

Showing him around our glaringly empty show-house, we do our various takes with the obligatory wide shots to capture our impromptu responses. These aren't rehearsed and therein lies part of the programme's strength. We and other counterparts would probably sound glib if we were too rehearsed. On the other hand, however, you inevitably think of what you might have said after the take is in the can.

After he does his one-to-one with Debs in the kitchen area, Kevin and I and camera crew troop upstairs for our interview. For once, the first take is rejected. Second time around, I come up with what they want to hear. My dream of getting up early, walking the dog, coming up here to write and perhaps wandering onto the balcony to derive inspiration from the birds in the trees, eating some lunch and then pottering for the rest of the day *à la* Graham Greene. Would that I could be as disciplined as he was. Pottering is justifiable if you put in a solid morning's creative work. I smile like a performing seal might do if it were able to smile. Everyone has been saying that I'm going to be some kind of national hero when the show is broadcast: that someone so inept should attempt such a feat and somehow bring it off. Like Eddie the Eagle, I guess. I certainly don't feel like a hero.

It's outside later on the freshly mown meadow that Kevin poses the hardest question of all. We are simulating a picnic, a kind of do-it-yourself *Déjeuner Sur l'Herbe* (though my wife sensibly keeps her clothes on). What have we learned from the whole experience? What **haven't** I learned! Both of us come up with stuff that will probably sound lame. Afterwards I think of all the things I should have said: how you can never plan *too* comprehensively; how everything takes longer and costs more than you bargain for; how sometimes you just have to upset people, but if you do, you can usually repair the damage; and – something which I never thought possible – how you can live happily enough with fewer possessions.

Finally, he asks us how we feel. I tell him in a rather more roundabout way that I'm shagged. Debs talks revealingly about not appreciating how unhappy and how smothered she felt towards the end of our sojourn in the old house – and promptly bursts into tears, because she's so happy now. I put a protective arm around my soppy wife. It would have been a great way to end the programme, but they fail to capture the touching moment because the camera's battery packs up at that precise spot.

Of course, though, the ending will be the traditional summation by the nation's favourite summarist. We mingle with the incidental crew members, joking good-naturedly about the kinds of things he might be saying to camera out on the balcony. We know by now, though, that Mr. Media approves of what we have done, so we can guess at what he'll be saying.

That evening, all of us – bar Kevin, who has sped off to yet another airport – meet up at the pizzeria on Martel's medieval market square for our farewell dinner. Tilley, Debs and I are all tired and hungry and feel a little stuck out on a limb. Nevertheless, we muck in pluckily and gather around our friendly neighbourhood Australian photographer to look at some of the lovely stills on his laptop. I remind him about sending us a few of his favourite selections. *Yeah, yeah mate. No worries.*

At the end of our meal, Sasha and Vicky present us with a couple of bottles of bubbly and a little oil and vinegar set for our new kitchen. The kitchen, that is, whose taps have not yet been plumbed in. We all embrace warmly and say our fond farewells.

There's a slight chill in the air as we all head off in opposite directions: the crew to their hotel, the family Sampson to their new and now vacated home. As an ex-actress, my wife should know what she's talking about when she tells me that it feels like the end of some long-running West End show.